HELL AND MADNESS;

GRACE AND SANITY:

The true biblical basis

for mental health

Pauline Holmes PhD

HELL AND MADNESS; GRACE AND SANITY: The true biblical basis for mental health.

First printing, 1992
Second printing, 1998

This edition published by Ransom Press, a division of Grace and Sanity Ministries, a not-for-profit religious corporation, 1645 Fairview Street, Berkeley, CA 94703. Mailing address: P.O. Box 191334, San Francisco, CA 94119.

Printed in the United States of America. ISBN 0-9634540-4-8

CONTENTS

PREFACE

Leaving behind a career path in academia and the philosophical stance of atheism, I became a Bible adherent in the process of learning how to be a psychotherapist. During my days in academia, I had sneered at Christianity. I wondered how people who appeared otherwise sane and intelligent could talk about God, particularly a personal God, or consider the Bible worth serious attention.

How wrong I was! Subsequent painful events in my own life, including a divorce, had the wonderful result of showing me there was a listening, intelligent, supernatural someone helping me. But the man who became my second husband led me to discover that this listener is the God of the Bible. My spouse has been a life-long explorer of the human psyche and the supernatural world who, after voyages in many false religions, had just returned home to the Bible at the point when I met him. I was able to benefit much, vicariously, from his experiences of how those false religions leave a person stranded spiritually, and as an outcome of that, abandoned emotionally.

Serious study of the Bible led me to a revelation which, if accepted by the mental health community, would revolutionize it. It is as follows. First, all humans know they are born with a stain on their nature. Second, they are also born with the knowledge that the consequence of this stain, or sin, is death. This death is separation from God leading to the eternal darkness of hell. Third, although humans are generally not conscious of it, their knowledge of this predicament causes universal psychological turmoil. In other words, the root of mental illness is that humans know they are doomed to go to hell. Confirmation of this has come from my private practice as a clinical psychologist.

Far-fetched as this view of reality may sound to anyone who does not accept it, its validity is established both inside and outside of the Bible. Supported by data from various sources, the present book makes the case that 1) the innate sense of being destined for hell is what causes mental illness, and 2) only the message of the Bible provides the necessary remedy that leads to sanity. In other words, mental health is only possible when we humans know that the God of the Bible provides refuge for our otherwise desperate predicament. The refuge lies in grace, i.e., God's gift of Christ, the ransom that buys us out of hell.

The book is for both clinicians and lay persons. Its thesis is not to be found elsewhere in the mental health literature. Though best understood by Christians, it can be of interest to all those familiar with psychological theory and research, comparative religions, and the phenomenology of mental illness. Due to its explication of universal phenomena, it is a book intended both for Bible-believers and for those still seeking God, whether or not they are conscious of it.

My purpose is twofold. One is to give a foundation for a truly Bible-based approach to counseling and psychotherapy, not just in the Bible-believing community, but in the general mental health field. The other is evangelical: to alert everybody to the danger we are in and point out the escape God has given us.

Introduction

THE BIBLICAL BASIS FOR

MENTAL HEALTH

THE BLIND SPOT AND THE JUGGERNAUT

Most humans have a huge blind spot concerning the fragility of their existence. The truth makes anyone who recognizes it want to shout, scream, and jump up and down in front of anyone unaware of it. During my father's boyhood at a silent movie house in a Cockney section of London, the entire audience would be uselessly bawling at the hero: "Look be'ind yer!"[1] He, of course, was oblivious to both the audience and the express train speeding up as he stood on the tracks. But this is no movie, and warnings do not always fall on deaf ears. At some point, we all must deal with the fact that the juggernaut of death is racing up behind us.

Some ask, so what if we are crushed by the juggernaut? Nothingness would be peaceful. However, the prospect of fizzling into nothingness is hardly appealing for those who love life, and we all do, deep down. But for the sake of argument, let us agree that death would be no calamity if there were nothing worse than extinction ahead. The real problem is this: there is a much worse possibility than extinction lying before us. The truth concealed behind the blind spot is what the Bible describes as the "bottomless pit" (Revelation 9:1), a place of eternal darkness, isolation and pain associated with "weeping and gnashing of teeth" (Matthew 8:12).[2]

Those who doubt that hell exists cannot afford to disregard the warnings. Despite popular misconceptions, the Bible is far from being the only source of admonition. Images of hell occur in religious belief systems and mythology too regularly for it to be dismissed. This is because a sense of the darkness that lies ahead is born in us.

9

I have found in my clinical practise that nobody is without a sense of something dreadful lurking in their path. No psychological theory can adequately explain this. Only Genesis can. The elements of a terrifying dilemma were programmed into us in the Garden of Eden. It is knowledge of impending doom in our collective unconscious,[3] inherited from our human ancestral parents.

Whether we are conscious of it or not, a shadow of fear, guilt, anger and despair has been cast over us. Fear is there because we intuit the punishment ahead; guilt is there because our imperfection tells us we deserve the punishment; and anger is there along with despair because we know we cannot extricate ourselves from it. This dilemma and the emotions it generates are the root cause of mental illness. Guilt lies deeper than the fear or anger; we go crazy trying to hide from it.

In some way every religion acknowledges that the human condition (imperfection) is a state of separation from God (perfection). Moreover, all say that this separation leads to eternal darkness. It happens that only one of the many proposed routes to connect humans with God and save them from this darkness is valid. Only the Bible does not pose an impossible task; the God of the Bible has made it easy.

Some think the Bible *causes* guilt through its articulation of imperfection, or sin. On the contrary, it explains what is already there. In fact, the Bible offers both the diagnosis and the cure, the bad news and the good news. Our sickness comes from our inability to avoid the juggernaut and what follows it. We are standing on the tracks in the way of impending death and the train driver wants to kill us. The cure is an escape which is absolutely without cost or effort to humans. All we need do is recognize God--that is, the God of the Bible. Why this particular God? Well, he[4] is the only one who offers a rescue as a gift. His gift is essential because humans have no bargaining power when perfection is the only legal tender. Our inherent flaws make us completely dependent on a dispensation from God.

PREMISES AND PURPOSE OF THE BOOK

The premises of this book are that God exists; he is the God of the Bible; the Bible is factually true from beginning to end; and what the first humans, Adam and Eve, learned in the

Garden of Eden has been inherited in the psyche of the human race.

God's law says that the price for (result of) sin (imperfection) is death (eternal separation from God ending in hell). Humans are doomed. Their sense of this produces existential guilt, the unconscious awareness of deserving eternal punishment. This guilt causes mental illness. Since humans cannot change their nature and perfect themselves, mental illness can only be healed by claiming the gift God gave us to cover sin. The Bible shows us he has done this by killing Christ in our stead. Without the knowledge of this "cover," or pardon, the emotions and self-blindness generated by our predicament cause psychopathology.

The purpose of this book is to lay a theoretical formulation that gives psychological counseling its true Biblical basis: fear of hell causes insanity; therefore only grace, or God's unmerited pardon, brings sanity.

PLAN OF THE BOOK

The book is divided into three parts. Part One, called "Hell and Madness," provides evidence for the basic thesis that the innate fear of hell is the root of all psychopathology; Part Two, called "Grace and Sanity," shows how and why only the Gospel, with its unique message of grace, can cure it; and Part Three, "Hell and Madness; Grace and Sanity" applies the hell/grace equation to the definition and cure of psychiatric disorders.

PART ONE

Part One of the book (Chapters One to Eight) defines the core mental health problem as our inherent knowledge of doom. This all-important thesis is supported by the Bible, mythology, psychological research, and the phenomenology of mental illness. The author's experiences in clinical practise provide illustrations.

Our journey in begins in Chapter One by delineating how the most essential elements of the human psyche--the sense of doom and the intimation of a rescue--are laid out in the book of Genesis, beginning in the Garden of Eden. From there we go into a variety of areas that support this. Many believe that the sciences conflict with the Bible but that is not the case.

Chapters Two and Three show that all empirical inquiry, including psychology, will ultimately prove the Bible to be true.

When viewed from the perspective of the Bible, psychological research, particularly the classic work of Freud and Jung (Chapters Four to Six), helps us to understand how our innate knowledge of doom affects us. Lacking the biblical underpinning, Jung and Freud had different overall perspectives than the one presented in this book. Nevertheless, their work is extremely useful in highlighting the psychodynamics of our archetypical life/death conflict.

In Chapters Seven and Eight of Part One there is a discussion of the ways in which psychotic disorders, particularly schizophrenia, are a showcase for our innate knowledge of doom. In particular, the spiritual truth underlying the so-called delusional "religiosity" is pointed out.

PART TWO

Fear of hell causes mental illness so grace must be its cure. But where is grace? In Part Two of this book, Chapters Nine to Twelve examine the existing approaches to psychotherapy and spirituality to show where they fail to offer grace. So-called Christian approaches that stray from the truth by preaching against sin are included in this investigation.

Chapter Thirteen deals with empirical research that demonstrates associations between various aspects of religiousness and well-being, especially psychological adjustment. Since its singular importance has not generally been recognized, the role of the Gospel has yet to be the focus of much study. However, there is a discussion of one research program that certainly points to the unique benefit of the grace of God.

PART THREE

Part Three deals with application. Chapter Fourteen applies our biblical diagnosis and remedy to most psychiatric disorders defined by the DSM-III-R. Chapter Fifteen tackles all the common arguments against sharing the Gospel in the counseling room. Finally, the book is summarized with some concluding remarks in Chapter Sixteen.

Notes

1. "Look behind you!"

2. All Biblical references are to the King James version.

3. The term "collective unconscious," borrowed from Carl Jung, is elaborated in Chapter Four.

4. Following the precedent of the King James Bible, from which all the Biblical references in this work are taken, pronouns for God are not capitalized.

Part One

HELL AND MADNESS

Chapter One

THE INNATE FEAR OF HELL

GENESIS AND GUILT

At the outset, it may be hard for the reader to see that the human mind cannot be fully understood outside of the context of the Bible. Harder still, even for some who consider themselves Christians, may be the fact that such understanding requires a literal belief in the Genesis account of Adam and Eve in the Garden of Eden. Yet Genesis explains all, and does so with beauty and economy. Genesis shows us that we humans have inherited innate knowledge of a universal dire predicament. Furthermore, this predicament is the root cause of every type of mental disorder.

From Genesis we learn that God gave a single command to the first humans he created: they were not to eat the fruit of a specific tree, the Tree of the Knowledge of Good and Evil. God said: "In the day that thou eat the fruit of that tree, thou shalt surely die" (Genesis 2:17). This death was was separation from God which led to physical death and the dark abyss of hell.

However, Adam and Eve naively listened to a competing source of authority: Satan, a fallen angel out to destroy the creation he could not have dominion over. Satan wanted God to lose the humans he made and loved. He knew disobedience would rupture their connection with their heavenly Father. So he told them the promised consequence of death would not apply if they ate the forbidden fruit. Appealing to their desire for power, he said: "Ye shall not surely die: For God doth know that in the day ye eat thereof, then your eyes shall be opened, and ye shall be as gods knowing good and evil" (Genesis 3:4-5).

LIES, TRUTH, AND LAW

In accepting Satan's advice, Adam and Eve broke with God. Once they disobeyed him, they immediately found the truth: they were doomed and Satan is a liar. God did not have to tell them this; they had ingested the Knowledge of Good and Evil, God's law. The law had become part of them and it told them the price for sin is death. In other words, the consequence of lawbreaking is alienation from God, meaning separation from the Tree of Life. Now they could put two and two together and make foreboding. They not only knew they were lawbreakers, they also knew they faced the terrible penalty of eternal darkness.

All of us face this penalty because we, too, are disobedient. Satan's lies--the promises of godhood, omniscience, and immortality--continue to appeal. Wanting to be gods, we rebel against God's authority. Implicitly, we do what Satan did before God kicked him out of heaven: try to build a "throne above the stars of God" (Isaiah 14:13).

Moreover, Satan's lies are the basis of all false religions. Their doctrines appeal to our rebelliousness. We think knowledge--enlightenment--will empower us. Instead it shows us how utterly vulnerable we are. In fact, "knowledge increaseth sorrow" (Ecclesiastes 1:18).

Genesis reveals our universal predicament. Paul, the apostle, puts it in a very simple way: "The wages of sin is death" (Romans 6:23). Disobedience lost our forefathers the protection afforded by their union with God. They were now wide open to Satan's onslaught, condemned for eternity. Their dilemma is our dilemma.

Indeed, everything Adam and Eve learned in the Garden of Eden has been passed on to their descendants, the human race. God's damning law was planted deep in our psyche. Interestingly, the word for law in the Danish language also means "doom." The knowledge of good and evil is God's law which tells us we are doomed.

GUILT

After disobeying God, Adam and Eve noticed their nakedness; they felt a need to hide. What they were experiencing was guilt. Guilt is the awareness of deserving punishment. Our ancestors' feeling was not sexual guilt but an existential type of guilt, a general sense of deserving punishment for missing the mark of perfection. The guilt was accompanied by a sense of their need for protection, a place where they could hide from punishment, a "cover."

Like them, we are all in hiding...physically, emotionally and spiritually. Because we have inherited God's law in our psyche, we know our sentence. But our flight from the truth means it may not be conscious knowledge. We feel bad about ourselves but have no idea why. Somewhere inside we carry tremendous guilt plus shame, terror, rage and despair because of these two ominous facts that are printed on our hearts: one, we fall short of God's standard and always will (i.e., we are sinners); and two, unless we are fortunate enough to have "ears to hear" (Deuteronomy 29:4) of God's rescue, we are stuck with the penalty.

In psychodynamic terms,[1] existential guilt, or the awareness of deserving eternal punishment, puts the psyche under enormous stress. Guilt sends us into whatever hiding our psychological defenses afford us until either the punishment occurs or there is a total reprieve. Our defenses aim to keep the conflict out of consciousness. They also strive, unsuccessfully, to lift the sentence off our heads. However, there is a price to pay for defenses: pathological patterns of behavior and thinking. These include self-punishment, self-purification, compulsive work, and delusions of grandeur.

Theologians and psychologists have made futile stabs at explaining our ubiquitous guilt outside of the biblical context. Adlerian psychology says guilt stems from a refusal to accept one's inferiority. Jungian psychology says guilt stems from a refusal to accept the "shadow," the darker aspect of being human. Martin Buber says guilt arises from our refusal to accept others. But all of these are outgrowths of the preexisting guilt. This is the situation: I cannot accept others until I accept my self; I cannot accept my self until I know my flaws no longer doom me; I only know my flaws no longer doom me when I have proof that God has forgiven me; but until I have that proof, I dare not look at myself.

HELL AND MADNESS

If we humans explore ourselves deeply enough, we become aware of the terror of a place of utter darkness. It is there in all of us regardless of familiarity with the Bible. We have all inherited a sense of the reality of an endless hell, the "lake of fire" (Revelation 19:20), or "gehenna" in Hebrew. Until this fright is put to rest our minds are bent out of shape by it. We humans cannot get rid of a feeling that we are completely vulnerable to the abyss, unable to stop ourselves from falling in.

Satan, envious of God and knowing he is destined for hell, actually stole the human race, thinking he would drag us all down with him.

How can we be at peace in such a predicament? We cannot. It produces an unending sense of affliction. God says that until we turn to him: "I will set my face against you, and ye shall be slain before your enemies: they that hate you shall reign over you, and ye shall flee when none pursueth you" (Leviticus 26:17). Also: "The Lord shall smite thee with madness, and blindness, and astonishment of heart" (Deuteronomy 28:28). And: "There is no peace, saith the Lord, unto the wicked" (Isaiah 48:22). "Wicked," of course, applies to all humans in their natural state.

Human race: Look be'ind yer! Burying our heads in the sand, rejecting the idea of Satan and eternal torment may enable us to survive in this world without completely caving in. But superficial ignorance will not save us, nor still the storm. This false respite offers existence but not life. It means forfeiture of psychological integrity.

Many of us make the mistake of thinking hell not only endurable but more interesting than heaven. It might even be fun, like an endless cocktail party in an overheated room accompanied by joke-cracking sinners, perhaps all our best chums. Nothing could be further from the truth. Eternal disconnection from God will not be bearable. It will be worse than anything we can imagine, with neither fellowship nor respite.

Living in the present world without God is bad enough. It is like being a trapeze artist performing without a safety net, no support to fall into. There is an indefinable sense of something missing, of insecurity, emptiness, and ungroundedness. Somehow, we always feel "wrong."

Traditional psychotherapy tries to assure us about our potency and goodness. But these affirmations bounce off like water from a duck's back.

Only a dilemma of this magnitude is adequate to explain the depth, pervasiveness, and content of all our human neurosis and psychosis. Even the more transient mental disorders stem from a sense of disconnection from God with only the prospect of eternal darkness ahead. In some fashion, all religions and psychotherapeutic methods attempt to heal this terrifying sense of being shut out in the cold, isolated and unprotected. The terms change but the intent is the same.

THE NATURE OF SIN

How we hate the "sinner" label, that finger pointing in accusation! Sin is accompanied by the resented burden of guilt. The Freud-based mental health profession helps us to blame "them" for the guilt...our parents, society, or that first grade teacher. We think "they" did it to us with "their" rigid standards and hypercriticality.

To combat this, we establish our own standards. We redefine "sin" to mean only the more serious transgressions which we consider avoidable. Psychological justification makes everything permissible. We are *not* sinners, we say. The erasure of the "s" word from our language has been noted even by the psychiatric profession.[2]

What is sin? To sin is to break God's law in thought, word, or deed. The Hebrew and Greek words for sin, "hattath" and "hamartia," respectively, are archery terms meaning "missing the mark," or "falling short." The "mark" is God, essentially the mind or wishes of God. The instant a sinful thought enters our head, we break connection with him. Our minds are not in the same place.

For its consequence of death to apply, sin does not have to be willful disobedience, and it does not have to be major. The minutest transgression, the tiniest impure thought, puts us on the wrong side of the law. Since one false step is all it takes, every one of us, from axe murderer to dedicated do-gooder, is in the same bind. "There is none righteous, no, not one" (Romans 3:10).

We are, as David said, "fearfully and wonderfully made" (Psalm 139:14), yet we have inherited a proclivity for disobedience. Sin is not only what we do, it is also what we say and think. Despite what all the non-Biblical religions tell us, we just do not have sufficient self-control to completely eliminate sin, particularly in our thinking process. Actions and tongue may be governable by us to some degree, but the stream of our consciousness is fed by dark springs. Sin is inevitable. Over and over again, the Bible states that man's heart is desperately wicked (Genesis 6:5; Romans 7:18, 7:25, 8:20).

Belief in human godliness, sometimes literal but usually implied, is the ultimate psychological defense mechanism, a common feature of both false religions and the delusional thinking of psychotics. Only as gods would we be be able to resolve our terrible dilemma through our own power, stepping outside of human nature. Only as gods could we escape hell by changing ourselves into creatures that did not miss the mark.

The directives, "Love thy neighbor as thyself" (Leviticus 19:18) and "love your enemies" (Luke 6:27) go against our selfish and unforgiving nature. When we apply these standards to our own thought and actions, we see how far short we fall. We cannot avoid it; God's love alone is perfect.

Evolutionists try to minimize our sinful nature by attributing it to the outmoded "reptilian" portion of the brain which will disappear further down the great chain of being, millions of years hence. But there is no evidence that ontogenesis, or the development of the individual, recapitulates phylogenesis, the evolutionary development of the phyllum. Nor is there evidence for evolution; the facts contradict it (see Chapter Two). Our nature is no better now than it ever has been.

Our nature is the problem: its egocentricity, its killer instinct, its selfish desire to avoid pain at all costs, its tendency to get lost in sensual pleasure, its laziness, its pride, its greed, its envy, and its covetousness. We are inherently self-centred and worldly.

However, there is one ultimate rebellion: to assert there is no higher authority than ourselves. It is the "sin unto death" (I John 5:16), since it implies rejecting God. This is what Samuel, the prophet, meant when he said: "For rebellion is as the sin of witchcraft, and stubbornness is as iniquity and idolatry" (I Samuel 15:23). But just like Adam and Eve, we fall into this trap. Often unaware of how dangerous our assumptions are, we conduct our lives as if we hold the reins that control our destiny.

THE CONSCIENCE

Our insides acknowledge the true predicament. Guilt, fear and rage seep up from an innate sense of the sentence our humanness puts us under. The conscience, God's inborn law in our hearts, does not rest when our nature transgresses. Psychological defenses hide the conscience and the guilt, but at the expense of our mental health.

In spite of what secular psychologists say, our sense of morality is not acquired through learning. However, learning can distort it like a veneer on the surface. Superficial layers of popular morality can separate us from God's law deep inside. Even so-called "Christian" morality often departs significantly from God's law. For example, God reveals in the story of Noah and Ham (Genesis 9:20-27) that he is far more upset about gossiping than drunkenness. He also shows us he considers pride (Psalm 10:4) and stubbornness (I Samuel 15:23) to be worse than either of these. Conversely, we humans are often willing to tolerate gossiping and stubbornness, we value pride, and we make temperance a condition for church membership. Yet the tongues of many smug "Christians" wag over someone with a weakness for alcohol, blind to their own transgression.

Secular humanists deny that moral sensitivity stems from God. They claim that doing what is right comes from innate human goodness. But that does not explain the existence of moral absolutes like "good" and "bad," nor why doing good feels good. Humanists are unaware that this speaks of an unconscious sense of accountability to God. And they invariably display huge, unacknowledged moral lapses as they deny sin to attain the illusion of their own goodness.

THE TORAH AND JESUS

Now we come to the good part: the rescue. God's law both dooms and frees. It is laid out in detail in the Pentateuch, or Torah, the first five books of the Old Testament written by Moses. The death and resurrection of Christ completes it.

Satan made humans disobey God's one prohibition, bringing down on themselves an impossible law that spelled doom. So God put a special provision in that law. He gave humans a key to the straightjacket, embedding possibility within impossibility.

For many reasons, it is hard for humans to grasp that the key is a gift. Yet grace is God's unmerited forgiveness, the gift of a total pardon to humans. This gift, for which God paid dearly, stems from his love for us, not from any deed or greatness on our part. God has given us tangible proof of this pardon. It is our ransom, the entrance fee to a relationship with him, the ticket out of hell that is essential to sanity. To make it tangible, he builds us a composite image of that gift throughout the Torah and Old Testament prophecies, then shows us the real thing in the Gospels.

God tells us what he wants of us, but acknowledges that we will be unable to do it perfectly--that sin is inevitable. His mercy is in giving us an easy "out" that still fulfills the requirement that the consequence of sin is death. This is the fundamental difference between the Bible and all other religions. God does not say we must be without sin before we can come to him. Rather, he gives us a provision for access to him as sinners. Since sin is inevitable, if we do not take the provision, we are permanent outlaws...lost, without hope.

Some think that the condensation of the law expressed by Jesus is softer than the version God gave to Moses. But this is not so. Jesus tells us "Thou shalt love the Lord thy God with all thy heart, and with all thy soul, and with all thy strength, and with all thy mind; and thy neighbor as thyself" (Luke 10:27). He is not making it any easier for us to keep the law than it would be to keep the six hundred and thirty odd commandments listed in the Pentateuch. Much of the Pentateuch addresses relatively "do-able" actions, rather than emotions we have no control over. Humans cannot love on command.

However, the point of the law, particularly Jesus' version of it, is to show us that we cannot save ourselves. As Paul states, the law is given to us to show us that "by grace are ye saved through faith: and that not of yourselves: it is the gift of God: Not of works, lest any man should boast" (Ephesians 2:8-9).

Comparing our behavior with God's standard certainly makes boasting impossible. Our taking his provision is the only thing that counts for righteousness as far as God is concerned. Perfect performance is neither expected nor is it an option. We have to go to God with a bent neck, not waving our credentials, which are as "filthy rags" (Isaiah 64:6). Our basic sense of unworthiness is no delusion, for it applies to our inability to pay the entrance fee to God and survive eternal darkness. If the price for sin is death, we cannot pay it and live. The only fee of any worth is the one God gave to us: Christ.

THE DAY OF ATONEMENT

The "gift" aspect of salvation is especially clear in the directives for the annual Day of Atonement. The people were asked to take a day of rest (i.e., a sabbath) while the priest made a sacrifice of burnt offerings in payment for the sins of the people (Exodus 30:10; Leviticus 16). This was to fulfil an agreement whereby God would forgive all their sins--the ones they knew about and the ones they were ignorant of.

Despite popular misconceptions about the God of the Old Testament, we certainly see no mean and vengeful old Yahweh here. Instead we see a loving lawmaker who provides an escape hatch in the law, a doorway that we lawbreakers can take to stay out of jail. This provision or cover was, and is, available at no cost to the sinner. No strings are attached.

It is critical to note that the required actions or rather, inaction, in no way *earned* the forgiveness. The definition of the Day of Atonement as a sabbath highlights the fact that no human effort can pay for sin. The human observance of this day of rest merely performed the function of signing a contract.

Why was an animal slaughtered? Bloodshed is absolutely essential. The law says that the price, or redemption value, for sin is death. The forgiveness contract must be signed with blood (found from Genesis on, but explicit in Leviticus 17:11, Matthew 26:28, and Hebrews 9:22). Blood ransoms us out of the hands of Satan, but it does not have to be our blood, nor can it be. The shed blood of any human, i.e., a sinner, cannot save anyone. That is why the pagan practise of human sacrifice is abhorrent to God. God lets us off the hook only through the blood of an unblemished substitute.

In the Old Testament, this substitute came from a specified group of animals. On the Day of Atonement, the shedding of the blood of the ram substituted for the blood of

humans.   Since it was to be observed once every year as an
"everlasting statute," humans obviously need constant cleansing.
We do not stop sinning.   The cleansing does not remove sin
from our nature, but removes the price of sin from our heads.
Without this pardon, we cannot approach God.   Blood is the
entrance fee; otherwise sin is the barrier.

Right from the start, God made it clear that *he* would
provide the substitute.   Adam and Eve found fig leaves to
cover themselves, but that did not suffice because there was no
shedding of blood.   God replaced them with animal skins.
Wearing the cover God gave them, Adam and Eve no longer
had to hide from him.

Humans cannot approach God without protective
covering.   Nor can we face life or ourselves without it.   Our
own flimsy psychological defense covering is just a bunch of fig
leaves; the cover has to come from God.   When Moses went
up to talk to God in Mount Sinai, God provided a cloud
cover, yet Moses returned glowing from the intensity of the
brilliant light emanating from God, the Shekinah glory (Exodus
33:10-11).   A cover is essential or we will be burnt to a crisp.

ONE STIPULATION

One of the many parallels between Adam and Eve's
original situation and our present one lies in the fact that God
only makes one reasonable stipulation on our relationship with
him.   Adam and Eve were given all the freedom in the world
except for one thing they were forbidden to do: eat the fruit
of a specific tree.   That was the only way they could rebel.
Nevertheless, albeit under Satan's influence, they committed that
one sin.

On the other hand, we who are strapped under a law
that makes it impossible for us to avoid sin, balk at the one
thing God asks us to do if we want to escape its terrible
consequence.   All we have to do is claim Jesus.   Despite
God's clear warnings, we got into a mess by doing the one
thing he asked us not to do in the Garden.   Now we refuse
to do the one thing that gets us out of our quandary.   Satan
has a strong role in that, too.   He blinds us to our
predicament and the easy escape God has given us.

Partly because the air is filled with false teaching about
the Bible, and partly because pride makes us want to control
our own destiny, we fail to see how easy God made it for us

to avoid hell. Even if we consider such a place or state to be only a slight possibility, we are utterly foolish if we reject the offer. As Pascal[3] pointed out, we have nothing to lose by accepting it, and everything to gain. On the other hand, we have nothing to gain by rejecting it, and everything to lose.

Jesus is the definitive covering for sin, our hell insurance. He fulfils all the metaphors and prophesies in the Old Testament with stunning accuracy. All we have to do is claim his death as the payment that buys us out of the separation from God that leads to hell (John 3:16; Romans 5:12-21)). When we go to God holding up the perfection of Jesus in front of our tainted selves, there is no barrier between us and God. Jesus took all the punishment that we deserve. We are under "no condemnation" (Romans 8:1), because God accepts his death in place of ours. He is the free pardon, the lamb of the Atonement whose blood was shed for us.

Moreover, he fulfils the requirement of the law that the sacrificed animal had to be "without blemish" (Exodus 12:5), or perfect and without sin. To fit that criterion Jesus must be God, because all humans are blemished.

Jesus said "I am the way, the truth, and the life: No man cometh unto the Father but by me" (John 14:6). In other words, without Christ as our cover or payment for sin, we are naked in our uncleanness and cannot come to God. Our sense of our own corruption tells us this. To state that we can reach God outside of Christ is to lie to ourselves.

From an intrapsychic perspective, reaching out for the free pardon is the one way to alleviate not only the guilt, but also the fear, rage and despair that otherwise torment humans. The guilt is dispelled when we have proof we are forgiven; the fear dissipates when we know we have a permanent rock beneath us; the rage is calmed when we know we have escaped from between a rock and a hard place; and the despair is replaced by hope. Now we have open access to God's loving ear and he sends the Holy Spirit to guide us. From this time on, our psychological defense equipment is redundant; psychological integrity is attainable. In fact, this is the only way we can be sound of mind.

ASLEEP ON THE TRACKS

However, the central importance of salvation from hell has slipped away from view even among today's Christian church attendees. In one study, members of different Judaeo-Christian denominations were asked to rank order the importance of salvation as compared to other values such as honesty, love, family security, a world at peace, forgiveness, and pleasure. Protestants ranked salvation fourth, Catholics ranked it thirteenth, and Jews and nonbelievers ranked it eighteenth. The Protestant ranking would have been lower if it had not been for the fact that the high proportion of Baptists in the sample ranked salvation first.[4]

Moreover, "salvation" for many who consider themselves Christians means being rescued from some sin, often an addiction, rather than from eternal darkness. In response to my question regarding whether or not her cocaine-addicted husband had been saved, one of my clients answered: "No, he's dead." We are falling asleep on the railway tracks.

WHY DIE THE FIRST TIME?

Because a just God keeps his promises, we all inherit the same fate as Adam: "Thou shalt return unto the ground; for out of it thou wast taken: for dust thou art, and unto dust shalt thou return" (Genesis 3:19). From the day of their rebellion, God cut off the Tree of Life from Adam and Eve, and our forefathers had to leave the Garden (Genesis 3:22).

Losing the connection with God not only meant physical death, it also meant losing God's protection from Satan. From that point on, humans have suffered physical decline, death, and darkness beyond that. Satan has been free to inflict upon us trials, tribulations, disease and confusion. His intention is to keep us lost by making us angry with God so we reject the door to salvation.

Some humans are born in hostile environments with the decks apparently stacked against them. They think: "A loving God would not have let me suffer like that." But, as the book of Job shows, God uses the work of Satan for his own purpose. Generally, we do not come to God willingly. He has to break our proud hearts many times over. Through that he forges us into stonger metal. Research shows that eighty percent of spiritually-committed people report that some crisis occurred prior to their commitment.[5]

God could have made faithful robots, but he gave us free will. He lets us suffer because he loves us and wants us to choose him; he is testing us. The choice to take his provision would be too easy if humans saw that those who did so never died nor suffered. We need to look at the larger picture. Instead of focusing on present ills or past hurts, our eyes need to be on the future, on the dire predicament our loving Father rescued us from. The fact that he uses suffering to achieve his ends is proven by Christ.

So claiming God's provision for sin does not restore us to our pre-Fall freedom. We all suffer physical death in this relatively brief pre-test for eternity, where the sheep are separated from the goats. But after death, physical life is restored to those who claim Christ.

WHAT IS MENTAL HEALTH?

Mental health is peace of mind about our eternal destiny through reconciliation with God. When we see the truth about our dilemma and reach out for the "life-belt" God has thrown to us, we can become sane. Our appreciation of the enormity of God's mercy initiates a major transformation inside us. Because he has given us proof that he loves us unconditionally, we cannot help loving him in return. We want to please God by doing what he asks; after all, his commandments are for our benefit. As our hearts of stone begin to change into hearts of flesh, helping others becomes natural. We can even find ourselves playing good Samaritan to an enemy. More than anything else, we want to warn others, friend or foe: "Look be'ind yer and claim Christ!"

Even so, the transformation is never total. At times we still find ourselves blindly giving in to our "secret faults" (Psalm 19:12), the darkness of our nature with its selfishness. However, the blanket pardon from God means we can stop hiding this and be relieved of the constant sense of unforgiven guilt nowadays called "low self-esteem." Perceiving God's mercy through his rescue enables us to see the cracked vessels we really are and internalize his compassion.

FREE AT LAST

"And ye shall know the truth, and the truth shall make you free" (John 8:32). In freeing us from the dark abyss, the truth of the Gospel frees us from psychological bondage:

It frees us from the constriction of internal defenses. We can openly engage with God in confession/repentance.

It frees us from the burden of layer upon layer of guilt, self-hatred, bitter rage, and the constant plague of fear.

It frees us to give and receive love.

It frees us to make decisions, to create, to take risks and act in faith because we know we have God's continuous support.

And it frees us from insanity and despair, putting our minds at rest and filling us with hope for the future.

Notes

1. "Psychodynamic" is a term originating in Freudian psychology. It has come to have a broader usage, referring to underlying emotional and motivational processes that operate below the level of consciousness.

2. Menninger, Karl (1973). Whatever Became of Sin? New York, New York: E.P. Dutton, Inc.

3. Pascal, Blaise (1958). Pensees. Translated by W. F. Trotter. New York.

4. Rokeach, M. (1973). The nature of human values. New York: Free Press.

5. Hall, C. M. (1986). "Crisis as opportunity for spiritual growth." Journal of Religion and Health, 25, pp. 8-17.

Chapter Two

WHY WE REJECT THE BIBLE

DESPITE ITS SCIENTIFIC BASIS

So...mental illness stems from an innate, universal sense of eternal damnation. This claim is based on the Bible's being literally true, from cover to cover. But is there evidence for this? And how many of us believe it?

Thirty one percent of all U.S. adults endorse the statement that "The Bible is the actual word of God and is to be taken literally, word for word."[1] The remainder express some degree of skepticism. Even many "Christians" ridicule the idea of complete, literal acceptance of the Bible.

The problem is that when humans begin to question the authenticity of the Bible, they have no idea where to stop. Each book in the Bible is a building block that adds to the credibility of its most important feature: the death and resurrection of Jesus Christ. What hope is there for any of us if we reject this center stone? This is the most important issue affecting the human race. Why do we fail to notice how important this is? Why do we spend so little time studying it?

Partly because we are too blind and afraid...afraid to find there really is nothing to hope for. However, our fear denies us access to surety. The fact is, when we explore the authenticity of the Bible, we discover the considerable support it has from other sources.

HUMAN CHARACTERISTICS THAT BLIND US

Before briefly surveying that support, let us consider several personal and cultural factors that Satan uses to lead many to reject the Bible before giving it a fair appraisal. These include fear, pride, pluralism, rebelliousness, scorn, cynicism, complacency, and ignorance.

31

FEAR

Adam's response to God after disobeying him was: "I heard thy voice in the garden, and I was afraid..." (Genesis 3:10). Our death sentence fills us with blinding fear.

There is a chicken/egg aspect to dealing with the fear. We have to see the bad news (our doom) before we can appreciate the good news (our free rescue). But we are afraid to see the bad news until we know the good news.

Somehow, a sense of God's total forgiveness must accompany a realization of the terrible danger we are in. Otherwise, fearing destruction, we block all thoughts of it from consciousness. We sense that a single transgression puts a gulf between us and God and this keeps us shut. False teaching makes us blame the Bible for the fear before giving ourselves a chance to learn that God's Word is the only refuge from it.

But once we are tucked under the safety of God's blanket pardon, we can loosen up and admit to that "one little sin." Our psychological defense apparatus begins to dissolve, gradually revealing all the other sins, big and small.

The more we see our depravity, the more we appreciate what God has done for us, and the more we love him. Although we will always be tainted, when we put on the cover of Christ we are connected with God. We are free to ask God to take charge of our pathological tendencies and meet all our needs.

The approach-avoid conflict

Benar[2] aptly describes the approach-avoid conflict we have regarding confession. On one hand, we want to confess because it relieves guilt and anxiety. It reestablishes a sense of connection with God.

Yet on the other hand, we run from it. The most important reason for this is not, as Benar, a Catholic priest states, out of our embarrassment in front of another human. Non-Catholics, who are not required to speak to a human confessor, avoid confession too.

The avoidance stems from two falsehoods: 1) God's forgiveness is not total; and 2) it is not given to us freely. The truth is 1) absolutely everything is covered, and 2) we do not have to earn or beg for it. By claiming Christ as the sacrifical lamb, the one who takes the blame for us, we are freed from all condemnation (Romans 8:1).

"Confess" comes from the Latin "con-" meaning "together," and "fatere" meaning "to acknowledge." It means "to acknowledge together." Confession is, in fact, an acknowledgement of what God already knows. In confessing we are agreeing with God instead of arguing with him.

So when we duck confession, we are trying to hide from God. It is a farce, because deep down we know when we have sinned and we know he knows. But we dare not consciously acknowledge sin knowing it damns us. It would be impossible for us to function from one moment to the next if we knew Satan's axe could fall at any time. So we hide behind the self-deception of psychological defenses. Sticking our heads in the sand, we leave our tails exposed.

The hiding and the terror abate when we perceive that God's forgiveness is a foregone conclusion. It is critical to understand that grace, the unmerited pardon, precedes repentance from sin, not vice versa.[3] If repentance were a prerequisite, grace would not be grace. It would not be unmerited. Grace comes first...the uniqueness of Christianity realized by relatively few.

It works this way: we cannot repent (reject sin) until we confess, we cannot confess until we see our sin, and we defend against seeing our sin until we are sure of being forgiven. But when we see the enormity of God's mercy towards us, repentance is natural. There is nothing forced about it; we are no longer under the gun. This is why salvation produces works, not vice versa. Works come out of the sense of freedom and gratitude towards God. No real transformation can occur otherwise.

Yet fear is the doorway to this freedom. The same fear that can keep us away from God is the entrance to salvation. "The fear of the Lord is the beginning of knowledge" (Proverbs 1:7). God gives us fear for a reason. Once we realize the bind we are in and see the open door of grace, it is clear that there is nowhere else to go. We are driven towards him.

PRIDE

Pride is another reason we reject or ignore the Bible. Nobody truly believes it possible for humans to shed all their flaws, to never miss the mark one *iota*. Nevertheless, pride makes us delude ourselves about our purity or power to attain it. Pride makes us fail to see the awesomeness of God and our dependency on him. We cannot stand the idea of being dependent on anyone or being in anyone's power.

Pride causes our downfall. Satan appealed to Adam and Eve through their pride. He told them they could have godly power and immortality if they ate from the forbidden Tree of Knowledge. But they went from freedom under God to enslavement under Satan. There are we all unless we claim the God-given pardon, Christ.

Claiming God's forgiveness means admitting we need it and dropping pride. Most of us refuse to do this until desperate. It is tough to acknowledge we are neither gods nor even "nice people" but flawed human beings who have no power over their destiny.

Perhaps we can achieve much through our own efforts. Unbelievers seem to be able to succeed. But the wicked only prosper temporarily. The fact is, the blessing of God's rain falls on the just and the unjust. A basically God-fearing nation receives a good portion of that rain. Many of us who became believers later in life can look back on our atheistic days and recall times we felt that a supernatural force was helping us. The invisible hand of God extends to all his children. None of us has a clear view of his involvement in "our" attainments. However, even if we could claim all responsibility for success in this world, the most important feat is beyond our capability. All our good works are minuscule compared with God's rescue from hell.

Self-inflation can be defensive. The grandiosity of a "false self" covers up the depravity we dare not face. Jung called this false self the "persona," believing its universality meant it was archetypical, or innate (see Chapter Four). But the false self is not innate. It loses its utility when we claim the safe cover of Christ.

For the most part, our propensity to glory in ourselves is not defensive. It is a basic element of our egocentric nature. Safe in heaven, Satan needed no defense, yet pride is what influenced the fool to try to build a throne higher than God (Isaiah 14:13). And until they disobeyed God, Adam and Eve had no need for defense.

False religion is filled with pride. Liberal "Christianity" is filled with pride. Said one prominent Methodist pastor in San Francisco: "I don't need anybody's blood to wash me clean."[4] Pride will keep us away from the truth that saves us.

PLURALISM

Ignorance of the Bible does not stop human beings from having strong opinions about it. These days a kind of pluralistic "openness" is valued as a "good." It is accompanied by a "holier-than-thou" condemnation of the "narrow-mindedness" of Bible-believers. These supposedly open-minded people would never dream of reading the Bible. Yet they declare they accept all "truths," all creeds, and all philosophical systems. And yes, they accept the Bible, too. They fail to realize that being open to the Bible means being closed to everything else. The God of the Bible tells us to reject every other source of spiritual knowledge, for Satan's influence is in all of them. Only the Bible offers a God-given reprieve from eternal darkness.

Nothing is examined in depth, particularly a person's own assumptions. To examine any non-biblical belief system in depth only exposes the holes (see Chapters Nine to Thirteen). The fact is, only the Bible can withstand scrutiny.

There are those who consider lack of closure on a religious belief system a sign of maturity.[5],[6] If that were applied to politics, "mature" people would find themselves unable to vote. Mature action must be based on commitment to some set of beliefs about the nature of reality, even if it is a provisional commitment where doubt plays a part. Gordon Allport characterized mature religious sentiment as "fashioned in the workshop of doubt...theoretical skepticism is not incompatible with practical absolutism. While it knows all the grounds for skepticism, it serenely affirms its wager." Allport goes on to state that in acting on the commitment to God, the doubts gradually disappear.[7]

REBELLIOUSNESS

Rebelliousness grows out of pride. It opposes rules, which ultimately means God's law. Question authority, it says, as it leads down the pathway of corruption.

Breaking away from moral absolutes permits the blinding, self-justifying influence of selfish needs and desires to dominate. It gives license to do anything a person feels like, because everything has equal validity and there is no higher authority than the personal ego.

Taking this to its logical extreme, rape, murder, and theft can become part of the terrain. Everything is beautiful in its own way.   Guilt feelings are an artifact of a judgmental society which takes its standards from that tool of manipulation, the Bible.   Such a statement was made by the existential psychologist, Rollo May, at a conference for pastoral counselors held in Berkeley, California.[8]

I can make it in hell, I'm tough, nobody can break me. Oh yeah?   Find out.   Spend eternity appreciating the stupidity of rebellion.

SCORN AND CYNICISM

"Blessed is the man that...sitteth not in the seat of the scornful" (Psalm 1:1).   To sit on that seat is to stay on the fence as a disdainful observer who cannot be a participator.   It is paralysis in the guise of personal freedom.   Nothing has meaning or value; nothing is fully embraced or trusted except nihilism, a rejection of all belief systems.   Scornful fence-sitting leads only to despair, isolation and powerlessness.   There is nothing to lean on and no basis for the faith which has to precede action.   The cynic cannot believe there is no catch in God's grace, that he does not have to pay for it.

To believe the Bible requires the openness of a child, the very opposite of scorn and cynicism.   Perceiving God's gift of ransom will give us the true sense of personal freedom, the freedom to move instead of sitting on the fence.

COMPLACENCY

Complacency is a kind of tunnel vision...a narrowed focus that avoids existential reality.   Just as long as we do not look at the juggernaut...

IGNORANCE

It is remarkable that ignorance of the Bible goes largely unnoticed by unbelievers.   In fact, this "Scripture-deafness" is consistent with prophesy (Matthew 4:12).   So many humans feel compelled, somehow, to possess a Bible but do not bother to read it.   At the "Great Books"-oriented small liberal arts college I attended as an undergraduate, the greatest book of all, the world's most widely-owned book, was not on the syllabus.

Not only are most of us ignorant about the Bible, we are also ignorant of the increasing evidence for its factual validity...

SCIENCE AND THE BIBLE

Many suppose that history and science contradict the inerrancy of the Bible. Not so. In all fields of study, even the occult, if there is apparent lack of support for the Bible it is only superficial. Close inspection reveals the chinks in the armor through which biblical truth shows. Consequently, science can be a tool to help us deepen our belief in the biblical truth that will save us. To prove this, let us dip into a variety of areas of empirical investigation.

THE BIBLE IS NO MYTH

There is growing trend among anthropologists and other students of folklore to treat the Bible metaphorically. They reject the factual and historical in it, while seeking the parallels it has with "other" mythology. Joseph Campbell,[9] for example, is an adept portrayer of the Bible as myth. Although there is truth in Campbell's view that the Bible has the same underlying message as folklore, this is because all myths point to the true facts in the Bible.

Campbell's misconceived notion of the message told by both the Bible and mythology is that humans can transcend the limitations of their earthly existence and achieve immortality. Jesus follows the line of the universal hero archetype, a blueprint for the godhood which, according to the Jungian psychology Campbell espouses, all humans can manifest (see Chapter Four).

For theorists such as Campbell, the factual basis to the Bible is irrelevant. The flood, the Exodus and the resurrection are merely symbols, unconscious templates which point the way for an upward human journey, a journey that in no way depends on the Creator's work of atonement.

However, it makes sense that the common flood "myth" found in many cultures has a historical basis. This is the "no smoke without fire" approach that can, and should, take us to believe the detailed account of a great flood in Genesis (7:10-24).

The underlying themes of the world's myths support the Bible as historically correct. The smoke of the myths agrees with the fire of the Bible. We miss the biblically-validating aspect of myths if we fail to conceptualize the Bible as fact.

The woman in the river

For example, in one mythical illustration described by Campbell,[10] we find a woman who seems to be helplessly caught in a river, with her torso half in the water and half out. Standing on one bank of the river is a shaman (priest) who is pulling her out of the water; on the opposite bank are several snakes in pursuit of her.

Campbell interprets this as signifying the journey each of us can make from the darkness of the unconscious submarine world into the light. But it would be more fitting to interpret the river as our existential dilemma, a breech that must be crossed. From a biblical point of view, this is an accurate notion of the human condition: no way out of our doom without a rescuer (the shaman in the present case) who in some way bridges the gap between God and man. The devil, frequently symbolized in snake form, waits to get us on the opposite side.

Campbell fails to mention the sharp contrast of the two banks of the river, one of which appears to represent safety, the other, doom. Also he makes no comment on the pivotal role of the shaman rescuer, a type of Jesus Christ. When we dismiss Campbell's interpretation, we see that what really comes out in the myth is our inherent knowledge that we depend on a God who comes to our rescue in human form.

The Bible is filled with metaphors for Christ, but that does not mean Christ is a metaphor and the resurrection not factual. Throughout the Bible, the book God wrote for humans, he uses what humans have found to be a basic principle of human learning, such as we see in the research of Piaget,[11] Bruner,[12] and Heidbreder,[13] and find systematized in Montessori education. This principle is that we derive abstract concepts from concrete experiences. God uses actual elements and metaphors to get the message of salvation into our minds. Without such tangibles, the concept of God's grace would be incomprehensible.

Campbell, Jung (see Chapter Four) and others correctly see archetypical programming in the thematic similarities of the mythology from widely spread cultures. Because they are blind to the message of the Gospel which is evident in myths, they deny biblical truth as being the source of archetypes. Instead, they postulate Satan's theme: that we are gods able to transcend mortality as we seek the enlightenment contained inside us.

The fact is, we walk around with the most amazing information programmed into us, dating back to the very first humans and the promises God made to them. As Jung pointed out, we do possess a "hero" archetype in our collective unconscious. This is based on the real one who laid down his life for us. This truth is more exciting than any of the myths and legends derived from it (see Chapter Four on biblical archetypes).

THE BIBLICAL BASIS OF ASTROLOGY

Likewise, studying the underpinnings of astrology points us towards biblical truth. It is common knowledge that the stars have been identified with the same zodiac signs for thousands of years. Less well-known is that the zodiac signs actually foretell Christ, both in the images viewed in the constellations and in the names of the brightest stars.

The Bible says that God named the stars (Psalm 147:4; Isaiah 40:26). Our planet is peopled with the descendants of Adam and Eve who fanned out after Great Flood (Genesis 10), carrying all the ancestral knowledge God put into them. Thus it is hardly surprising that the Hebrews, the Aztecs, the Babylonians, the Norsemen, the Egyptians, and the Chinese all recognize essentially the same meanings of constellations and have identical names for the stars.[14]

The stars tell a story of doom and redemption. Each constellation makes a different statement about Christ. The heroic Orion, for example, has one foot raised to crush the head of a serpent, consistent with the first biblical prophesy on Christ. God told the serpent, Satan: "...it (Christ, the seed of the woman) shall bruise thy head (plan), and thou shalt bruise his heel (body)" (Genesis 3:15).

In Job, reportedly the earliest-written book of the Bible, several stars are mentioned by name, including Arcturus, meaning "he comes," a reference to the Messiah (Job 38:31-32).

It is clear that the biblically prophetic meaning of the stars was widely known at the time Christ came into the world. The wise men of the east used the heavenly timetable and map to learn of the birth and location of the Messiah that the stars foretold (Numbers 24:17). But this was not astrology, the worldly practise of attempting to read the course of individual human lives from the stars. The biblical theme on which astrology was founded has been contaminated by an overlay of the occult, an outcome of Satanic influence. Astrology has become the fatalistic worship of stars as the guiding forces in our lives. This is a form of idolatry, the reason why the practice of an "observer of times" was forbidden by God (Deuteronomy 18:10).

THE EVOLUTION HOAX

Says Julian Ripley: "It hardly seems wise to base a philosophic outlook on the meaning of life upon the generalities of contemporary science, no matter how well founded these may appear to be at the moment."[15]   Yet even though Darwin's theory of evolution lacks scientific foundation, the civilized world has adopted it as if it were fact. Even the popular theory of reincarnation feeds off it, with its notion of the evolution of the soul.

Despite the fact that what Darwin called the "theory" of evolution is generally treated as established fact, the scientific community is producing more and more data which conflict with the evolutionary hypothesis. These data lend increasing support to the Genesis account.[16]

Actually, devolution, rather than evolution, accords with our laws of thermodynamics, which predict entropy in a closed system. With energy running down in our universe, we would expect decreasing differentiation and specialization. Counter to the law of entropy and without a mechanism to explain it (teleology assumes a master planner), evolution defines the "ascent" of man. The most complex life forms appear last in the "great chain of being," an order which happens to coincide with the Genesis account of life appearing on the earth.[17]

As far as the fossil evidence goes, a series of creations is a better fit to the data than any of the evolutionary theories, particularly with regard to the concept of "punctuated equilibrium." Due to lack of any evidence of intermediate forms, punctuated equilibrium describes sudden "evolutions" of new life forms in local geographical areas. The new life forms are radically different from anything else in existence, and their appearance cannot be resolved with a slow and gradual evolutionary process which requires fossil evidence of links in the great chain.

Evolutionists can give no explanation for the apparently sudden, dramatic appearance of a totally new creature. It just sort of happens as an exciting facet of the "evolutionary" process. Yet punctuated equilibrium, which has no adequate causal explanation outside of a supernatural one, is now widely accepted by eminent anti-creationist scientists such as Stephen Gould.[18] In a most unscientific manner, these theorists try to bend evolutionary theory to fit something that looks exactly like creation. It seems that only blindness could stop scientists from seeing how much closer is the phenomenon of punctuated equilibrium to Genesis than any hypothetical evolutionary process.

Recent research in genetics similarly supports the Genesis story of the creation. Since there is such detailed similarity in the genetic structure of all members of the human race, and since this genetic structure is radically different from that of even the "closest" great ape, it points to the human race having descended from one original "Eve." What is even more remarkable is that this Eve presumably had a genetically identical mate. So there were two genetically identical mutants popping into existence in the same place at the same time, an event bearing great resemblance to a miracle. The same genetic research postulates that this appearance was relatively recent, perhaps one hundred thousand years ago. This is much closer to some Bible historians' stabs at dating Adam and Eve six thousand years back than any previous "scientific" date for the advent of humans.[19,20]

Furthermore, recent research on the history of language points to Hebrew as the basis for all existing tongues. Linguists have concluded that the ancient root language they call "Indo-European" originated in Anatolia, resting place of Noah's ark. This lends further support to the Bible account of the first humans and their descendants in Genesis.[21,22]

If we did not know, somewhere inside us, that God created the universe, the findings of a 1991 Gallup Poll would make no sense. In spite of the ban on teaching creationism in our public educational system for most of the present century, 47 percent of all Americans report that they believe God created man in his present form within the last 10,000 years; another 40 percent favor the idea of a God-guided evolution over millions of years.[23]

THE BIG BANG

Scientists claim to have reconstructed the events that took place during the first few seconds after the hypothetical Big Bang. However, they are still unable to explain this incredible creative explosion as a non-supernatural event. They think that because they *seem to* have been able to extrapolate back to a little from a lot, they will therefore be able to extrapolate even further back from a little to nothing. But this contradicts the first law of thermodynamics. Nothing can come from nothing.[24]

To detractors, the Genesis account of the creation seems implausibly geocentric, proof of the immaturity of its writer. It does not follow the steps scientists hypothesize, but describes the creation of the sun, moon and stars following the creation of the earth. However, the facts show that the earth *is* special. No other heavenly body appears to support life as we know it. Moreover, the scientific community knows nothing with any surety. We are finding that other planets do not behave in the manner predicted by current scientific theories. Neptune, for example, has two moons that go in a direction opposite to all the other moons. It is clear that we do not know enough to refute the biblical view of the creation. There is now a growing body of research in the area of creation science that supports the Bible's account.[25]

SCIENTIFIC VALIDITY AND GOD'S WORD

How well does the Bible stand up to scientific scrutiny? Can we say the Bible is an accurate measuring instrument of God's word according to scientific standards? There are several accepted criteria for determining the scientific validity of a psychological testing instrument. To answer the question we have just posed, we can apply four of these criteria to the Bible: concurrent, predictive, face and construct validities. This may appear an unorthodox way to attempt to establish the authenticity of the Bible as God's word, but the truth is that we can, and must, use our minds as well as our hearts in this matter.

CONCURRENT VALIDITY

Concurrent validity requires that there be agreement between the instrument in question and other measuring instruments sensitive to the same phenomenon during the same time period. If the Bible has concurrent validity, we should be able to find independent witnessess who report the same facts that are recorded in Scripture.

Through archaeological discoveries, increasing amounts of evidence show that biblical historical accounts coincide with accounts found in other ancient documents.[26] In the last century, some of our knowledge has been unlocked by the discovery of the Rosetta stone, the key to the hieroglyphic writings of early historians.

Consider the flood. Inscribed on twelve tablets written by king Gilgamesh in a form of Akkadian dated to 1700 B.C., an epic story of a flood was found in the ancient library at Ur at the turn of this century. The events described bear much similarity to the Genesis account; only the names are changed.[27]

Consider also the Exodus. Other historical documents coincide with the Biblical account of the sudden departure of thousands of Israelites from Egypt.[28] Aside from the Bible, we have not found a historical account stating that God was responsible for this. Yet without supernatural intervention, it is very hard to explain why a Pharaoh with an ambitious building program would suddenly let go of thousands of useful slaves, complete with flocks of animals, gold and jewelry.

Detractors have claimed the very personage of Jesus Christ to be a myth, but several early historians made reference to him. Among the non-Christian ones were the Jewish historian, Flavius Josephus,[29] and the Roman historian, Cornelius Tacitus,[30] both of whom described the false charges leading to the cruxifiction.

So far, nothing suggests the Bible to be historically inaccurate. It has concurrent validity because other historical accounts agree with it.

PREDICTIVE VALIDITY

If the Bible has predictive validity, then the prophecies in it cannot err. The reader is invited to discover, through personal biblical inquiry, that they do not. Bible prophets accurately described both events that would take place soon after their words were uttered, and events that would take place many hundreds of years later.

The first type of prediction established the authenticity of the prophets, ensuring an immediate audience. The second type, concerning Christ and end times, were for the salvation of humankind. With the exception of events connected with end times that still await us, every other prophesy has taken place as predicted.

Anyone who pays serious attention to the Bible prophets and studies history has to regard the Bible as a supernatural source of information. The only other possible explanation for the degree of accuracy displayed by Bible prophecies is that they were written *post hoc*, but there is considerable evidence against that.[31]

The Gospel according to Matthew conveniently refers us back to the Psalms, Micah, Isaiah, Zechariah and other prophets for a host of uncannily accurate predictions concerning events in the life, death, and resurrection of Jesus. The prophesies about Christ date from as far back as God's previously mentioned promise to Satan in the Garden of Eden (Genesis 3:15): "And I will put enmity between thee and the woman, and between thy seed and her seed; it shall bruise thy head, and thou shalt bruise his heel." The Bible gives us the genealogy between Eve and Jesus (Luke 3:23-38)[32] so that we make no mistake that Jesus was the seed of the woman who bruised the head of the seed of Satan. In other words, Jesus thwarted the entire plan of Satan, whereas Satan only managed to maim the body of Jesus, symbolized by his heel.

Such consistency in the fulfilment of prophesy means that according to the criterion of predictive validity, the Bible is an accurate measuring instrument. It measures, or describes, something of a supernatural order operating over thousands of years: the word of God.

Now, even if we have doubts about reportage, and concern ourselves *ad nauseam* with whether or not Moses really wrote the books biblically attributed to him, this prophetic aspect of the Bible cannot be dismissed. It should warrant attention from those among us who are even slightly curious about the world. Yet we humans are largely blind to Bible prophesy. If curious about the future, we take our information from the devil's minions. These are the world's "scientific" forecasters who present extrapolation as if it were revelation, not to mention the more obviously occult stargazers and spirit channelers.

Our blindness to the importance of Bible prophesy only makes sense if we factor in the prophecies concerning this very phenomenon. For example, Isaiah (6:10) related God's intent to "Make the heart of this people fat, and make their ears heavy, and shut their eyes; lest they see with their eyes, and hear with their ears, and understand with their heart, and convert, and be healed."

FACE VALIDITY

Face validity refers to whether or not an instrument bears an immediately discernible resemblance to the underlying construct it is supposed to tap. If the Bible is the word of God, we expect to see miracles in it, and, of course, we do. With few exceptions, the credibility of all writers of the Bible is established by miracles God performed in front of or through them.

Scorners try to explain these away as natural phenomena, but they are unsuccessful, especially concerning the one miracle that counts most. The cornerstone on which all the importance of the Bible rests is the resurrection of Christ, which has not been refuted as a historical event. In fact, the few serious attempts to do so have led to the very opposite; hard-headed detractors have become firm believers.[33]

Much as anyone may try to argue against the resurrection, we cannot get away from the fact that none of Christ's foes ever came up with a contradictory account that stuck. The chief priests paid the Roman guards to spread a story (Matthew 28:11-15), but that was as far as it went. They could easily have produced a mutilated body that they claimed to be his. We have no report of their trying this. The reason they did not seriously try to contest the resurrection was because the return of Jesus was seen by so many of his followers. These followers were completely transformed by the experience. Mice turned into lions. For example, Peter, who once hid his connection with Christ, became an eloquent spokesman for him (Acts 2:14-38).

CONSTRUCT VALIDITY

Lastly we have construct validity, a complex concept bearing on many facets of the fit between instrument and data, including soundings from other types of validity and reliability. We focus here on two aspects of construct validity: internal consistency and parsimony.

Internal consistency refers to the degree to which an instrument taps a unitary concept. Many people see the Old and New Testaments as conveying two entirely different messages. This is not so. The Bible is internally consistent in the sense that a series of witnesses all report the same theme throughout the Old and New Testaments. The theme is that although we are doomed by God's law, there is potential redemption through claiming his provision for sin.

The second aspect of construct validity of interest to us is parsimony, which appears to be an inherent facet of the human mind. Parsimony has been the subject of considerable research by the Gestalt school of psychology.[34] In the 1930s, researchers in Gestalt theory determined some principles by which the human mind perceives and organizes information. Parsimony is collectively defined by the basic perceptual tendencies towards closure, good figure and Pragnanz (a combination of meaning, simplicity and completeness).

Parsimony is a major standard for the applicability of a construct or theory to a set of facts. The most parsimonious theory is generally the one that gets the most votes. That is, the one that is most inclusive, explains data in the simplest and most elegant way, and gives a sense of closure. God has given us a parsimonious eye for a reason: so that we will find him when we look around us. His handiwork is everywhere. "God did it" is the most parsimonious explanation for the origins of the universe, the coming of life to this planet, the history of mankind and the structure of the human psyche. What is simpler yet more inclusive than the Bible's account of a Creator? So far, we have been unable to refute it. As we will see in the following chapters, the sin/death equation is the most parsimonious explanation for psychopathology.

Overall, based on consideration of these criteria borrowed from psychological test construction, the Bible has every appearance of being a valid instrument of God's word.

SUMMARY AND CONCLUSIONS

The core mental health problem is a universal, innate sense that humans are destined to spend eternity in darkness. This claim can only be as as true as the Bible. However, it is commonly assumed, even among many who consider themselves Christian, that the Bible is largely myth. This is dangerous. It leads us to question the truth of Christ as the payment for sin; it will lose us our salvation.

In this chapter we looked at some human characteristics that Satan uses to makes us refuse to take the Bible seriously. These are fear, pride, pluralism, rebelliousness, scorn, cynicism, complacency, and ignorance.

We went on to see that our ignorance is vast. Not only does it apply to the Bible, but also to science. The physical and social sciences are generally considered irrelevant or antithetical to the Bible. In fact, not only the sciences but also some occult practises support the Bible as factual. This is true of myths and folklore; astrology; fossil data and genetic exploration; the laws of thermodynamics; history; and psychological research and theory. Over and over, the Bible fulfils the major criteria for the scientific basis of a measuring instrument. It measures, or taps, God's word.

Notes

1. Princeton Religious Research Center (1990). Religion in America. Princeton, New Jersey: Author.

2. Benar, C. A. (1989). "Personality Theories and Asking Forgiveness." Journal of Psychology and Christianity, 8(1), 45-51

3. "Repent" is translated in the Old and New Testaments from words with two different meanings. (1) The Hebrew "shub" and the Greek "metanioa" both imply turning or changing the mind; (2) the Hebrew "naham" and the Greek "metamelomai" imply regret, or sorrow. According to the first meaning, repentance does precede grace: we must turn our heads to look at God so as to perceive grace. Regret and sorrow come after we are freed by grace to see ourselves as we really are.

4. Personal communication from Cecil Williams at a Sunday service at Glide Memorial Methodist cathedral on August 3, 1987.

5. Batson, C. D., and Ventis, W. L. (1982). The religious experience: A social-psychological perspective. New York: Oxford University Press.

6. Meadow, M. J., and Kahoe, R. D. (1984). Psychology of religion: Religion in individual lives. New York: Harper and Row.

7. Allport, G. W. (1950). The individual and his religion: A psychological interpretation. New York: Macmillan, p. 72

8. Rollo May stated, in a speech during a workshop for pastoral counselors at Calvary Presbyterian church, Berkeley, May 11, 1987, that "guilt is a product of fundamentalist religion."

9. Joseph Campbell (1972). Myths To Live By. New York: Viking Penguin, Inc.

10. Joseph Campbell (1988). The Power of Myth. New York: Doubleday, page 157.

11. Piaget, Jean and Inhelder, B. (1969). The Psychology of the Child. New York: Basic Books.

12. Bruner, Jerome S., Olver, Rose R., Greenfield, P. M. et al. (1966). Studies in Cognitive Growth. New York, New York: Wiley.

13. Heidbreder, E. (1945). "Toward a Dynamic Psychology of Cognition." The Psychological Review, 52(Whole No. 1).

14. Fleming, Kenneth C. (1981). God's Voice in the Stars. Neptune, New Jersey: Loizeaux Brothers, Inc.

15. Ripley, Julian (1964). The elements and structure of the physical sciences. New York, New York: John Wiley and Sons, Incorporated, p. 235

16. Morris, Henry (1976). The Genesis Record. San Diego: Creation Life.

17. Peck, M. Scott (1978). The Road Less Travelled. New York, New York: Simon and Schuster, Inc., p.265. Peck points out the incongruence between evolution and entropy.

18. See Newsweek, March 29, 1982, p. 45, for a discussion of the debate following Stephen Jay Gould's assertion that punctuated equilibrium is an evolutionary phenomonon

19. "How we came from Eve" (April 29, 1990). San Francisco Examiner, pp. 15-16.

20. Ackerman, P. D. (1990). In God's image after all. Grand Rapids, Michigan: Baker Book House.

21. For example, we know that certain Hebrew abstract formulations are common to Babylonian and Aramaic languages. The code of Hammurabi of Babylon, written around 2,000 B.C. displays Hebraic linguistic influences.

22. "The Mother Tongue" (Nov 5, 1990). US News and World Report, pp. 60-70.

23. "The Creation." (December 23, 1991). U.S. News and World Report, pp. 56-64.

24. The first law of thermodynamics refers to the conservation of energy in a closed system. According to this law, it is impossible for any form of energy to emerge from no form of energy.

25. For example:

Gange, William (1986). <u>Origins and Destiny</u>. Dallas, Texas: Word Publishing.

McArthur, John (1991). <u>Voice of Calvary</u> tape series, Box 2000, Eugene, Oregon, 94702.

Sunderland, Luther D. (1988). <u>Darwin's Enigma: Fossils and Other Problems</u>. Santee, California: Master Book Publishers.

Schroeder, G. L. (1991). <u>Genesis and the big bang.</u> New York, New York: Bantam Books.

26. Keller, Werner (1981). <u>The Bible as History</u>. New York, New York: William Morrow and Company, Inc.

27. Ibid, Chapter 4, p. 50.

28. Ibid, Chapter 10, p. 118.

29. Josephus, Flavius (early second century). <u>Antiquities</u>, xviii, 33.

30. Tacitus, Cornelius (A.D. 80-84). <u>Annals</u>, XV, 44.

31. For example, the book of Daniel purports to be a first person account written during his lifetime, after the Babylonian captivity in 605 B.C. Evidence Daniel was written before the events prophesied therein can be found in the fact that Ezekiel, purportedly writing after 586 B.C., refers to Daniel by name, that Daniel uses the Babylonian calender in his writing, and that his account provides details of Babylonian history that could only be known to an insider at the time the events occurred. One such detail is his use of the term "Chaldean" to designate a class of wise men and advisors, a fact only known from the later discovery of Babylonian records.

32. There is some fuzziness about the exact parentage of Mary. Although Luke gives Heli as the father of Joseph, Joseph's father is given as Jacob by Matthew. Since Mary was reportedly a cousin of Joseph, it is possible that Heli was her father rather than Joseph's.

33. McDowell, Josh (1972). <u>Evidence that demands a verdict: historical evidence for the Christian faith</u>. San Bernardino, California: Campus Crusade for Christ International.

34. Wertheimer, M. (1958). "Investigations of Gestalt Theory" in D. C. Beardsall and M. Wertheimer (Eds.), <u>Readings in Perception</u>. Princeton, New Jersey: Yale University Press, pp. 115-135.

Chapter Three

PSYCHOLOGY BEARS WITNESS

TO THE BIBLE

Psychology. Liberal Christians love it;[1] conservative Christians hate it.[2] However, neither position is tenable; this is not an all-or-nothing situation.

Psychology has an important role in helping us understand the Bible. It demonstrates how events in the Garden of Eden have shaped the human psyche. In particular, it shows how our unconscious sense of condemnation affects us. For example, the concept of an "unconscious defense mechanism" explains our universal existential blindness. Some highly relevant factual and conceptual babies are left behind when the secular, theoretical bathwater is drained out.

However, the utmost caution is needed when dealing with psychology. "Christian" psychologists often defend their exclusive use of psychological concepts with the statement that "all truth is God's truth." It is true that all truth is God's truth. But to avoid mentioning salvation through Christ in psychotherapy is to dismiss its importance. It is a lie by omission. Much of what we consider "truth" is just that.

Plenty of Christians are afraid to stand up for Christ out of fear of social ostracism and economic downfall. "We have a business to run," was a defense I heard at one major "Christian" counseling enterprise in the San Francisco Bay area.

There is also the problem that "at the present time there is no acceptable Christian psychology that is markedly different from non-Christian psychology."[3] Up to now, Christian psychology has leaned on secular psychology for theory. If the Bible is used at all, it is to support such ungodly theory, rather than vice versa. The fallacies in psychological theory are laughable until we realize how many people are deceived by the web Satan has woven.

A BIBLE-BASED MODEL OF THE PSYCHE

Our theory says that psychopathology arises from a human psyche which has innate knowledge that the price for sin is death. This biblical model of the psyche goes hand-in-hand with a uniquely Gospel-based cure of mental illness.

Figure One depicts "before" and "after" perceiving the Gospel. In the drawing of the human figure, God's law sits in the centre of the sin nature. In diagram A, lacking the presence of Christ to completely resolve it, the dark, dooming law inside the blindfold individual's heart has painful jagged edges. He is rolling downhill in darkness towards the pit. In diagram B, the presence of Christ in the law keeps him on a continuous level surface out in the light with his eyes open. The jagged edges of the law are smoothed and softened by God's forgiveness. There is harmonious interplay between the law and the sin nature, whose hold on the person is reduced.

Figure One: The human psyche before and after Christ

Diagram A: before   Diagram B: after

Is is possible to prove this model? Should, indeed, scientific proof have to be provided, considering that most, if not all, psychological theory rests upon inferences and ideas that are purely speculative and hypothetical? The fact is, if I am not called upon to provide any more proof than any of the accepted theorists in the field of psychotherapy, all I need do is come up with a convincing theory. However, it is likely that if the mental health profession is to recognize its true biblical foundation, a lot more evidence will be required than in the case of any secular theory. As pointed out in the previous chapter, we humans have a stubborn resistance to the Bible. The parsimoniousness of the sin/death = mental illness equation may not be enough to convince us.

The model certainly fits the data. Chapters Seven, Eight, and Fourteen cover the ways in which the sin/death equation is manifested in all major psychiatric disorders. Here we look at two examples of the explanatory potential of this theory outside of psychiatry. These are 1) our maladaptive attributional tendencies; and 2) our pervasive low self-esteem.

ATTRIBUTION THEORY AND FEAR OF HELL

Attribution theory deals with our perception of who or what makes things happen, what causes the events in our lives. It has provided a fertile ground for research.[4]

A GENERAL BLAMING PATTERN

It is interesting that we humans display a general tendency to view ourselves as responsible for positive outcomes and outside forces as the source of negative ones.[5] We are more willing to take the credit than the blame. In fact, we go to great lengths to not look bad, either to others or to ourselves. Why? Pride is undoubtedly an element in this, but the tendency makes most sense as a defense. Refusal to acknowledge the flaws which make us deserve hell is an unconscious defense against our deadly sentence. Instead, we blame some outside force. It is nothing new: Adam blamed Eve for the Fall.

Except among those who know the Gospel (see below), the local exceptions to this overall tendency are equally off the mark. Severely depressed people over-attribute negative events to themselves, believing they are responsible for all the world's ills. As for positive events, they are blind to them.[6] Another variation is that people with an internal locus of control tend to see themselves as the cause of all good and bad: super-controllers. Conversely, externally-oriented people tend not to see themselves responsible for *anything*.[7] However, externals are more likely to attribute failure than success to external factors.[8]

In general, our psychological defense apparatus distorts our view of causality. We are blinded to our own shortcomings. This tendency has no survival value; it blocks learning. Denying our mistakes, we are condemned to repeat them over and over.

BLAMING GOD

This general blaming tendency is reflected in people's relationship with God. Many are angry with God without being conscious of it. Considerable evidence exists that people generally make attributions to God in circumstances that are important and have what they perceive to be negative outcomes.[9,10,11] As they see it, pain and misery in no way stem from the free-wheeling activities of Satan, nor from their own actions.

It is hard to comprehend that God uses hardship as a teaching tool for our benefit. Events go from bad to worse because we are too angry with God and too blind to turn towards him. However, as the Bible displays, God uses Satan to test us (see the entire book of Job). He puts us through the refining fire and helps us come out stronger. "All things work together for good to them that love God" (Romans 8:28).

The fact that people who have a highly developed sense of God do not display these blaming tendencies certainly supports the idea that they stem from existential defensiveness. Research shows that the closer people report feeling to God and the higher they score on the (Biblical) Fundamentalism scale, the more they tend to attribute positive events to him rather than negative ones.[12,13] Individuals with these same characteristics are also less likely to blame bad outcomes on other factors outside themselves.[14] This suggests that when people know the mercy of God, their attributions are reality-based. They are freed to face their human flaws and learn from mistakes. *The provision of Christ (solution) enables us to face reality*

LOW SELF-ESTEEM IS EXISTENTIAL GUILT

At the same time that humans avoid seeing themselves responsible for bad things that happen, they nevertheless seem unable to feel approval for themselves. We have recognized the "low self-esteem" plague, and there is a great deal of research and theorizing about it.[15] It is such a problem that there is, at the time of this writing, even a state-funded task force trying to remedy low self-esteem in California.

The problem goes far deeper than most realize. What we call low self-esteem is really existential guilt, or guilt over missing the mark. The fact is, we cannot love ourselves when our very human nature puts us under a death sentence. With doom hanging over us, our beauty as creatures made in God's image escapes us. Existential guilt produces constant feelings of being condemned, "wrong," unworthy, trapped and unloveable. This is why so-called low self-esteem is a component of every mental disorder listed in the Diagnostic and Statistical Manual of Mental Disorders (DSM-III-R).[16]

The apparent exceptions are those disorders involving grandiosity, narcissism, and delusions of omnipotence. But these exceptions prove the rule. The self-esteem manifested in these disorders is defensive: unrealistically inflated or delusional.

Low self-esteem is also common to the nonpsychiatric population. We know there must be something wrong with the constant feeling of dislike or downright loathing we feel towards ourselves, and we want to get rid of it. Yet if the available therapies were able to cure it, we would expect the inhabitants of California, that therapy-conscious state, to be better off than they are. Despite its extremely high proportion of psychotherapists, Marin county, for example, has one of the highest suicide rates in the United States.[17]

GOD IS THE LOOKING GLASS

Social science has shown that our concept of ourself is influenced by the way we think others see us: the "looking glass self."[18] But we make a big mistake if we assume that human attitudes are the foundation for self-esteem. Research shows self-esteem to be linked to a person's concept of God.[19] The Bible has been telling us this for thousands of years. It shows us our relationship with God is the foundation for all other relationships. Only the assurance of God's grace, his gift of a pardon enabling us to escape the consequence of missing the mark, will allow us to feel acceptance and compassion towards ourselves and others.

The way we think other humans see us is contaminated by our perspective on our self as we think God sees us. Until we have proof of God's love in the form of Christ, we assume he hates us. We make that projection into the darkness that separates us from him. Our mistake is in believing that God damned us instead of Satan.

Lacking God's love, we cannot believe other people could possibly love us. We block out love and let in hurt. Support and praise from others go unnoticed. Criticality or abusiveness sink in as they resonate with our existential guilt.

Compounding the problem is the fact that when we perceive only the malevolence which comes from others and none of the benevolence, our defensiveness makes us abusive. We cannot receive any love nor give any, but we can wound. Needing a relationship of some kind, we settle for a mutually abusive one unless it becomes too painful. If it ends, we blame the other for hurting us; we do not see our own role.

GOD AND FAMILY RELATIONS

All our relationships are diseased when we do not know Christ. The widely-lamented breakdown of marriage and the family in this nation is a result of a retreat from the Bible, the only source of knowledge of God's love. As each new generation slips further away from the Bible, it also moves further away from self-compassion, compassion for others, and the moral compass. Husbands and wives reflect their self-rejection in their marital relations, and parents with their children.

Child abuse is on the rise. Abused children who do not know God are doubly wounded. Ignorant of God and innately filled with existential guilt, they are wide open to the hurts coming from their parents and impervious to whatever affection may come their way. They feel under constant attack, both from the outside and from the inside. It is no wonder that increasing numbers of children display conscienceless, sociopathic tendencies. We are raising a generation of killers.[20]

However, even the most loving, God-filled parents cannot cure their child's searing, gut-wrenching existential guilt. For one thing, even a loving parent, acting out of his dark side, will sometimes treat a child unfairly or abusively. But the inconsistency of human love is not the real problem. The real problem is human love cannot keep anyone out of hell. It cannot provide a sense of being forgiven at the deepest level. Only God has power to stay execution. For each human being, only the love of the one "other" of genuine significance, i.e., God, can plumb the depths. God's love can over-ride hurt from all the rejections and abuses suffered at the unpredictable hands of even the most loving human significant other.

THE GOSPEL AND THERAPY

Therapy that does not convey this cannot produce fundamental change. If we do not go to the source of our self-loathing--guilt over missing the mark--we never reach its permanent solution. We rightly feel self-rejection until we begin to look at ourselves through God's compassionate eyes. It is essential that we know we are forgiven, safe for eternity.

Research on coping shows that our sense of God's attitude towards us is related to many aspects of our functioning. People who report a high degree of faith in a God they see as loving and providential involve that faith in the way they deal with life and score higher on a number of measures of positive coping. They cope much better than those view God as punishing and desirous of passive dependency.[21]

Such findings show that the focus on low self-esteem is a red herring. Yet even the Christian mental health community has blindly taken up its the banner.[22] The ambiguous term ought to be dropped from our psychological vocabulary. "Esteem" can mean "regard highly," and only God is worthy of high regard. In fact, some Christians have been found to reject positive statements of self-esteem because their realistic view of themselves as sinners does not permit them to agree.[23] A "sense of God's compassion" would be a better term for the ideal perspective on the self. This takes the emphasis off the person and places it on God and his gift to a flawed but forgiven sinner. This is the starting point for sanity. Only after humans perceive the gift of salvation can they fully appreciate the beauty and uniqueness of being human.

SUMMARY AND CONCLUSIONS

The purpose of this chapter has been to show that psychology amplifies and supports our understanding of the biblical model of the human psyche. Figure One pictures this model in terms of "before" and "after" the presence of Christ enters the psyche to resolve the sin/death conflict.

Psychology describes our human tendencies, the Bible

interprets them. Two examples of the parsimoniousness of our Biblical model were given: 1) our blaming patterns; and 2) the low self-esteem plague that has shown itself to be basically incurable through secular psychotherapy.

Such psychological examples show us that our Bible-based model of the human dilemma explains what makes humans tick as nothing else does. Only through this model can we fully understand human functioning.

Notes

1. Tyrrell, Bernard J. (1982).   Christotherapy, II.   Ramsey, New Jersey: Paulist Press.

2. Bobgan, Martin and Deirdre (1987).   Psychoheresy: the psychological seduction of Christianity.   Santa Barbara, California: Eastgate Publishers; see also Hunt, Dave and McMahon, T. A. (1985).   The Seduction of Christianity. Eugene, Oregon: Harvest House Publishers.

3. Bobgan, Martin and Deirdre (1987).   Psychoheresy: the psychological seduction of Christianity. Santa Barbara, California: Eastgate Publishers, p.5

4. Kelley, H. H. (1967).   "Attribution theory in social psychology."   In D. Levine (Ed.) Nebraska Symposium on Motivation, 15, Lincoln, Nebraska: University of Nebraska Press, 1967; see also Bandura, A. (1989) "Human agency in social cognitive theory." American Psychologist, 44, 1175-1184

5. For example:

Johnson, T. J., Feigenbaum,R. and Weiby, M. (1964).   "Some determinants and consequences of the teacher's perception of causation."   Journal of Educational Psychology, 55, pp. 237-246.
Streufert, S. and Streufert, S. C.   (1969).   "Effects of conceptual structure, failure, and success on attribution of causality and interpersonal attitudes." Journal of Personality and Social Psychology, 11, pp. 138-147.

Wortman, C. B., Constanzo, P. R., and Witt, T. R. (1973). "Effect of anticipated performance on the attributions of causality to self and others." Journal of Personality and Social Psychology, 27, pp. 372-381.

6. Seligman,m. E. P., Abramson, L. Y., Semmel, A., and von Baeyer, C. (1979). "Depressive attributional style." Journal of Abnormal Psychology, 88, pp. 242-247

7. Rotter, J. B. (1966). "Generalized expectancies for internal versus external control of reinforcement." Psychological Monographs, 80(Whole No. 609).

8. Davis, W. L., and Davis, D. E. (1972). "Internal-external control and attribution of responsibility for success and failure. Journal of Personality, 40, pp. 123-136

9. Metalsky, G. I. and Abrahamson, L. Y. (1980). "Attributional styles: Toward a framework for concetpualization and assessment." In P. C. Kendall and S. D. Hollon (Eds.), Assessment Strategies for Cognitive-Behavioral Interventions. New York: Academic Press, pp. 13-58

10. Miller, D. T. and M. Ross (1975). "Self-serving biases in the attribution of causality: Fact or fiction." Psychological Bulletin, 82, 213-225

11. Snyder, M. L., Stephan, W. G., and Rosenfield, D. (1978). "Attributional egotism." In J. H. Harvey, W. Ickes, and R. F. Kidd (Eds.), New Directions in Attribution Research, Vol. 2, Hillsdale, N. J.: Lawrence Erlbaum Associates, pp. 5-34

12. Gorsuch, R. L. and Smith, C. S. (1983). "Attributions of resopnsibility to God: A function of religious belief." Journal for the Scientific Study of Religion, 22(4), pp. 339-352

13. Spilka, B. C. and Schmidt, G. (1983). "General attribution theory for the psychology of religion: the influence of event-character on attributions to God." Journal for the Scientific Study of Religion, 22(4), pp. 326-329

14. Pargament, K. I. and Sullivan, M. (1981). "Examining attributions of control across diverse personal situations: A psychosocial perspective." Paper presented at the 1981 convention of the American Psychological Association, Los Angeles, CA.

15. For example: Lays, Julie (1990). "The Serious State of Self-Esteem: the California Task Force on Self-Esteem." California State Legislatures, 16(6); and California Task Force to Promote Self-Esteem and Personal and Social Responsibility (1988). Sacramento, CA (1130 K St., Suite 300, Sacramento, 95814): The Task Force.

16. Diagnostic and Statistical Manual of Mental Disorders (Third Edition-Revised) (DSM-III-R) (1987). Washington, DC: American Psychiatric Association.

17. Allen, Nancy (1973). Suicide in California 1960-1970. Sacramento, California: Department of Public Health.

18. Mead, G. H., Mind, Self, and Society. Chicago: University of Chicago Press, 1934

19. Benson, P. and Spilka, B. (1973). "God Image as a Function of Self-Esteem and Locus of Control." Journal for the Scientific Study of Religion, 12, pp. 297-310.

20. Ewing, Charles Patrick (1990). Kids Who Kill. New Jersey: Lexington Books.

21. Hathaway, W. L. and Pargament, K. I. (1991). "The Religious Dimensions of Coping: Implications for Prevention and Promotion." Prevention in Human Services, 9, 2, pp. 65-92.

22. Ellison, Craig W. (1984). Self-esteem. Blue Jay, California: Christian Association for Psychological Studies.

23. For example: Strunk, O., Jr., (1985). Dealing with proceptive counter-transference-like issues: The factor of psychotherapeutic ideology. In E. M. Stern (Ed.), Psychotherapy and the religiously committed patient. New York: Haworth, pp. 129-134.

Chapter Four

JUNG AND BIBLICAL ARCHETYPES

WHEAT AND TARES

Carl Jung (1875-1962)[1] and Sigmund Freud (1856-1939)[2] were system builders who imposed order on the workings of the human mind. These theorists dived below the surface and attempted to navigate in the murky depths of the psyche. The theories they came up with are unacceptable in the overall sense. However, their exploration of the unconscious realm has produced much that helps us understand the psychological importance of Scripture. Among the tares there is good wheat that enables us to understand the psychological impact of our terrible demise. The rest can be thrown away. Fact can be separated from fiction by using the Bible as the standard of comparison.

This chapter concentrates on Jung, who has gained great popularity a world which increasingly recognizes the spiritual aspect of mental health. He is the most established psychological theorist to openly espouse a spiritual perspective.[3] From liberal Christians to Buddhists to New Age, in pastoral or "transpersonal" counseling centers and training programs across the country, Jung's work is gaining acceptance.

THE TARES IN JUNG'S WORK

Jung explored his own psyche, the minds of his analysands, and the collective minds of whole societies. His material was dreams, myths, fantasies, symbolism in art, introspective accounts of experiences during meditation, and psychotic and neurotic phenomena.

However, the tares in his work lie in his interpretation of this material. Jung sought the help of a spirit guide named Philemon.[4] His failure to heed God's prohibition to "consult with familiar spirits" (Deuteronomy 18:11) may have been unwitting. But since he was familiar with the Bible, it may have been defiant. Whatever the reason, it led him into the lie that humans are partakers of a divine nature which can conquer death. This implicitly denies the breech due to sin. It is the very twofold Satanic lie that lured Adam and Eve: "Ye shall not surely die" (Genesis 3:4) and "ye shall be as gods" (Genesis 3:5).

The purpose of God's prohibition towards seeking spirit guides is not only to protect us from actual demonic possession, but also to prevent exposure to the Satanic lie. So-called "spirit guides" are perfectly capable of posing as dead Auntie Jane, who stole the family fortune, cursed God up to her last breath, and was not even nice to cats and dogs. Through a medium such as the Ouija board a spirit can give some uncannily accurate about Auntie, then report that she is in a beautiful, peaceful place. Spirit channeling exposes us to demons posing as "angels of light" (II Corinthians 11:14); they provide the false reassurance of a fool's paradise.

Even worse, Jung fell into a blasphemy that derives from his assertion that humans are God: if we are both good and bad, and we are God, then God is bad as well as good. Obviously no peace of mind can come from this. There is no basis for believing anything good lies ahead nor any security if the "numinous" force, as he called it, of the universe may capriciously subject us to evil. It is actually a terrifying thought that God could be no less evil than we are. However, God's Word shows the lie in this (Mark 10:18).

The famous passage from Psalm 82 is often quoted out of context by Jungians and others attempting to make a case for the deity of man: "I have said, Ye are gods: and all of you are children of the most High" (Psalm 82:6). We should note that the writer, King David, did not actually direct this towards all humans; it is aimed at those in authority. More importantly, we should pay attention to the following verse: "But ye shall die like men, and fall like one of the princes" (Psalm 82:7). We have some godly qualities but lack the most important one: power over the demise resulting from our ungodliness.

THE WHEAT IN JUNG'S WORK: ARCHETYPES
Besides the tares, there is some good wheat in Jung's work. Essential to Jung's psychology, and to a psychodynamic model in general, is the notion of the unconscious mind.

What is the unconscious mind? In theory it is a part of the thinking process that humans are, by definition, not consciously aware of, although it governs most physiological and psychological functions. Psychodynamic theory sees the unconscious as the source of the basic human drives. It is also a place for concealment or containment of facets of the human personality that cause insoluble conflict and the threat of potentially overwhelming guilt and fear.

Jung divided the unconscious into two main areas: the "individual unconscious," specific to the individual, and the species-wide "collective unconscious." His collective unconscious contained information universal to humans in the form of innate themes or "archetypes," Jung's most useful concept from a biblical point of view.

He took off with Freud's observation that there appeared to be "archaic remnants" in the dreams of his analysands. These archetypical remnants were mental forms whose presence could not be explained by anything in the person's own life. He went on to focus on these apparently innate, unconscious elements, believing them to be of divine origin.

NATIVISM

The archetype is a nativist concept. Nativism, or the concept of innate ideas and faculties, conflicts with the learning theories that dominated psychological theory and research in the early part of this century. Nevertheless science is producing increasing evidence for a genetic basis for many of the human characteristics that were once considered to be learned. Studies of identical twins separated at birth and raised separately are coming up with astounding similarities in their adult tastes, habits, timetables, career choices, illnesses and other human facets we formerly attributed to environmental influences.[5]

Nativism is not popular in our "egalitarian" society, where we have tried to prove that environmental differences alone account for the disparities we see in the worldly status of humans. A sense of equality is part of our basic equipment, but we seek it in all the wrong places until we find the right one: the eyes of God.

However, nativism is not a new idea. It has long been recognized that some type of inherent wisdom is present in humans. For centuries philosophers have proposed innate elements in the human mind. Plato saw archetypes as pure forms in the mind, of which existing things are imperfect copies. This seems to deny the reality of a perfect God, but does acknowledge the human impossibility of attaining perfection.

Descartes defined three principle innate ideas: God, the self, and matter. His was a "no smoke without fire" notion of the archetype: ideas are based on objective reality. The innate idea of God comes from the reality of God, which is no less perfect than the idea. However, Descartes' God is distant and impersonal, having set the universe in motion and stepped into the background.

JUNG'S ARCHETYPES

Through his occult practises and the study of mythology, which for Jung included the Bible, he developed a "smoke without fire" notion of the archetype. Having no factual, historical basis, they are ideals, divine guides, an internal pantheon capable of moving humans towards transcendence of their mortal limitations. The process of change occurs as the person opens up to the archetypes within.

Jung came up with the following major archetypical elements in the human collective unconscious: the anima/animus, or female and male elements; the shadow, or dark side; the persona; the hero; the abstract processes of initiation and transcendence; the journey; death and rebirth; and adversity. In a part of the collective unconscious Jung called the "superconscious," there was a place of connection with the godhead, which inspired the process of archetypical transformation.

Later in this chapter we will discuss the parallels between Jung's archetypes and ones in the Bible. However, two immediately obvious omissions in Jung's archetypology are hell and God's law with its death sentence. These omissions explain how Jung could put transformation and immortality in human hands rather than in God's hands.

Kelsey's more recent definition of archetypes has some biblical themes but it, too, leaves out the same all-important aspects. Kelsey's archetypes are good, evil, Satan, angels and demons. For Kelsey, these are not an objective reality but innate unconscious determinants of human behavior.[6]

THE BIBLE AND THE UNCONSCIOUS

Is there Biblical acknowledgement of the unconscious mind? Yes. The story of David, Bathsheba and Nathan, the prophet indicates this (II Samuel 11). No human has been more consciously aware of God's law than David, who extolls his love for it in several of his Psalms (Psalms 1:2, 19:7, 40:8, 119). Yet apparently David was not conscious of wrongdoing in his theft of Bathsheba, the wife of Uriah, the Hittite, nor in his subsequent arrangement for the man's death. That is, until God used Nathan to expose the sin to him in the story of a rich man who stole a poor man's one little sheep.

At the conclusion of the story, David exclaimed that the rich man deserved to die. Nathan returned with "You are that man." Only then did David fully see the wickedness in his own actions, and he experienced great remorse. This shows how we are perfectly capable of hiding our eyes from seeing the wrongdoing we commit, even when we know what wrongdoing is.

In the many Biblical accounts of prophetic dreams, such as those of the Pharaoh of Egypt during the time of Joseph (Genesis 37:5), and of Nebuchadnezzar in the time of Daniel (2:3), are examples of God's use of the unconscious mind to transmit information. In those cases, God prevented understanding for his own reasons, rather than this being simply a function of the person's psychological defense equipment.

ARCHETYPES FROM GENESIS

An astounding blueprint entered the human race in the Garden of Eden. The events in the Garden were written in the psyche of our first ancestors and passed on to us. Knowledge of the existential dilemma and the main cast of characters associated with it exists inside us in an unconscious way without our ever having learned about this. It is information carried by humans from their conception, memory traces of real events and prophesies from God.

Since it is impossible to step inside the human mind and inventory its contents, we can only make inferences about it by observing what humans say and do. The presence of the following archetypes from Genesis is supported by the same types of information source used by Jung, sometimes with the addition of large-scale scientific research to which Jung did not have access. The first four archetypes follow the order of events in the Garden.

THE ARCHETYPICAL AWARENESS OF GOD

A 1988 Gallup poll found that ninety four percent of Americans say they believe in God.[7]   Moreover, researchers have found that people who have not recently been active in formal religion spontaneously turn to God in a crisis situation.[8] Can there be so much smoke without fire?

For Adam and Eve, a sense of the existence of God, their maker, must have preceded their awareness of even themselves. God was fashioning them before they could think. The same is true for all of us. True, our nature separates us from God. But although we feel this separation, it does not remove the sense of his presence.

One thing I have found in exploring my clients' stance towards the existence of God is that no one is neutral. The issue is charged with strong emotion. If there really were no God, would we feel so strongly? Unbelievers assume that the uneasy feeling of blasphemy that goes with the denial of the existence of God must have been inculcated by organized religion. They keep trying to stamp out God using reason, but it is never completely effective.

Often we experience a sense of God without being aware of it, or calling it that. It can be a feeling that someone who cares is always watching or listening. The sociological term "generalized other," which defines the totality of the "them" to whom we mentally refer, is largely a perception of God.[9]   Even the humanist idea of the inherent good of man is really a perception of God waking the conscience. When a humanist honestly scrutinizes his desire to operate according to higher principles, he finds that this is not just pragmatic or utilitarian. There is actually a recognition of a higher audience.

And just who is the "perfect lover" of our fantasies, the one who can read our mind, who knows our very soul?   That is no one else but God. We make the mistake of seeking that type of intimacy from our human partner when we do not know God.

If a sense of God is innate, it makes sense that it will be displayed by those who are more open and intuitive. This description best fits children, females, primitive peoples, artists, and certain psychotics.   In all these groups there does tend to be an above average acceptance of the supernatural realm.[10]

Naturally, skeptics will attribute this to lack of intelligence among these groups, but there are contraindications to that.   Paranoid schizophrenics, for example, who have a strong preoccupation with the supernatural, often display superior intelligence on the Wechsler scales.[11]   In Chapter Eight, there is a discussion of psychotic "religiosity," a preoccupation with the supernatural that has not been explained by environmental influences.

"The fool hath said in his heart, There is no God." (Psalm 14:1).   Some of the world's foremost "brains" have concluded that there must be a supreme being...Galileo, Newton, Einstein and Stephen Hawking are just a few examples.

However, the sense of the supernatural is not necessarily godly.   Humans can easily be led astray by it if the influence of the Bible is absent.   The mystical experience of being connected with something out there can lead us to believe we are a part of God.   Made in the image of God, we begin to believe we are god, playing ourselves into Satan's hands. As we will see in Chapter Ten, Jung is only one of a long line of deceived deceivers who promote this belief.

The Bible helps us realize that true awareness of God is the opposite: it is an overarching feeling of accountability, awe, fear, and separation.   Psychologists have said that the central problem of our time is alienation.[12]   This is true, but it is not alienation from other people.   It is alienation from God, deadly in its consequence.   Until we know Christ as our free entrance, we experience distance between us and God.   Our intuition tells us there is a power greater than ourselves, but we need more than just intuition to find it.   We need the facts the Bible shows us.

THE SATAN ARCHETYPE

The devil, or Satan, was the second source of authority to appear to Adam and Eve.   His appearance was deceptive, evil posing as good.   Like Satan himself, archetypical representations of him come in many guises.

The snake

Satan took the form of a serpent or snake to seduce humans into rebellion. Following this, God cursed snakes. He promised enmity between the snake and the woman, and between the descendants of both (Genesis 3:15).

It is not surprising that snakes seem to be intrinsically connected with Satan in our minds. Freudians treat the snake as a phallic symbol, and a fear of snakes as a fear of sexuality. But this fails to account for the fact that fear of the snake is still the leading form of simple phobia in the United States.[13] Are we all so afraid of the male sexual apparatus even after the so-called sexual revolution in this country? Hardly. Nor do the objective facts about the dangerousness of snakes completely explain the prevalence of the fear. What better explanation than that God put that fear of snakes into us in fulfilment of prophesy?

It is interesting that the snake, as a symbol of deity, is widely seen in pagan religions, all of which whisper the same enticing lie as the original serpent. Topiltzin, in the legend mentioned in Chapter Three, sails away on a raft made of snakes, a key to the Satanic theme.

The ancient pagan practise of goddess worship, popular today among New Agers[14] often has the snake associated with it as a fertility symbol.

Moreover, the snake on a pole used as a symbol for healing in modern medicine comes from the Bible. God punished the complaining children of Israel by sending in snakes to bite them. When they repented, God told Moses to make a "fiery serpent, and set it upon a pole, that every one that is bitten, when he looketh upon it, shall live." (Numbers 21:8). The conquered snake on the pole symbolizes God's victory over Satan, a metaphor for Christ taking us back to God's first reference to him in Genesis (3:15).

Mother nature

Satan encourages us to worship false gods. These include elements of the creation, rather than the invisible Creator. God's curse on the earth after Adam and Eve's disobedience particularly highlights the futility of worshipping it. The pagan appeal of Mother Nature or Mother Earth is that gentle Mommy has no hell to send us to. We want to cling to Mommy and avoid Daddy's enforcement of the law. But the law is inside us, telling us what we face. We cannot have Mommy (mercy) without Daddy (judgment), and we cannot avoid Daddy. The devil's lie that we can dispense with Daddy only deceives us temporarily, lulling us into a slumber from which we cannot afford to wake unless we know the price for sin is paid.

The trickster

Satan has to resort to cunning, and the evil trickster is a common figure in mythology. He is found among the pantheon of heavenly gods, such as the Norse god, Loki. He also appears in the earthly supernatural realm: trolls, the siren, faeries, elves, the "big, bad wolf," etc.

The dragon

Another image of Satan found in both the Bible and mythology is the dragon. The book of Revelation describes the archangel Michael and his host of heavenly angels defeating the dragon, Satan, and his host of fallen angels (Revelation 12:7). Some of the most popular children's fairy stories involve a prince who slays a dragon as a rite of passage.

We appear to have inside us this knowledge of "the prince of the power of the air" (Ephesians 2:2), an intrinsic awareness that Satan and his crew are all around us. This becomes even more apparent when we look at psychotic phenomena (see Chapters Seven and Eight). Even our universal fear of the dark derives from this. God is associated with light, the devil and his demons with darkness: "For we wrestle not against flesh and blood, but against principalities, against powers, against the rulers of the darkness of this world, against spiritual wickedness in high places" (Ephesians 6:12).

THE ARCHETYPICAL SIN NATURE

Our dark nature is inborn. We may be capable of altruism but it is impossible to escape the extent to which sin motivates us. Although made in God's image, we get in trouble when we try to think like gods and reject God's authority. It opens the flood gate to our inherent evil.

Jung versus the Bible on sin

Jung and the Bible both see an inherent, ineradicable stain in our character. For Jung, the destructive power of this darkness comes only from its unseen quality. Like the dark side of the moon, it is fear-inducing because it is unknown. It has no death sentence attached to it.

For Jungians, the work of psychotherapy is to defuse the fear of the shadow by acknowledging it. This permits its peaceful coexistence with the "light" side. The positive and the negative, or the yin and the yang, can exist side by side in harmony, enclosed mandala-fashion by one big circle representing unity and wholeness. Thus there is no need of a power higher than or outside of ourselves to provide a rescue, no need for God's pardon in the form of Jesus Christ.

However, Jung's "journey," "initiation," and "transcendence" archetypes imply distance or a barrier between man and God. The difference between Jung and the Bible lies in how this obstacle is removed. Jung says by man; the Bible says only by God.

Egocentricity

Much of the sin in our lives stems from egocentricity, or selfism. God's two basic commandments, to love him and to love our neighbors as ourselves, oppose our predisposition towards self-worship.

Confirmation of the inborn nature of self-centredness comes from the considerable research by the Swiss child development psychologist, Jean Piaget, and his followers.[15] Young children appear to be literally unable to adopt a perspective other than their own. By adulthood we have developed the ability to take another's point of view. However, we tend not to do so unless specifically motivated-- often by self-interest. Research has shown that although adults are capable of displaying altruistic behavior, this typically only happens when they empathize with the other person. The rest of the time they will act according to self interest.[16]

The joys of the flesh are an ever-present trap. What is worse is that our thoughts tell us we are killers, momentarily wishing for the demise of those who have wronged us even briefly...that driver of the car stealing the much-sought parking space just as we are delicately manoeuvring our way in. Counseling on a hotline for stressed parents, I discovered how often parents other than myself had thought about pushing their child over a cliff at some time, much as we all love our offspring. Moreover, we find ourselves committing adultery with our eyes when we are out in public, and our first response to finding a cash-filled wallet on the sidewalk is "keep the money." Human nature is not pretty.

Inherent good, inherent aggression?

In spite of all the research by sociobiologists, anthropologists, and humanistic psychologists seeking evidence that humans are basically good, there is no scientific evidence of this. Research suggest otherwise. Consider, for example, Milgram's laboratory experiments demonstrating human adults' willingness to knowingly administer what they perceived to be painful electric shocks upon request to unseen victims.[17] Our tendency for violence is seen in a general preference for aggression over cooperation during the "prisoner's dilemma" game, even though cooperation would benefit both players.[18] It does not take much to induce us to hurt others: "For their feet run to evil, and make haste to shed blood" (Proverbs 1:16).

Children are no more innocent and pure than adults. Right from the start, aggression is much more the norm than cooperation. We see this, for example, in the social learning theorists' extensive laboratory experiments on preschoolers where, despite their opportunities to model nonaggressive behavior, children persistently exhibit aggression.[19] Some of the earliest research on moral behavior has been on children. One finding has been that even when they say stealing or cheating is wrong, elementary school children will do these things if they think they do not face punishment.[20]

Since the role of experience still cannot be discounted, such research does not prove humans are innately bad, but makes it impossible to argue in favor of innate goodness. All the evidence suggests that humans are a violent species and want to deny it. In vain we search the world for the gentle, peace-loving people who can prove to us that our violence and corruption are the product of the sick society we live in. Yet fossil remains of our ancestors are filled with evidence of murder: smashed skulls. If our society is sick it is because its individuals are sick, with a congenital disease.

Jesus told us who we really are: "That which cometh out of the man, that defileth the man. For from within, out of the heart of men, proceed evil thoughts, adulteries, fornications, murders, thefts, covetousness, wickedness, deceit, lasciviousness, an evil eye, blasphemy, pride, foolishness: All these evil things come from within, and defile the man" (Mark 7:20-23).

These human qualities are part of us until we die. Only the knowledge of a blanket pardon enables us to be bold enough to face the truth about ourselves. Our "shadow," as Jung called it, has a deadly consequence. It can only be encountered and accepted through the safety of God's pardon, the doorway of Jesus Christ. Only with that safety can we allow ourselves to see the full extent of our darkness and come to terms with it.

THE LAW ARCHETYPE

The claim that the Gospel is the *only* route to mental health rests on the inborn nature of God's black and white dooming law. This cannot be emphasized enough. It is of fundamental importance to whether or not grace is essential for mental health. If the law were not written in our hearts, we would have no need for the God of the Bible in order to be mentally healthy. The sin/death equation would be foreign to us. We could be contentedly ignorant until our lives are over.

However, the evidence suggests otherwise. For one thing, the legal systems of the entire world are based on similar principles incorporating the concept of a "natural law" ordained by a power greater than humans. For another, guilt is a pervasive force in the human psyche. Freud saw that. Existential guilt, deep and without focus, implies a law which says we fall short of the glory of God in our very humanness. It is only cured by the assurance of God's forgiveness for who we are.

Beside this guilt is the fact that all religions address the same universal problem: separation between man and God. There is no more reasonable explanation for this than the existence of an innate sin/death equation.

For centuries, philosophers and scientists have questioned the existence of an innate moral law. In support of the innatist position, Immanual Kant[21] postulated an *a priori* "categorical imperative," an internal command to do what is right and an immutable sense of duty. In recent years there has been increasing empirical evidence for this.

Lawrence Kohlberg

The work of the psychologist, Lawrence Kohlberg, points to an inherent moral code.[22] In the research by Kohlberg and his associates, an invariant sequence of six stages in the development of moral judgment were found across several cultural groupings.

In the first four stages, morality is based on a selfish fear of social consequences, a basic concern to save one's own skin. The fifth stage displays a sense of the importance of maintaining the social order for the good of all. The most advanced sixth level of judgment, which Kohlberg called a "Universal Ethical Principles Orientation," is one in which the individual's own conscience is the only criterion of moral conduct. Morality is based on his higher sense of right and wrong without regard for selfish needs, social consequences, or even the social order.

Kohlberg belongs to the "cognitive developmental" school of theorists. This school maintains that the role of experience is to draw out, through an interactive process, what is already there below the surface in blueprint form, waiting to be activated. The moral code requires the opportunity for moral decision-making to stimulate its development. The fact that Kohlberg found the sequence of stages to be universal and invariant suggests that the code is innate.

The work of this school is often used to support the secular humanist position that man is good. According to this position, the "right" socialization experiences will expose the deep godliness of man, the "wrong" experiences will prevent it from surfacing. Man does not need to be taught to do good. He merely needs to be allowed to unfold in a stimulating, loving environment. Without such an environment, his goodness will stay inside.

From a Biblical perspective, there is truth in this. But the "right" experience that will soften our hearts, expose God's law and motivate us to do good is the grace of God. Human socialization has a role in this only if it is under the direction of God. And even with the assurance of God's saving grace, man continues to have the innately corrupt elements in his psyche.

Unsurprisingly, Kohlberg found that few of the adults he studied reached stage six. Among those who did, most did not function at this stage all the time. A person has no reason to

obey his conscience unless he also has a sense of being accountable to God, albeit possibly an unconscious one.   When a sense of God is absent, the temptation to break the law has no prohibition other than personal discretion or whim.   Using rationalization and other psychological defenses, we humans act in our own self-interest and become a law unto ourselves.
Only the fullness of knowing God's love inspires us to follow his law.   And even those who know this love have self-serving blind spots.

Sociobiology

Sociobiology is also finding increasing evidence for an elaborate system of inherent values in the human genetic structure.[23]   Such findings do not prove that God's law stating "the price for sin is death" is born into us.   However, as we show elsewhere in this book, this theory makes the best sense of the observable regularities in human thinking and behavior.

The Bible

The Bible certainly says God's law is inborn: "For when the Gentiles, which have not the law, do by nature the things contained in the law, these, having not the law, are a law unto themselves, which *show the work of the law written in their hearts, their conscience also bearing witness,* and their thoughts the meanwhile accusing or excusing one another." (Romans 2:14-15).

The law God gave to Moses is written in the first five books of the Bible, the Pentateuch or Torah.   It articulates what humans already know at an unconscious level, although not at the same level of specificity.   Reading the law shows us why we have always felt uncomfortable about certain thoughts and actions.   This knowledge is not acquired through Bible study.   Rather, the Bible brings this innate knowledge up to the level of consciousness.

The law itself contains an acknowledgement of how unconscious our sin may be.   But according to God's directive to Moses, we are guilty even when we break the law and "wist it not."   Humans can break the law by accident or by unconscious intent and still face the sentence (Leviticus 5:17).   If this makes God seem tight, we must remember that he wants us to be sure to see we cannot make it without him, so we will seek his refuge.

Humans are never truly in ignorance of God's law. Conscious awareness of it may be dim or absent. Its voice can become "weak" (I Corinthians 8:7), "defiled" (Titus 1:15), or "seared," as in the case of the psychopath (I Timothy 4:2). Nevertheless, unconscious conviction of it is fully present. Psychological defense mechanisms, detailed in Chapter Six, perform the task of concealment. As in the story of David and Bathsheba described earlier in this chapter, defenses can keep actions conveniently separate from moral evaluation.

The hidden defense artillery silences the internal judge by pushing him out of sight. Then we can allow ourselves to perform those actions that are morally questionable. Yet this is always accompanied by unease, adding another layer of guilt to strain the defenses...and the judge will have his say, eventually.

THE PARADISE ARCHETYPE

Humans have been seeking Paradise ever since our ancestors were forced out of the Garden. We picture a happy society where everyone coexists in a state of love, the ultimate family and high school reunion. As a child I was sure I would wake up one day in a fresh, flower-filled world, where my previous existence would seem like a bad dream. There is a memory trace of a perfect world in our collective unconscious. This explains our fascination with Shangri-La and Utopia. Yet all human attempts to remove the flaming sword which bars access to the Tree of Life and a perfect world have led to failure. Only the recognition that we will have it after death enables us to stop insisting we must have it here.

When the explorer Cortez was moving up into California from farther south, he was seeking the mythical fountain of youth. In our preoccupation with eternal youth, is there more than a defense towards death? Perhaps it, too, stems from an innate sense of the youth God will restore in heaven.

THE HELL ARCHETYPE

The nursery rhyme says: "This is the way the old men go. Hobble-dee, hobble-dee, hobble-dee, and down into a ditch." Our sense of Paradise is the glimmer of light in the midst of foreknowledge of the dark pit. Why were Adam and Eve afraid when they knew they were going to die? It was because they somehow knew about a place of utter darkness resulting from their separation from God. This is the ultimate abandonment, the reality basis of existential guilt and anxiety, the abyss underneath waiting to swallow us up.

We innately sense two things. One is a place or state of utter darkness and desolation; the other is continuity past this lifetime. Unfortunately, our psychological defense apparatus generally keeps the two separate, at least at a conscious level.

In our complacency, we assume that we will continue in some desirable state, certainly a state no worse than the present one. The widespread popularity of accounts of "near-death" encounters with angels and white light attests to our search for evidence of this.[24] But we are foolish if we believe a near-death experience can be equated with an after-death one. Satan bolsters the lie that there is nothing to worry about, sending visions of those "angels of light."

Besides, not all near-death experiences are so positive. In my own practise I have listened to some hellish "near-death" accounts from individuals who professed to have neither a current religion nor any religious education earlier in their lives. Nevertheless they reported post-major-surgical experiences of "visiting" a place that was dark and fearful, filled with malevolent presences.

Imagery about this place of terror keeps coming up in our mythology, dreams and other aspects of our awareness. The underworld theme is found in the Greek myths of Ceres and Persephone, the Minotaur, and many others; it occurs in the myths of all societies.

A 1990 Gallup survey found that three out of five people say they believe in hell. However, only a small percentage think they have excellent or good chances of going there, even among those who profess to have no religion. A higher proportion, almost four out of five, say they believe in heaven.[25] The same survey showed that the proportion of "hell-believers" has actually risen during a period of at least thirty years in which mention of hell has been almost absent from the pulpit. This certainly lends credence to the presence of a hell archetype in the collective unconscious. It also suggests that humans deceive themselves into thinking they will not go there.

The sense of the dark abyss or "black hole" is a key feature in existential psychotherapy.[26,27] It is treated in that school as if its importance lies only in the here and now, rather than being seen as an intimation of what is ahead. Yet existential psychotherapy views separation anxiety, most apparent in children but also common in adults, to be a form of death anxiety.[28]

If there is no hell, why does research show attitudes towards death to be prevalently negative? Except among Christians, positive expectations about death appear to be unknown in the literature but we hear plenty of negative ones, such as death-related depression. This depression has been shown to have five factors: despair, dread, sadness, depression, and finality.[29] Moreover, lurking death anxiety is demonstrated by adults who, though claiming they have no fear of death, exhibit significant response delays and changes in galvanic skin response when presented with death-related topics and words.[30]

If hell were a myth, it would make no sense that all religions conceptualize some form of it. Like existentialism, Hinduism and Buddhism have temporary hells. The Bible and its man-made derivative, the Koran, have permanent ones. Jesus described hell as a "furnace of fire: there shall be wailing and gnashing of teeth" (Matthew 13:42), and as "outer darkness; there shall be weeping and gnashing of teeth" (Matthew 22:13). The gnashing of teeth Jesus describes in all his references to hell indicates the rage we will feel at having been given a chance to escape, and having thrown it away: "There shall be weeping and gnashing of teeth, when ye shall see Abraham, and Isaac, and Jacob, and all the prophets, in the kingdom of God, and you yourselves thrust out" (Luke 13:28).

We may argue that a loving God would not subject us to eternal darkness. But we cannot know God's motives, and such an idea only tempts us into thinking hell might be worth risking. Rebellious as we are, only the prospect of unending torture will make most of us turn our faces towards God in more than a passing way.

THE RESCUER ARCHETYPE

This brings us to the question of whether or not there is a rescuer archetype to bring a sense of closure to our archetypical dilemma. In other words, did God give us an innate conflict without also providing an innate conflict resolution mechanism?

It certainly appears not. Evidence suggests there is a rescuer archetype, Jung's "hero." Its presence is most clear in the thinking of disturbed people. For example, Walsh states that: "Belief in an ultimate rescuer is seen in many patients with disturbed personality and behavioral patterns (severe passivity, dependency, masochism) and in some patients who feel especially vulnerable to loss and depression."[31]

This does not mean that belief in a rescuer is pathological. On the contrary, psychopathology is a doorway to the collective unconscious (see Chapters Seven and Eight for a discussion of this in psychosis). Through phenomena that surface during mental illness, we can learn a great deal about what goes on in all of us.

The first Biblical reference to the rescuer is in God's curse on the serpent (Satan): "And I will put enmity between thee and the woman, and between thy seed and her seed; it shall bruise thy head, and thou shalt bruise his heel." (Gen 3:15).

The seed of the woman refers to the genealogy of Jesus Christ, descendant of Eve, who truly bruised the head, or plan, of Satan, the inhabitor of the serpent. Because of God's gift of Christ, Satan's plan to send the entire human race to hell was destroyed.

Mythology gives us plenty of evidence for innate knowledge of a rescuer, God in human form. Yet mythology inevitably brings a Satanic twist to this. The mortal human becomes the hero who attains godhood and immortality. In mythology the hero is clearly not everyman. There is usually something special about his birth. It is of a supernatural order, setting him apart from others. Through communication with the gods he becomes a god himself, winning immortality through self-sacrifical bravery.

The events defining him often bear a remarkable resemblance to those we are told about Jesus. Consider the various legends on the Toltecs' most glorious king, Topiltzin, who lived around 900 A.D.[32] According to different stories, the following happened to Topiltzin: he burned himself in a funeral fire; his heart went into the underworld for four days and returned as the morning star; and he parted the sea and walked away through it, finally sailing away on a raft made of snakes.

By 900 A.D., factual accounts of Christ could have reached the Americas so this legend may not be purely archetypical. Although it contains many striking similarities to accounts of Christ, the Satanic twist is there. Jung makes the mistake of regarding such legends as indications of man's innate ability to save himself.

Based on mythology, Jungian theory emphasises the pivotal role of the "hero" in a misguided way, as a role for the self.[33] Jung-inspired "hero" and "warrior" workshops have been popular in recent years. It appeals to our pride to believe that we can rescue ourselves if we act boldly. However, deep inside we know that no amount of bravery will enable us to pay the price for sin. Laying down our own lives will not buy us out of our dilemma. The price for sin is disconnection from God and only God can free us by paying it.

The Genesis reference to God's provision of a rescue is obscure but God has a habit of using riddles when he wants to test us. He has planted a germ of knowledge in our psyche, beginning with the image of the seed of the woman bruising the head of the seed of the serpent.

The Topiltzin legends indicate our innate sense of the central role of a god-man, a savior. Our unassuageable thirst for rescue stories and human heroes mirrors our unconscious need for Christ. But our human heroes let us down. The sports star discloses the presence of a sexually-transmitted disease; the movie star becomes a paunchy, alcoholic wreck. And our pictures do not fit the reality of the events around the life and death of Jesus Christ. We do not see him physically unattractive, with no white horse or sword, led like a dumb lamb to the slaughter, dying a cursed death with pierced hands and feet (Isaiah 53; Zechariah 9:9; Psalm 22:16).

Judging by the universality of blood sacrifices, we are innately aware that the shedding of blood is essential in some way for our atonement: "for it is the blood that maketh an atonement for the soul" (Leviticus 17:11).

However, knowledge of the specific details of the atonement must come from Bible study. We are dependent on God not only for the rescue, but also for the information that makes us feel secure about it. God is looking for a certain kind of response in us, a willingness to seek and to listen, perhaps.

OTHER ARCHETYPES IN GENESIS

The following three archetypes are in the minor league in the sense that they do not bear on our existential dilemma, yet they explain much about the difficulty of life in this world. All three are prophetic curses which show us that when God makes a promise, he keeps it.

Childbirth

God placed an unequivocal curse on all women through Eve. In my atheistic days I used to ponder over why childbirth (and also, by extension, menstruation) had to be a painful affair. It seemed to go against evolution because humans seemed to have a much more difficult time with it than any other living thing.

Genesis explains this as a curse on women that went into effect from the time of Eve. God said "I will greatly multiply thy sorrow and thy conception; in sorrow thou shalt bring forth children;" (Gen 3:16). That has borne true. Moeover, "the curse" is a term women still use in reference to menstruation.

Male domination

The next archetype is a stumbling block for feminists. Yet why else would it be that, despite the feminist revolution of the sixties, women continue to be second class citizens?[34] According to Genesis, it results from another of God's curses on Eve. Eve was told "thy desire shall be to thy husband, and he shall rule over thee" (Gen 3:16). It is in the collective unconscious of women to focus their attention on men and to allow men to dominate them. This is the source of all the problems women have in their relations with men.

For many years, scientists have debated over whether sex differences are due to nature or nurture. There is little contesting that male and female societal roles *are* different. Back in the 1930s, the sociologist Talcott Parsons described the male role as "instrumental," in contrast with the "expressive" role of the female.[35] Men do; women feel.

Science has discovered small differences in the construction of male and female brains that suggest an innate basis for male-female differences in cognition and personality.[36]

For example, females have more connections between right and left brains in the corpus callosum. The left brain is said to be more instrumental, analytical, and action-oriented than the right, which is more expressive, receptive, imaginative, intuitive, and spatially-oriented.[37]   This could explain why men tend to be more single-minded and less emotionally expressive; they may be able to shut out right hemispheric functioning and stay with the left hemisphere. On the other hand, if women are more likely to use both sides of the brain, this could explain why they think more globally and intuitively. It also makes sense of their somewhat reduced ability to produce a cognitive structure, which could be described as "structure hunger," a lack of firm boundaries as compared to men.[38]

In research on electrical activity in the brain, women are found to have larger "evoked potentials" than men, an indication of greater sensitivity to certain stimuli. Women's increased sensitivity, intuition and receptivity may explain why they seem to be more open to the spirit world, and thus more likely to accept non-Biblical forms of spirituality than men. The first woman certainly fell for the Satanic seduction.

Moreover, most of the Greek and Roman demons are female, e.g., Hecate, the Harpies, and the Gorgons. These myths seem to express a widespread unconscious recognition that the receptivity of the female makes her an easier target for Satanic deception than the male. This explains the current trend towards feminist spirituality, with its rejection of Christ and espousal of the female as goddess.[39]

Receptivity and sensitivity are not inferiority, however. Men are not superior, just different. God is not a sexist. Women, last to appear in God's order, may be superior in certain respects. A man and a woman complement each other. Each needs what the other has so that both can be more effective. Doing needs to go hand in hand with feeling. The female benefits from the male's leadership, his ability to take action. The male benefits from the female's sensitivity and emotional clarity. His ability to lead is enhanced by the woman's sensory apparatus, her antennae.

The problem arises when humans reject God. Then male leadership becomes domination. Domination of females by males derives partly from the ungodliness of man. A man without God believes he is under no other authority than his own. His natural hardness inclines him towards exploitation.

The problem also stems from the ungodliness of the woman, whose experience of her own powerlessness and vulnerability makes her cling to a man who abuses her. Without God, each member of the couple is striving to get more from the other than the other has to give. "Getting" is the motive for the relationship, rather than "giving."

Both the woman and the man need to know that the relationship, desirable as it is, it is not essential. This comes from perceiving that God will provide for all our needs. He will make up for our inherent deficits. In a male-female couple, when each leans on God, there can be interdependency without addiction. When each depends on God more than on the other, each can appreciate the complementary nature of the relationship and not resent the role differences. There is no fear about giving.

Jung conceptualized male and female principles to be present as archetypes in the collective unconscious of all humans. He called these the "animus" and "anima." The Jung-based theory that domination of the female by the male would end when the male's internal female, the anima, and female's internal male, the animus, surfaced has some truth. But the male only develops his expressive side, and the female her ability to take action, when each knows they can lean on a forgiving God who has total control of reality.

If humans, both male and female, are made in the image of God, God must incorporate both male and female aspects. Interestingly, one Jungian analysis of the behavior of Jesus in the four gospels finds equal amounts of "anima" and "animus" behavior.[40] The silly Jungian purpose is to show us we can all be androgynous like Jesus, for we are all assumed to be part of the godhead. The anima/animus archetypes are seen as enabling each human to develop equally strong maleness and femaleness.

But this is to deny the value of the inherent differences. A biblical view of the animus/anima, if such exist, is that they are a blueprint for both a literal reality and a spiritual one. The presence of the opposite sex archetype makes us seek to establish a partnership to round us out: a "help-meet" (Genesis 2:18). Second, it shows us our relationship to Christ, the bridegroom who unites us with God and prepares a heavenly home for us. In a sense, men play a female role towards Christ just as women do, a surrender.

Clearly, no human means will stop male domination/female subjugation if God established it. The only solution for both sexes is to claim the payment for sin provided by the God of the Bible. Only then can women be free from psychic enslavement to men, and men from exploiting women. Then genuine intimacy will be possible. Women cannot liberate themselves; only God can liberate them, in this world and the next.

Thorns and thistles
    The third archetypical curse involves the hardship to be involved in obtaining food. God's curse on Adam particularly highlights the uselessness of the pagan practise of praying to Mother Earth, or Mother Nature. God told Adam the ground was cursed because of him. From then on, there were no more convenience foods; there was no more simple reaching up to pick fruit from the trees during a stroll through the garden. Food would have to be produced through hard labor, which would bring sorrow (Gen 3:17). There would be thorns and thistles to contend with, and bread would be eaten only after much sweat. This hard life would be ended by a return to the dust that man was taken from. Not a pretty picture.
    The bumper sticker reads "Life is hard, then you die," cynical but true on an archetypical level. It would be a cruel joke if there were no God to call upon and only the prospect of death and hell ahead.
    God has warned us to expect hardship. But Satan bolsters the belief that life should be easy. This fuels our anger about the difficulties and injustice in this world. Satan wants us to shake our fists at God and turn away from him.
    The good news about our situation is that it is temporary and we have a Comforter in the midst of the sorrow of life. God can be called on to fight our battles, and he will blow strength into us via the Holy Spirit.
    These curses that God sent on down through the generations show us that he keeps his promises. This reassures us that God's promise to provide the payment for sin is true.

SUMMARY AND CONCLUSIONS
    Despite the tares, Jung's most useful contribution to us has been his work on the archetype, an innate unconscious template guiding human thought and action. The archetype

construct explains how everything of importance that Adam and Even learned in the Garden of Eden influences the human race.

Humans inherit a time bomb in the form of the most important archetypes: 1) knowledge of the existence of God and his dooming law; and 2) a sinful, lawbreaking nature that cannot avoid the law's deadly sentence.   However, God also put knowledge of a rescuer in the human psyche, a Savior through whom the bomb is dismantled.

Other archetypes from Genesis that add to this theme of despair followed by hope are: Satan, hell, paradise, and some specific prophesies affecting our day-to-day life in this world.

There is a major difference between a Bible-based view of archetypes and every other view of them.   Jung and other theorists see archetypes as symbolic of human potential for transcendence of earthly limitations.   The Bible shows us they are representative of an objective reality outside of human control.   Familiarity with God's Word is essential if we are to perceive the true meaning of the archetypical images that exist in our collective unconscious.   Only the Bible offers the essential closure to end the war between the archetypes.

Notes

1. Jung, Carl (1928).   "The Psychology of the Unconscious." In Collected Works, Volume 7, pp. 1-117.

2. Freud, Sigmund (1900).   The Interpretation of Dreams.   In Standard Edition, Volumes 4 and 5. (First German edition 1900).

3. C. J. Jung, Memories, Dreams, and Reflections.   (1965). New York, New York: Vintage Books.

4. C. G. Jung (19--).   VII Sermones ad Mortuoso. (Published anonymously), documentation of Jung's occult experiences.

5. Mittler, P. (1971).   The study of twins.   Harmondsworth, England: Penguin Books.

6. Kelsey, Morton T. (1982)   Christo-Psychology. New York: Crossroad, pp. 136-137

7. "Hell's sober comeback." (Mar 25, 1991). US News and World Report, pp. 57-64.

8. Cobble, J. F. (1985). Faith and crisis in the stages of life. Peabody, MA: Hendrickson Publishers.

8. Cooley, Charles Horton (1922). Human nature and the social order. New York, New York: Scribner Publishers.

10. For example: Frank, Jerome (1974). Persuasion and Healing New York: Schocken, p. 83. Frank states that adolescents are the age group most prone to sudden conversion. For a discussion of a difference between American Indian and mainstream American perspectives see Sue, D. W. (1980) Counseling the Culturally Different. New York: Wiley. For a discussion of male/female ways of knowing see Luthman, Shirley Gehrke (1972). Intimacy: The Essence of Male and Female. San Rafael, California: Mehetabel and Co.

11. Ogdon, D. P. (1977). Psychodiagnostics and Personality Assessment: A Handbook. Los Angeles, California: Western Psychological Services, pp. 10-19.

12. Karier, C. J. (1986). Scientists of the Mind: Intellectual founders of modern psychology. Urbana, Ill: University of Illinois Press.

13. Doctor, R. M. and Kahn, A. P. (1989). The encyclopaedia of phobias, fears and anxieties. New York: Facts on File; and Goodwin, Donald W. (1983). Phobia: the facts. New York, New York: Oxford University Press.

14. For an explanation of the New Age movement: Hunt, Dave and McMahon, T. A. (1985) The Seduction of Christianity: Spiritual discernment in the last days. Eugene, Oregon: Harvest House Publishers

13. Piaget, Jean (1923). The Language and Thought of the Child. Cleveland and New York: The Wworld Publishing Company.

16. Batson, C. Daniel (1990). "The Human Capacity for Caring." American Psychologist, 45, pp. 336-346

17. Milgram, Stanley (1963).   "Behavioral study of obedience." Journal of Abnormal and Social Psychology, 67(4), pp. 371-378

18. Campbell, R. (Ed.) (1985).   Paradoxes of rationality and cooperation: prisoner's dilemma and Newcomb's problem. Vancouver, British Columbia: University of British Columbia Press.

19. Bandura, Albert (1973).   Aggression: a social learning analysis.   Englewood Cliffs, New Jersey: Prentice-Hall, Inc.   An extensive review of laboratory studies of aggressive behavior produces no evidence that although physically aggressive behavior is influenced by situational factors and modelling, this is not an innate part of the human repertoire.

20. Hartshorne, H. and May, M. A. (1928).   Studies in deceit. Book I.   General methods and results.   Book II.   New York, New York: Macmillan Press.

21. Kant, Immanuel (1873).   Critique of Pure Reason and Other Writings on the Theory of Ethics.   London.

22. Kohlberg, Lawrence (1971).   "Stages of moral development as a basis for moral education." In C. M. Beck, B. S. Crittenden, and E. V. Sullivan (Eds.) Moral education: Interdisciplinary approaches.   New York, New York: Newman Press.

23. Sperry, R. W. (1988).   "Psychology's mentalist paradigm and the religion/science tension." American Psychologist, 43, pp. 607-613

24. Moody, R.A., Jr. (1975).   Life after Life.   Harrisburg, Pa.: Stackpole Books.

25. "Hell's sober comeback," (March 25, 1991).   U. S. New and World Report, pp. 57-64

26. Frankl, Victor (1988).   The Will to Meaning.   New York, New York: Penguin Books.

27. Grotstein, James S. (1990). "Nothingness, meaninglessness, chaos, and the "black hole," Part 2: The black hole." Contemporary Psychoanalysis, 26, 3, pp. 377-407.

28. Yalom, I. (1980). Existential psychotherapy. New York: Basic Books.

29. Templer, D. I., Lavoie, M., Chalgujian, H. and Thomas-Dobson, Shan. (1990). "The measurement of death depression." Journal of Clinical Psychology, 46, 6, pp. 834-839.

30. Feifel, H. and Branscomb, A. (1973). "Who's afraid of death?" Journal of Abnormal Psychology, 81, pp. 282-288.

31. Walsh, Stephen J. (1984). "The Existential Approach in Psychiatry." In Review of General Psychiatry, H. H. Goldman (Ed.), Los Altos, CA: Lange Medical Publications, p. 533

32. Brandon, William (1961) The American Heritage of Indians, New York, New York: Dell Publishing Company, p. 48

33. Campbell, Joseph (1949). Hero with a Thousand Faces. New York, New York: Meridian Books.

34. Sanoff, A. P. (Feb 12, 1990) "The mixed legacy of women's liberation." U.S. News and World Report, p. 61

35. Black, Max (1961). The social theories of Talcott Parsons: a critical examination. Englewood Cliffs, New Jersey: Prentice-Hall.

36. For a discussion of this see "Just How the Sexes Differ," (May 18, 1981). Newsweek, pp. 72-83

37. Christen, Yves (1991). Sex differences: Modern Biology and the Unisex Fallacy. New Brunswik, New Jersey: Transaction Publishers.

38. For example:
Luchins, A. S. (1942). "Mechanization in problem-solving--the effect of Einstellung." Psychological Monographs, 54, 6.

Guetzkow, H. (1951). "An analysis of the operation of set in problem-solving behavior." <u>Journal of General Psychology</u>, <u>45</u>, pp. 219-244.

39. Bolen, Jean (1984).   <u>Goddesses in Everywoman: A New Psychology of Women</u>.   San Francisco, California: Harper and Row Publishers.

40. Stahlke, Paulette E. (1990).   "Jungian archetypes and the personality of Jesus in the synoptics." <u>Journal of Psychology and Theology</u>, <u>18</u>(2), pp. 174-178.

Chapter Five

FREUD'S CONTRIBUTION TO A

BIBLICAL MODEL OF THE PSYCHE

WHAT'S RIGHT ABOUT FREUD?

Sigmund Freud's ideas permeate the mental health profession. He has made a tremendous contribution to our understanding of psychological functioning.[1] However, atheist Freud might be surprised to find his ideas used to illuminate the psychodynamics of our crazy-making attempts to deal with an innate sense of doom. Nevertheless, through Freud we can see why accepting Christ is the only route to mental health. So much is right about Freud:

1) his analysis of the structure of the psyche;
2) his idea of a dynamic unconscious aimed at resolving a basic conflict;
3) his delineation of our psychological defense network;
4) and his view of guilt as the basis of psychopathology.

Yes, Freud saw that humans are in a perpetual state of guilt-ridden internal strife.

WHAT'S WRONG?

Yet so much of Freud is wrong. His major departure lies in his exclusive focus on the human world. Although he wrote at a desk covered in idols of Eastern gods and goddesses,[2] he argued that all religion is a kind of universal obsessional neurosis, if not an outright delusion.[3] Failing to perceive the biblical focus on active walking in faith, Freud saw a passive, defensive purpose to religion that he called "regression in the service of the ego." His refusal to consider the reality of the spirit, right in line with the Darwinism of his time, limited his perspective to inadequate human solutions.

FREUD'S MODEL VERSUS THE BIBLICAL ONE

Freud conceptualized a three-way division of the psyche, or mind, into: the "id," the "superego," and the "ego." This is a useful model from a biblical perspective, except the respective parts would be "sin nature," "God's law" and ego.

Agreement: In both Freudian and Bible-based views, mental illness is due to conflict between the two elements of the psyche corresponding to human nature and morality.

The "middle-man" ego uses crippling psychological defenses in a vain attempt to eliminate the conflict. The ego's work is done largely below the level of consciousness. Although the Bible shows us the ultimate powerless of the ego (Latin for "I"), Freud's depiction of its role in creating psychological defenses helps us understand the way our mind distorts and hides from the existential dilemma.

The Bible-based model and the Freudian one agree that until this conflict ends, the human mind is constantly engaged in it. Attempts are made to resolve it at best, hide from it at worst. This is a conflict- or tension-reduction model.

Disagreement: Despite the parallels between the Freudian and biblical models, the true conflict is powerful beyond anything Freud imagined. It involves man's relationship with God and Satan, not man's relationship with himself or other humans. Eternity is its major concern, not this lifetime. In Freudian theory, the fight is between the innate id and the learned superego. It is a battle to be fought and won on an intrapersonal, human level by changing the way we think. The Bible, on the other hand, shows us a war between the sin nature and an innate dooming law. It is a clash that humans cannot win through mind manipulation.

Humans flee, internally, from the edge of destruction although they unconsciously know they cannot escape through their own means. They hopelessly run on a conveyor belt which pulls them towards a dark precipice.

The major differences and similarities between the Freudian and biblical models are summarized in Table One.

THE ID VERSUS THE SIN NATURE

According to Freud, humans are born with a "pleasure principle," or drive for sensual fulfilment which, early on in his theory development, centred on eros, i.e., sexuality.[4] Sexual pleasure is the primary goal of a wild, violent, childishly

Table One: Freudian and Bible-based models

===

Freudian model	Bible based model

1. Id

    <u>Similarity:</u>
    Innate

2. Superego

    <u>Similarity:</u>
    Clashes with id to produce
    guilt, psychopathology

    <u>Differences:</u>
    Learned
    No death sentence attached

3. Ego

    <u>Similarity:</u>
    Has task of resolving conflict
    between id and superego.
    Uses defense mechanisms.

    <u>Differences:</u>
    Conflict is worldly.
    Human means can
    resolve it. Psycho-
    analysis can
    soften superego, channel
    id, develop healthier
    defenses.

---

1. Sin nature (SN)

    Innate

2. God's law

    Clashes with SN,
    produces guilt,
    psychopathology

    Innate
    Death sentence

3. Ego

    Conflict is between
    SN and conscience.
    Uses defense
    mechanisms.

    Existential crisis.
    Human means <u>cannot</u>
    resolve it.
    Only a dispens-
    ation from God can.
    Psychological def-
    enses become
    redundant.

demanding, selfish, inherent nature: the "id." Freud went as far as to describe it as a "ravening wolf,"[5] just as Jesus described the inner workings of the hypocritical Pharisees (Matthew 7:15). This is the Freudian equivalent to the sin nature which, although mistakenly narrowed down to sex, otherwise parallels it closely in its innate origin and guilt-arousing function.

LEARNED SUPEREGO VERSUS INNATE LAW

Both Freudian and Bible-based views see the basic product of the conflict between the law (superego) and human nature (id) to be guilt, a sense of deserving punishment. This guilt and the anxiety associated with it cause; mental illness.

In Freudian theory, guilt results when the demands of the unruly id come up against the restricting superego, or "reality principle:" the internalized beliefs and mores of society transmitted primarily through the father. The overly harsh superego is acquired through the socialization process. Therefore it can be unlearned and replaced by one that is kind and tolerant. Then there will be an end to guilt.

However, this is where Freud and the Bible profoundly disagree. The Bible shows the law to be an immoveable object. It cannot be softened or purged from our hearts. There is no way Freudian methods can eliminate conflict. The terrible guilt that makes humans mentally ill is not relieved by altering the law, but through knowledge of a dispensation God placed in it. Conflict is ended when humans perceive that the "sin equals death law" contains a God-given reprieve.

The Oedipus complex

It was clear to Freud that the superego (law) was present from early childhood. He blindly assumed that its task entails only sexual prohibition. This led him to conclude that it must be learned when the child first experiences genital eroticism at approximately the age of three. To explain why the child would swallow a painfully thwarting moral standard, he devised a strange theory.

In the bizarre classical Freudian theory of the Oedipus complex, which still has wide acceptance, the young boy takes on the superego as a defense. According to the theory, the castrating father stands between the male child and the supposed first object of his genital lust, his mother. The boy identifies with the feared father, internalizing his moral value code. This wards off the sexual impulses towards his mother that would doom him if acted upon. Now he is protected from being castrated by the father, the rival towards whom he has homicidal impulses just like Oedipus in the Greek tragedy.

Does this not sound far-fetched? Yet many of the people who reject the factuality of the Bible swallow this unwieldy Freudian formulation of the superego without even blinking.

Ad hoc research I have conducted over this issue in my practise has produced some confirmation that men have sexual thoughts towards their mothers. But none have reported that this was accompanied by a fear of castration from his father. Moreover, the same men reported sexual thoughts towards other female members of the family.

"Cut off"

It is likely that the Oedipal formulation was a result of Freud's unconscious awareness of a dire consequence for transgression. Funnily enough, the expression "cut off" can be applied both to Freud's idea of the ultimate punishment and the biblical one. Freud's arrival at this formulation displays unconscious awareness of the sin/death equation. In liberal Judaism, there is no belief in the resurrection of the body despite clear references to it throughout the Old Testament.[6] An afterlife is to be attained primarily by having children. So castration for Freud, who came from that liberal tradition, unconsciously connotated loss of an afterlife.

The castration complex was Freud's attempt to explain the origin of the harsh internal critic who tells us of the imminent "cut off" from life. But Genesis shows us the true nature and origin of this critic: the archetypical fruit of the Tree of Knowledge of Good and Evil.

Penis envy

Note that there is no strong counterpart to the Oedipus complex for the girl. In spite of Freud's formulation of the Electra complex, the girl's hypothetical incest-related fear of her mother has no great significance. Instead, she, too, identifies with paternal values more strongly than maternal ones. The mechanism is "penis envy," a desire for the power symbolized by the male sexual apparatus.

Freud was close to the mark in seeing guilt arising from

a law given by the father. His mistake lay in making the innate law from God a moral code learned from the human father. The Father in heaven became the father on earth.

Freud did hit on something of importance here, though. That is the idea of a sex difference in the dynamics of God's law. It makes sense that because he is more violence-prone, the male acquires his sense of accountability to God through fear. This is less true for the female. Naturally less violent and more nurturing, she is less likely to see herself as a sinner and less fearful of God because of that. Her increased spiritual receptivity[7] inclines her to identify with god, failing to perceive the need for Christ. This would explain why the God of the Bible generally favors men as spiritual leaders.

Taken as a whole, Freud's formulation of the superego has the fabulous quality of a delusion, in itself a defense towards the universal fear that Freud, himself, could not confront.

Generic superego acquisition

Post-Freudian generic psychodynamic theory has a broader concept of superego acquisition. The child identifies with the morality of significant others, motivated by such factors as reward and perceived power.[8] It is true that humans do learn some moral values in this way. What they acquire is only superficial, however, and creates confusion if it contradicts the deeper, inherent knowledge of God's law.

THE EGO VERSUS GRACE

The third division of the psyche in the Freudian model, the "ego," is the middle-man with the task of resolving the conflict between the id and the superego. Freud saw that the ego could not alter the superego without outside help. It was to be modified through extensive psychoanalysis. Nor could the ego radically transform the innate id. Mostly what the ego had at its disposal was subterfuge: concealment, distortion, or rechanneling through defense mechanisms.

Ego defense mechanisms

Not realizing the true purpose of defense is to ward off a sense of imminent doom, Freud and his followers nevertheless made brilliant analyses of the elaborate network of contructs carrying out the ego's task of concealment and distortion.

Walls are erected to contain, hide and divide the naughty id. The id is only allowed to come out and play when it is disguised as a little angel, or when the vigilant superego is distracted, persuaded to step back temporarily, or permanently changed through the work of psychoanalysis--a practical impossibility from a biblical standpoint. The conscious sense of transgression *must* be avoided at almost any cost; the truth about its consequence is potentially overwhelming.

At best, defense produces a superficial semblance of sanity. Underneath is intrapsychic conflict leading to psychopathology. Instead of having an appropriate outlet, the unacceptable, guilt-laden drives, thoughts and memories fester behind the defensive walls, hidden from conscious awareness. Anxiety and a host of other emotions are concealed or "bound" too. These elements attempt to surface but they are contained, a phenomenon Freud called "resistance." The emotions do great damage as they are acted out in a distorted fashion at an unconscious level. They produce the many, varied forms of psychopathology. Since they cannot be resolved outside of grace, they cause unending pain. In the following chapter the defense gambits are discussed in some detail.

Ego control

The other ego mechanism is control or taming of the id impulse (sin nature), to be discussed in the next chapter.

THE BASIC CONFLICT ACCORDING TO FREUD AND HIS FOLLOWERS

Although there are grains of truth in their ideas, Freud and his followers have missed the mark about the nature of the conflict which causes all the defense. What follows are six mistaken attempts to reach the crux.

1. SEXUALITY AS THE ROOT

In the early Freudian model, the basic conflict lay between the sexuality of the id and the mores of the superego.

2. LIFE AGAINST DEATH

However, Freud found that conflict remained in his patients after years of psychoanalysis, long after their sexual issues had apparently been resolved. So he changed his notion of the id and added two basic drives: an aggressive survival instinct in conflict with a death instinct.

This was because Freud realized that the violence in man was not attributable to thwarted sexuality. It was a separate drive, an aspect of his desire for survival, life. Yet since he also found so much self-punitiveness in humans, he also conceptualized a drive for extinction.[9] But what he was seeing was no death instinct. It was a powerful defense mechanism: man chasing his own tail, unconsciously trying to pay for sin by punishing himself.

Note that this conflict was unresolvable. Two inherent, opposing drives in the id were always going to be at odds. A latent death wish could not be channeled in a way that did not thwart the desire for life. This was the closest Freud came to recognizing the real bind humans are in.

Implicitly, Freud was concluding that man's basic conflict was not to be healed through Freudian psychoanalysis, and he was right. Psychoanalysis, or any other type of psychotherapy, can only plug holes in a dam that shores up a huge black reservoir. Since Freud failed to bring the God of the Bible into the picture, he could only come so far along the road.

Furthermore, this life versus death idea of Freud's did not gain much acceptance. Only a couple of his followers developed it. Others came up with different ideas about man's basic conflict.

3. LIFE AS DEATH

Norman O. Brown[10] was one theorist who thought he could close the gap between Freud's life and death drives. He postulated that the life wish, expressed through sexuality, was also a death wish. The "little death" of the sex act was a return to the womb of peace and safety, reentry into Paradise. Sex was both life, through procreation, and death, through self-annihilation.

The problem is, even for those who are not enamoured of life, this lacks intuitive validity. Honestly confronting the reality of death, we cannot help but be aware of how much we want to continue being "us" for eternity. We want our children and our parents, all our loved ones, to go on being "them." In fact, we cannot envisage a state of not being.

For those who find life overwhelmingly painful, death can seem a welcome escape as long as it is a state of peace. But the belief that death is always peaceful is a delusion fostered by Satan. Hell is real and genuine escape is found only in through Christ. If the "little death" of sex is used as a psychological defense, an escape, it becomes addictive because it never produces closure. The more we seek it, the less satisfying it is. We know deep inside that there is no peace to be found in death *per se*.

4. UNLOVING HEARTS

Karen Horney said "the conflict born of incompatible attitudes (towards other people) constitutes the core of neurosis and therefore deserves to be called basic."[11] To paraphrase this biblically, Horney found evidence that humans have little love for their neighbors. She saw this unlovingness as the basis of guilt. Not true. In truth, breaking the commandment to "love thy neighbor as thyself" (Matthew 19:19) does lead to guilt but this is far from being the core problem. Unlovingness is but a symptom of our sense of separation from God.

In another attempt that was more on target but still off the mark, Horney defined basic anxiety as the feeling a child has of being isolated and helpless in a potentially hostile world.[12] This is exactly the human condition outside of connection with God.

5. FEAR OF EXTINCTION

Anna Freud, daughter of Sigmund, took the position that the basic conflict was powerful, but there were not sufficient data to make any hypotheses about its nature. She acknowledged that she had no idea what was really the root of our human turmoil: "What it is that the ego fears either from an external threat or from a libidinal danger cannot be specified; we know that it is in the nature of an overthrow or of extinction, but it is not determined by analysis" (Freud, 1946, p. 85). This is the closest and most honest neo-Freudian stab at identifying our unconscious fear of hell, about the best anyone has ever managed without seeing the truth in Genesis.

6. PSYCHOSOCIAL COMPETENCE

Erik Erikson theorised about "psychosocial" development, postulating a drive towards competence and fulfilment in family relations and work throughout the life span.[13] He deemphasized the role of any one basic conflict or drive, proposing instead a series of conflicts, or developmental tasks, each building on the last.

Erikson's theory is of interest because it reflects a popular misconception. He saw the initial conflict as one between a basic sense of trust versus mistrust. In theory, this will affect a person's religious orientation later in life. To be able to trust God, the child must have been able to trust his caregivers in infancy. In other words, good parental care is the foundation for a good relationship with God.

But the idea that our concept of God is primarily a projection of the father or mother has been discredited. God-image and parent-image are linked, but the relationship is not strong, and we do not know which way the influence goes.[14,15] Moreover, self-image has been found to be a stronger independent predictor of God-image than parent-image.[16]

The closer humans get to God, the more possible it is that they will be alienated from their human parents. Jesus said "Think not that I am come to send peace on earth: I came not to send peace, but a sword. For I am come to set a man at variance with his father, and the daughter against her mother, and the daughter in law against her mother in law." (Matthew 10:34-35). In fact, generally we only look to God when our human relationships go bad and we are crazy with loneliness. But if we think God as cruel as humans, we will be unable to go to him.

The truth is, God's love can reach us regardless of caregiver deficits in our childhood. Confronting our dilemma and God's rescue will enable us to see the sun of God shining behind the dark clouds of bad parenting, or even fallible "normal" parenting. God is the only parent who is completely trustworthy.

PSYCHOANALYSIS VERSUS THE GOSPEL

Our existential conflict is outside the human domain; so must its treatment be. The healing impact of the Gospel departs radically from psychoanalysis in many ways.

Psychoanalysis strives to cure neurosis on two fronts: one, by changing the superego, the law man carries around inside himself; and two, through the psychological manipulation of his guilt-provoking basic drives.

But the problem is that the law is innate. We are stuck with it. So according to a Bible-based view, mental health is achieved not by changing the unchangeable law which God put in man's heart, but by knowing--that is, knowing in our hearts--of God's dispensation within that law. Once the Holy Spirit has opened us up, the tempering of our egotistical drives is the fine tuning. But this fine tuning can only "hold" when the basic fear is quieted. Otherwise the rumblings from deep inside keep pulling us out of adjustment.

Of course, as Anna Freud stated, our true conflict is so deep it does not come out in Freudian psychoanalysis. It is only free to surface when there is the reassurance that God paid the price for sin, that we are protected from what we fear the most. It is only safe to look over the edge when we know we cannot hurt ourselves falling. Vertigo, incidentally, is only another of God's ways of reminding us of the abyss beneath.

Psychoanalysis aims at the humanly impossible, a drastic restructuring of the psyche. This is a "born again" experience without God, returning to the emotional infancy of the pre-Oedipal stage before the "bad" superego penetrated the psyche. The aim is to replace it with a permissive superego and an ego stronger in its tasks of defense and control.

Freud focused on changing the individual but some of his later followers, such as Herbert Marcuse, thought that society had to be changed before the individual could change.[17] Little did they realize that a humanistic revolution removes a corrupt, repressive government only to unfetter the sin in the populace.

In terms of defense, the Freudian goal is to replace less functional, primitive defenses with more functional, sophisticated ones. "Sublimation" is the best defense, a transformation of the guilt-producing sex and aggressive drives into a drive to create products beneficial to society.

In classical psychoanalysis and, to a lesser extent, in more time-limited psychodynamic therapy, these processes are thought to drastically restructure the psyche: catharsis, insight, working through...undoing the effects of the past. In theory, the harsh parental standard can gradually be replaced by a liberal one. But in practise...? Impossible.

Major areas of disagreement between the biblical and Freudian approaches lie: A. in the treatment of guilt; B. in the role of experience; C. in the conceptualization of fixation and stages; D. in the the understanding of child abuse; E. in the need for defenses; and F. in the role of the future versus the past.

A. TREATMENT OF GUILT

Not surprisingly, Freud found guilt persisted in his patients after many years of attempting to erase moral absolutism.[18]   Undoubtedly the superego (law) contains learned elements which are potentially reversible, but these are only a small part of the problem.   The crux of the problem is that the supposedly internalized critical parent is inborn.   The ineradicable conscience will always criticize our transgressions and give us the awareness of deserving punishment, i.e., guilt.

The Freud-based mental health establishment tells us we can reason our way out of guilt, call bad good, and become psychologically healthy.   But we cannot.   Guilt is the bruise indicating the wound.   The wound is not removed when we take medication to reduce that bruise.   The reverse is true. Like the bruise, guilt is a necessary part of the healing process. Without guilt there will be no confession, no claiming the payment for sin, and no sense of being forgiven by God.

There are two sources of guilt.   One is an overall sense of missing the mark, the other has to do with specific transgressions.   We have no control over the first, and some control over the second.   Either way, guilt is inevitable. Therefore its cure must be the all-accepting nature of God. God accepts us, simply as a result of our claiming Christ.

Research shows that in the right context, guilt is beneficial.   It is associated with indices of healthy psychological functioning for those who know grace.[19]   However, the same research shows that if the assurance of grace is absent, guilt is not such a positive sign.

All too often, Freudian therapy separates us even further from reality, providing a detour from the truth. Rationalization and intellectualization are its major products, particularly among the "YAVIS (Young, adult, verbal, intelligent, socioeconomically advantaged)" clients who are its ideal candidates.

Expensive psychoanalysis takes humans back over the past to weed out those hypercritical parental "introjects."   After a whole lifetime there can be no substantive progress, just more guilt and confusion under the defenses.   The same applies to the less ambitious short-term psychodynamic therapy.   The innate sin/death law keeps telling us we are doomed.

B. THE ROLE OF EXPERIENCE

To be sure, the sin/death equation implies a diminished role for past experience.   However, experience is not irrelevant. Interaction with the world, especially the family, affects the type and severity of psychopathology.   Defenses are affected by experience; so are emotional reactions, beliefs, expectations, opinions, attitudes, and habits.   Genes also play a part in the nature of the illness, but that does not concern us at present.

Consciously or unconsciously, we learn a great deal from significant others about how to handle our existential conflict. Seeing irrationality or unfairness in our parents, we vow to avoid repeating their mistakes.   Yet we find ourselves engaged in many of the same familial defensive patterns.   Those old patterns happen to be there to avoid something even worse: exposure to underlying, potentially overwhelming existential guilt and anxiety.

Through psychotherapy the old patterns can be replaced by some new patterns that may look better, feel better, and enable us to function better.   A house built on sand can be shored up for a while.   Maybe it can stand for a long time, if it is not subjected to much stress.   Stress has a way of thrusting our lack of foundation closer to the surface of consciousness.   The defense walls give way and if we do not seek God at that point, the result is collapse into illness.   Only the Gospel gives us a foundation of rock.

C. FIXATION AND STAGES

Just as Freud theorized, humans keep striving for closure, or tension-reduction.   No peace is possible until we reach it. Research has shown that an unfinished task exerts a hold, interfering with new learning.[20]   This helps explain the phenomenon Freud called "fixation," an emotional arrest caused by an unresolved conflict related to a stage in psychosexual development.

Assuming that there is a reality to Freud's concept of an invariant sequence of developmental stages, each new stage or task is a voyage into the unknown.   For Freud, sexual energy was the propelling force moving the individual through the stages, each building on the last. Neurosis resulted when this process was thwarted. The harsh superego would forbid the id's appropriate "object libido," or the channeling of the erotic drive into some satisfying mode of expression. The id might stay bottled up or find an inappropriate but safer outlet behind psychological defense cover. Guilt and anxiety were bi-products.

The fact is, nobody can feel safe enough to willingly embark on a developmental voyage unless there is a sense of God's support. Fear of the unknown triggers the deeper fear that must be avoided. This means that humans without God are emotional dwarfs, only moving forward to a new stage when forced to do so by circumstances, never fully reaching that stage.

Some researchers in the psychology of religion have found stages in the development of religious faith.[21] But from a biblical point of view, there is only one transition of importance. This is the transformation from unbeliever to believer through a perception of hell and the God-given rescue. Only the believer can become mature in those qualities psychology calls "adult," known biblically as the fruits of the Holy Spirit (Galations 5:22; Ephesians 5:9). These include patience, persistence, integrity, wisdom, love and commitment. Once the ego acquires the message of grace, God's freely available, everlasting defense, those forward leaps essential to psychological growth can be made in confidence.

D. UNDERSTANDING THE ABUSED CHILD

The fact that bad experiences can intensify the pre-existing guilt and deepen psychopathology is never clearer than in the case of the extremely abused child. This child adopts some particularly pathological forms of psychological defense which become characterological. They include identification with the aggressor; infantile regression; dissociation, which can lead to multiple personality disorder; self-mutilation; substance abuse: and massive repression, including repressed rage which leads to psychosomatic and conversion disorders.

The basic reason why a child is so scarred by abuse is that he perceives this to be the punishment for the sin he finds in himself. Since he knows he will continue to be a sinner, he expects abuse to be his life story. He even feels anxious when it is not happening because he comes to depend on it as a means of atonement.

The abuse triggers murderous rage and hatred in the child that can lead him to become an abuser himself. Even though rage seems justified on a rational level, God's law in the child's heart tells him it is wrong: "He that despiseth his neighbor sinneth" (Proverbs 14:21). The additional guilt from rage creates the need for massive defense. At the deepest, unconscious level, the child's anger is towards the God who must have abandoned him. He rejects God and is blinded by the obsession of getting revenge, stuck in the past. One thing can change all this: the sense of being undeservedly rescued from a sure drowning, safe in God's arms forever. A painful past pales in comparison with the escape from eternal darkness.

E. CAN WE DISPENSE WITH DEFENSE?

Unsurprisingly, the traditional mental health definition of normalcy, or even superiority, in psychological functioning involves a certain degree of defensiveness. A low score on the defensiveness scale of the Minnesota Multiphasic Personality Inventory (MMPI) is generally considered symptomatic of pathology.[22] That is because the root conflict has never been cured through the secular world of psychotherapy, and the MMPI is a part of that world. Outside of a relationship with God through Christ, we humans will always have a need to psychologically defend against guilt and anxiety, a need to believe that we are good guys when we are not.

According to a Bible-based view, the purpose of all the psychological defense equipment so cleverly identified by the Freudian school is to defend against potentially overwhelming guilt and terror over the prospect of hell. Ego defenses are a psychological "cover," ultimately ineffective but pervasive equipment. Defenses are the sand we put our head in as we try to escape the ravages of our inner turmoil. The overworked ego of a nonbeliever can snap at any time, opening the flood gates towards the panicky sense of imminent doom. His ego is a poor, weak, inefficient intermediary, unable to produce the state of peace we call mental health.

Secular psychotherapy aims to help the person develop "healthy," sophisticated defenses in place of primitive, dysfunctional ones. Lacking knowledge of the Gospel, humans have to have defenses. Unless threat is removed, we go insane without them. Research supports this. An inverse relationship exists between defensiveness and the lifetime prevalence of serious psychiatric disorders.[23]

However, there is no need for psychological armour when there is no threat. If all is forgiven, all can be known. A biblical model of the healthy person is one who has no use for psychological defense. The ego of a believer is freed from the need to resolve the conflict between the id and the superego. Christ is the intermediary who has already achieved reconciliation between man and God, or more specifically, between man's sinful nature and God's law. Only our failure to comprehend this and our pride (see Chapter Two) maintain the defense front.

E. FOCUSING ON THE FUTURE NOT THE PAST

Psychoanalysis focuses on the past. However, only when we stop looking at the past can we move forward. Otherwise we humans stand paralyzed, like a pillar of salt. The future is what concerns us, because without a rescue, we must spend eternity in darkness.

All the problematic elements of our lives begin to get resolved with the easing of the root conflict. We no longer face the death penalty for the slightest infringement of God's law, nor any longer carry the burden of guilt.

The role of the ego in Bible-based psychotherapy is to acquire knowledge of the Bible, resonating its warning and internalizing its blessing.

SUMMARY AND CONCLUSIONS

Freud offers us much good wheat among the tares. His formulation of intrapsychic conflict helps us understand the psychological dynamics of our existential dilemma. The Freudian model sees the need for reconciliation between the id and the superego to attain mental health. The biblical model agrees with this, but in a way that is profoundly altered by the elements of the conflict.

In the biblical view, the conflict is driven by avoidance of eternity in hell. In the Freudian one, the conflict is driven only by worldly gratification. The critical difference is that the biblical counterpart of the superego is God's innate law which tells humans they are doomed by their ineradicable sin nature. This is an archetypical intrapsychic conflict that only God can resolve: escape from hell through reconciliation between imperfect man and the perfection of God. The Gospel, and only the Gospel, offers mental health.

There is nothing new to Christian psychotherapy about incorporating the tripartite Freudian model of the psyche.[24] However, none of the previous Christian theorists have postulated that God's deadly law, the structural equivalent of Freud's "superego," is inherited by all humans as the root cause of psychopathology. They have therefore not gone as far as saying Christ, as God's gift of a dispensation within his law, is both necessary and sufficient for mental health (see Chapter Twelve for a discussion of Christian approaches to mental health).

The Bible-based definition of the basic conflict implies a fundamentally different approach to psychotherapy than the Freudian one. The focus needs to be on the future rather than the past, on the relationship with God through Christ rather than the relationship with the family.

Notes

1. Freud, Sigmund (1935). Autobiography. New York: Norton; see also Freud, Sigmund (1961). Complete Psychological Works (Standard Edition, translated by J. Strachey). London: Hobarth Press.

2. Wulff, David (1991). "The Life of Sigmund Freud." In Psychology of Religion. New York, New York: John Wiley and Sons, p. 263.

3. Freud, Sigmund (1953). The Future of an Illusion. New York: Liveright.

4. Freud, Autobiography.

5. Freud, Autobiography.

6. Central conference of American rabbis (approx. 1900). Pittsburgh, Pennsylvania. "We reject as ideas not rooted in Judaism the beliefs in bodily resurrection and in Gehenna and Eden as abodes for everlasting punishment and reward."

7. For an exposition of this, see Luthman, Shirley Gehrke (1972). Intimacy: The Essence of Male and Female. San Rafael, California: Mehetabel and Co.

8. For example: Freud, Anna (1946). The Ego and the Mechanisms of Defense. International University Press; Rapoport, D. (1959). "The structure of psychoanalytic theory: A systematizing attempt." Psychological Issues, 6, International University Press.

9. Sigmund Freud (1927).   The Problem of Lay Analysis. New York: Brentano.

10. Norman O. Brown (1959).   Life Against Death: the psychoanalytic meaning of history.   Middletown, Conneticut: Wesleyan University Press.

11. Horney, Karen (1945).   "The Basic Conflict."   In Our Inner Conflicts.   New York: W. W. Norton and Company, Inc., pp. 34-37

12. Horney, Karen (1937).   The Neurotic Personality of Our Time.   New York: W. W. Norton.

13. Erikson, Erik (1950).   Childhood and Society.   New York, New York: Norton Publishers.

14. McDargh, J. (1986).   "God, mother and me: An object relational perspective on religious material."   Pastoral Psychology, 34, pp. 251-263.

15. Bradley, C. (1988, April).   "The most preferred parent hypothesis as a determinant of God concept."   Paper presented at the meeting of the Southeastern Psychological Association, New Orleans, LA.

16. Spilka, B., Addison, J. and Rosensohn, M. (1975). "Parents, Self, and God: A Test of Competing THeories of Individual-Religion Relationships." Review of Religious Research, 16, 154-165.

17. Marcuse, Herbert (1955).   Eros and civilization: a philosophical inquiry into Freud.   Boston: Beacon Press.

18. Freud, Sigmund (1940). "An Outline of Psychoanalysis."
In <u>Standard Edition, Vol 23</u>, 1964, pp. 139-207.

19. Watson, P.J., Morris, R. J. and Hood, R. W., Jr. (1988).
"Sin and self-functioning, Part 1: Grace, guilt, and self-
consciousness." <u>Journal of Psychology and Theology</u>, <u>16</u>, pp.
254-269. This is the first of a series of five studies by these
authors. The work shows that guilt is not necessarily related
to maladjustment. For a subsample of students in a Christian
college, guilt was associated with indices of adjustment.

20. Zeigarnik, Bluma (1927). "Uber das Behalten von
erdedigten und unerledigten." <u>Handlungen Psychologische
Forschung</u>, <u>9</u>, pp. 1-85. Research showing that people recall a
greater proportion of interrupted than completed tasks.

21. Worthington, Everett L. (1989). "Religious Faith Across
the Life Span: Implications for Counseling and Research." <u>The
Counseling Psychologist</u>, <u>17</u>, 4, pp. 555-612.

22. David Lachar (1987). <u>The MMPI: Clinical Assessment
and Automated Interpretation</u>. Los Angeles: Western
Psychological Services. A low score on the defensiveness scale
of the MMPI is often associated with psychopathology,
malingering, or a cry-for-help.

23. Kane, R.D., Merkangas, K. R., Schwartz, G. E., Huang, S.
S. et al. (1990). "Inverse relationship between defensiveness and
lifetime prevalence of psychiatric disorder." <u>American Journal
of Psychiatry</u>, <u>147</u>, 5, pp. 573-578.

24. Frank B. Minirth (1977). <u>Christian Psychiatry</u>. Old
Tappan, New Jersey: Fleming H. Revell Company.

Chapter Six

THE FREUDIAN FIG LEAVES

VERSUS THE GOD OF GRACE

Freud defined two tasks for the ego: defense and control. Both are discussed in this chapter, but the first one is of most interest to us. Ego defense explains how we humans can be so blind to our terrible dilemma. It also shows us how psychopathology arises out of our need to escape from it.

The second task, ego control, is a more conscious process of restraining and rechanneling id impulses. However, control of the id is very limited until grace has entered our spirit.

DEFENSES: PSYCHOLOGICAL FIG LEAVES

Like lava inside a volcano, the truth keeps wanting to erupt into consciousness, but our psyche resists it. Satan wants to keep it this way. If we cannot see the truth, we will not reach out for our God-given rescue. At times the resistance is conscious, but most of the time we are blind to our blindness.

The complex arsenal of invisible psychological defense mechanisms has considerable intuitive validity. There is also research evidence for its presence.[1,2] The very intensity and pathological side effects of the arsenal make it cost ineffective unless its purpose goes way beyond the concerns of this world. So much psychic energy is poured into the ego's varied and colorful menu of defenses that it is clear that they are there to fight something terrible. Until we know God has given us the only valid defense, the shed blood of the lamb, what else can our poor little ego do? This extensive fig leaf armour only makes sense as equipment used to ward off a dark destiny. The ego uses these tools 1) to hide and 2) to atone.

HIDING

One element of the ego's work is to hinder us from conscious knowledge of our existential position. Walls are erected inside us; and "every city or house divided against itself shall not stand" (Matthew 12:25). Behind the walls, various tools of distortion are employed to keep the truth from surfacing. This "divided self," a term R. D. Laing used for schizophrenia, actually has a much wider application. It describes the lack of psychological integrity due to separation from God.[3]

ATONEMENT

The other line of defense strives for resolution of the conflict at an unconscious level. The ego's defenses do what they can to pay for sin with the limited means they have available: works, suffering, self-purification, and the like.

WHY DEFENSES?

What do defenses really achieve? We want to be at peace, to escape from the existential guilt that eats away at us. The defenses allow us to pretend. The problem is we can run, but we cannot hide for very long. The fig leaf armour often stretches to snapping point. It requires constant repair.

God's sin/death equation applies to thoughts as well as actions. This means not only is it dangerous to act; it is dangerous to think and feel. The conscious knowledge of breaking the law can be terrifying. It brings the imminence of death and our absolute powerless towards it right into the forefront of our awareness. Existential doom is the true source of the "fear of abandonment" that brings many people into therapy. Until we are assured that God has forgiven every one of our transgressions, all elements of our life/death conflict must be keep out of consciousness. We must not see we are lawbreakers; we must blind ourselves to the law; and we must not believe in eternal darkness.

The tricky thing to keep in mind is that guilt often causes symptoms that seem unrelated to any existential concern. Examples are compulsive thoughts or actions; psoriasis; self-loathing; fear of success; and many others that will be described in this and later chapters. Moreover, defense mechanisms are not mutually exclusive by any means. They operate in concert. In fact, all mental disorders can be characterized by a particular constellation of defenses. So can "normal" personalities; we all use defenses to some extent.

The list we have here is not exhaustive. Creative as God has made us, we keep coming up with new ways to hide from the truth. Just as habitual liars learn to become increasingly subtle, there seems to be a developmental process in defense-building. This tool of Satan, the "father of lies," (Acts 5:3) moves towards increased sophistication and specialization. However, under acute stress, the more advanced defenses can give way to the clumsier, global, primitive ones. When even these fall apart, there is a state of breakdown into acute mental illness...unless we claim Christ as our defense.

A "primitive/sophisticated" dimension is frequently mentioned in the psychodynamic literature.[4] Consequently, the defense panoply has been divided for present purposes into two major categories. The first consists of primitive defenses: eliminators; acting out; regression; and delusions and fantasy. The second includes the more sophisticated ones: compartmentalizers, analyzers, pseudo-atoners, and deflecters.

PRIMITIVE DEFENSES

The primitive defenses tend to be more dysfunctional. They arise earliest during development and generally act in a massive, indiscriminate way. Their ranks include the "eliminators," which push material away from consciousness. Also in this category are regression; delusions and fantasy; and acting out.

ELIMINATORS

The first step in the defense process is to push guilt-arousing information out of consciousness. Eliminators remove threat from view, sweeping it under the carpet. On a continuum from more to less conscious, we have suppression, or conscious avoidance ("I know it's there but I won't look at it"); denial, or conscious negation ("It's not a problem"); and repression ("I have no idea it's there").

Repression

Repression causes elements of a conflict to be pushed or kept completely below the surface of consciousness. On the surface, there seems to be a simple loss of memory...quite innocent. Guilt-triggering single events or whole periods of a person's life can be conveniently forgotten, buried.

If the person has been the subject of extreme physical or sexual abuse, the most deeply buried part of the experience will be his or her own guilt, whether it is based on transgression (examples are a true sense of complicity, or murderous rage towards the abuser) or not (a false sense of having somehow caused the whole episode). When this memory loss is obvious, it is called "psychogenic amnesia."

The archetypical material described in Chapter Four, particularly our innate sense of being doomed to spend eternity separated from God in pain and darkness, is kept captive below the surface. Only the safety of the Gospel frees it to become conscious, except when it comes shooting up unexpectedly in the form of dreams, panic attacks, visions, and the phenomena we call psychotic.

OTHER PRIMITIVE DEFENSES

Eliminators push knowledge away; their effects are not immediately obvious. Other primitive defenses give rise to more noticeable changes in behavior and personality.

Regression

One way to deal with guilt is to go back to infancy, or a reasonable facsimile of it. Pseudo-infancy creates the illusion of non-responsibility. It is a state of decisionless withdrawal and passive inertia, avoiding blame for the present, future, or past: "I do not know what is going on; I have no control; I do not make any decisions; therefore I am not subject to punishment."

Earlier stages of development are stored away in our memory. They can be revisited, these apparent safe havens. Like a babe in the womb, we let ourselves go back to them and be passively carried along even though that means surrendering to another's control. Somewhere inside us we know that God does not hold children accountable. On both emotional and behavioral levels, we attempt to stay below that age of accountability.

In decision-making of any kind, the problem is not just that the fear of making a mistake triggers the sense of eternal condemnation. There is also the fact that without a mechanism to connect us with God, we have no sense that he will be there to support and sustain us in the unkown terrain ahead. Regression offers a means to deny the need to make a decision. It is a hole to hide in.

It may be a mini-hole, a regressive pocket. A person functions at a normal level in one area of life and at a primitive level in another, fixated in that area of functioning.

The "Peter Pan" syndrome has been on the increase in the last few years.[5] Adult-aged humans act like children, avoiding commitment and responsibility. But this type of regression is mild compared to some of its other forms: dementia, substance abuse, and acute psychosis. All of these involve a global escape from consciousness into childlike dependency.

This piece of deductive humor on the wall of a restaurant expresses the thinking process of regressive escapism: "When I get drunk, I sleep; when I sleep, I don't sin; when I don't sin, I go to heaven; so let's all get drunk and go to heaven." The fallacies are, one, that we are pure in our sleep, as if some of our darkest impulses do not come out in our dreams, and, two, that we have to refrain from sin to get into heaven. However humorous, this is a sad example of the pervasiveness of the legalistic thinking that leads to defense.

Delusions and fantasy

Daydreaming, television-watching, movies, and novels provide the refuge of passive fantasy, a hypnotic escape to the imagination. Active fantasy, as found in the creative arts, can have both an escape and a control function. It gives the illusion we can bend reality to fit our needs. The process of making a graphic representation of a monster seems to give a person power over it, robbing it of its power over the person.

A delusion is a more pathological type of fantasy characteristic of psychosis, a fantasy that the psychotic consciously appears to believe. Yet there is a curious aspect to delusional thinking to be discussed more fully in Chapters Seven and Eight. On the surface, delusions are clearly gross distortions of reality. But underneath this there is a true perception of existential reality, a sense of doom that is consistent with the Biblical picture. Delusions of malevolent controlling forces reflect a sense of Satan; messianic delusions reflect a sense of the need for godhood to escape eternal torment.

Acting out

As if we can defy God! But we still try. The law-breaking, defiant, deviant actions of a person who is acting out attempt to deny the authority of the one who put the law in our hearts. We humans try to prove to ourselves there are no repercussions for law-breaking, that God is not watching, and that we are not under a deadly sentence. The louder the internal voice of condemnation from the conscience, the more a person acts out in denial of it.

Research has substantiated the shame-based origin of this defense.[6] The inner impulse gives the order to drown shame by rebelling. The unconscious anger and rebellion is towards God when Satan, who led humans into their predicament, should be its recipient. God has provided the only way out.

The main course of acting out is often followed by the dessert of pseudo-atonement. The purge follows the binge. Existential guilt and anxiety are alleviated for a while until again there is the need to prove there is no dire consequence for law-breaking.

Often the acting out is in connection with an out-of-control habit a person is struggling with. There is a moment when the urge to exercise the habit is overpowering, and momentarily there is a loss of sight of all the reasons for restraint. Nothing is a clearer indication of our inability to control our nature and our need for Christ.

The more deeply a person becomes involved in acting out, the more serious the transgression and the more buried the conscience. The psychopath is an extreme case. He has no conscious sense of the law, yet feels compelled to break it to empower himself.

Although causality has not been established, studies showing the monotonous brainwave patterns and low levels of serotonin in psychopaths[7] suggest that their behavior has an element of thrill-seeking. They seem to be trying to relieve boredom and depression. The thrill-seeking may take a pathological form because the psychopath has typically been harmed by a childhood of physical abuse and a lack of bonding with parents. He seeks his kicks through mistreatment of fellow human beings, apparently excited by his power to manipulate and deceive them in the process. He must assert his complete independence of God and everything God stands for. This is why Satan worship is common among psychopaths.[8] His underlying sense of condemnation tells him he is hopelessly lost. This he tries to disprove by going further down the path of crime.

SOPHISTICATED DEFENSES

There is a huge cost to the primitive forms of defense. Global repression, regression and acting out can have a tragic impact on the quality of life.

Consequently, some more specialized, sophisticated defenses tend to develop over time. The benefits are that there is reduced "defense spending," i.e., less emotional/behavioral disruption. But they are more insidiously harmful in their blinding effects.

These are grouped here as the compartmentalizers, the analyzers, the pseudo-atoners, and the deflectors.

COMPARTMENTALIZERS

Just as a bomb is only dangerous when all its components are properly connected, certain defenses have the task of compartmentalizing or separating elements of our conflict from one another.

Isolation

The defensive function of isolation is to keep threatening material superficially disconnected from the conscience. In the example of David used previously, he knew the law, but he made himself blind to the moral meaning of his actions. In his conscious thought, his actions were isolated from the law. He could pretend he was safe from guilt and punishment; thus he allowed himself to continue on his corrupt course.

He did not consciously see the meaning of what he had done to Bathsheba and Uriah until God showed him through Nathan, the prophet. Nathan knew David would not accept direct criticism. It would only arouse defensiveness. So he told him in an indirect way, through the story of the rich man taking the poor man's one little sheep. He had to use an analogy in the form of a parable to hold up a mirror that David would accept.[9]

Isolation acts locally, turning items of conscious thought into islands separated from moral evaluation. One sin leads to another behind these blind spots. David went from stealing a man's wife to having the man killed. Guilt was there, but it lay below the surface where he would not feel the stabs from his conscience.

Dissociation

Dissociation is a withdrawal from one state of consciousness into another. In its less pathological form, it is a common defense...the sudden shift of attention away from a threatening thought, the abrupt transition in a conversation. In psychotherapy sessions with unbelievers, the topic of death is most likely to produce to produce this response.

There are two highly pathological forms of dissociation. One is the "fugue" state often depicted in movies. Here, the split is so complete that the person loses all sense of his true identity, as if waking up in a new world, reborn as a new person.

The other is the Multiple Personality Disorder (MPD). A psychological-biblical explanation for MPD is that the ravening wolf of the sin nature and its consequence is kept at bay by breaking him down into some lesser wolves. At the first sign of threat, one personality is shed for another. Transgress as Mr Hyde, slip back into Dr Jekyll when the first intimation of guilt appears, and have no conscious sense of being a bad guy.

The mechanism for both of these serious conditions has been described as self-hypnosis, but it is likely that demonic agency is a factor in many cases (see Chapter Eight).

MPD and other dissociative phenomena are common among adults abused as children, particularly incest victims. To avoid the guilt feelings and the sense of existential powerlessness triggered by the incident, the defense wipes the experience out of consciousness. However, its toxic influence remains. Adults abused as children tend to enter dissociated states as abusers and/or abusees.

Idealization and devaluation

Idealization is a defense permitting us to see only the good in ourselves and others; devaluation is the opposite. "Good" and "Bad" are kept in separate boxes. Knowing the consequence of the tiniest flaw, we humans strive to find perfection in another. If that person can be perfect, so can we.

We seek someone to adore without reservation. Our innate sense of God makes us do that. If we do not have God, we idolize some human. We blind ourselves to their shortcomings, telling ourselves that any flaws we see in them are shadows cast by others. Eventual recognition of the truth takes us to the opposite pole; the angel becomes a devil to be shunned.

Rejection of that other human being is a mirror of an internal process. Seeing their imperfection only reminds us of our own. If they cannot be perfect, neither can we. In rejecting them, we strive to reject our death sentence. Then we go and seek someone else to idealize, repeating the pattern.

ANALYZERS

Analyzers capitalize on the human mind's ability to erect false beliefs or objective detachment around a guilt-arousing thought.

Rationalization

Rationalization works hand-in-hand with isolation. As a more conscious mode of defense, it redefines either sin or the law to justify transgression.

David could have rationalized his seduction of Bathsheba with the argument that she enticed him by taking a bath in a public place, on the roof of her house. This made it right for him to send his soldiers over to fetch her to the palace. She was asking for it. And then, when she found she was pregnant, he had to cover up his part in it in some way...for her sake. But this was adultery, punishable by death according to the law God gave Moses.

Rationalization desensitizes the conscience by turning wrong into right, each time on a grander scale.

Intellectualization

Intellectualization is a mind/body split, a separation of cognition and emotion, a loss of spontaneity. On the rare occasions when the intellectualizer does express feelings, it sounds like a conversation about somebody else. He lives in his head not his heart.

Although a mild form of intellectualization is common, this type of detachment is found in an extreme form in schizophrenia. There can be an acute separation of thoughts and feelings. Affect is often inappropriate; the schizophrenic may laugh as he describes the death of a close relative.

Intellectual dissociation is actually a goal of Eastern religions. The premise is that detachment and objectivity stop the darker emotions from producing guilt. In theory, we can perceive that our darkness is just an illusion, or simply accept it. But in reality, we can do neither. Emotions are no more an illusion than the person who experiences them, and guilt is a reflex that shows us our darkness is not acceptable to us.

The dissociative process involves progressive loss of contact with the inner self. It leads down the path to insanity.

PSEUDO-ATONERS

Pseudo-atonement is a futile unconscious attempt to get out from under the hell sentence through one's own efforts. It stems from the merciless perfectionism of an innate law that needs the light of God's forgiveness to shine in. In fact, the ritualism of all non-Biblical religions involves this type of defense (see Chapter Ten for a comparison of perfectionism with grace). Since Freud saw no mercy in Christianity, he dubbed it a "universal, obsessional neurosis." But in truth, true biblical Christianity is the only religion that does not deserve this title (see Chapter Ten).

As we will see, pseudo-atoners account for a wide range of eccentric and pathological human behavior.

Turning against the self

As stated in Chapter Five, Freud found masochism and self-sabotage to run so strongly through the psyche that later in his career he postulated a basic self-destructive drive, a drive towards extinction. Subsequently his daughter, Anna, removed masochism from among the inherent drives and put this tendency where it belongs: among the ego's defense mechanisms.[10]

"Turning against the self," as Anna Freud called it, is the donning of the hair shirt, a prominent component of false religions which promote suffering rather than grace as a route to salvation. It is a mechanism associated with i) self-mutilation; ii) abusive relationships; iii) self-sabotage; and iv) a number of sex differences. The last category includes sex-linked physical illness, particularly the auto-immune type in which the body's defense against illness attacks the very organism it was designed to protect.

Self-punishment is a perplexing tendency both for those stuck in it, and for others around them. Its function is to temporarily reduce existential guilt and anxiety. The guilt in the collective unconscious says humans deserve to suffer. Deep inside, we anticipate a terrible punishment but do not know what, or when. As in the case of a child told to expect a good hiding when his father comes home, it is a relief to be penalized. At least the suspense is reduced.

We unconsciously try to take control of the existential situation by seeking hurts, rejections, abandonments, and failures. To have anything good happen makes us uncomfortable. It arouses a sense of unworthiness, undeservingness. Our guilt makes punishment and failure feel appropriate. As stop-gap measures, they are recurrent and the personality becomes organized them.

i) Self-mutilation

Making oneself bleed through superficial skin wounds is a common "martyring" phenomenon in Major Depression and Borderline Personality Disorder. This certainly points to an innate sense of the essentialness of blood atonement.[11] Sometimes even suicide is viewed as a way to pay, but self-sacrifice will not rescue us from eternal darkness. If the price for sin is death, atonement can only come through one who has no sin. Only God has the power to atone for us. But even though we know this in a deep, unconscious way, we still find ourselves seeking suffering until we fully know of God's ransom.

ii) Abusive relationships

We fall into abusive relationships where we unwittingly encourage the other person to mistreat us. Consciously perceiving the sickness in one such relationship but not knowing our unconscious motive and its remedy, we may escape from it only to drop into a worse one. We can never get enough mistreatment, because no amount of our own suffering can pay the price for sin, no matter how miserable we make ourselves.

iii) Self-sabotage

On the brink of success, often after many years of hard work, there is a silly mistake or the omission of the last step. We can set ourselves up for failure in an elaborate fashion, the higher the climb, the harder and more punishing the fall.

iv) Men, women, and self-punishment

It has long been noted that women tend towards more diseases of the nervous system than men.[12]   Seemingly, they handle guilt differently. In particular, they display more psychological disorders that involve self-punishment; they are far more likely than men to be classed as having one of the two "new" personality disorders: the masochistic and self-sabotaging disorders.[13]

Women are also twice as likely as men to suffer depression, a disorder in which guilt is highly conscious.[14] Consistent with the archetypical curse discussed in Chapter Four, they display disorders reflective of powerlessness and dependency on males: hysterical personality disorder;[15] conversion disorders and neurasthenia;[16] and agoraphobia.[17] Also, more auto-immune diseases are found in women, who have a stronger immune response than men. Devised to make it less privy to outside invaders, their immune system attacks their own body.[18]   Emotionally and physically, their guilt leads them to attack themselves.

Men are more likely to project guilt outward as anger and blame. They become abusers rather than abusees, scape-goating others. Even the first male did this. Adam tried to excuse himself for disobeying God by placing the responsibility not only on Eve, but also on God for having given him Eve for a wife (Genesis 3:12).

Undoing

Undoing, or self-purification, is another way to seek atonement. This involves behavior that has a symbolic quality of cleansing. In its extreme form it is found in the elaborate rituals of Obsessive-Compulsive Disorder. It is no wonder that Freud called this disorder a "private religion."[19]

The Bible certainly gives us some pictures of the defensive nature of undoing. We see the guilty Pontius Pilate washing his hands, one of the most popular activities of obsessive-compulsives. But neither washing the hands nor any of the other compulsive rituals cleanses us from sin.

In Obsessive-Compulsive Disorder, the rituals tend to increase in number, as if adding one more will achieve the cleaning job that all the others cannot. For a while, each new ritual brings relief, but when its placebo effect wears off, another is sought.

In Bulimia, purging aims to atone for sin. But sin cannot be removed from our nature. Intellectually we may see that, yet we unconsciously continue to try to wipe ourselves clean and evade the deadly punishment. Our only escape is to put on the raiment of white linen that God gives us in Christ (Revelation 19:14).

Sublimation

Freud considered sublimation, the theoretical unconscious transformation of the problematic sex drive into a creative drive, to be the healthiest form of defense, one that could benefit civilization. Fulfilment of the sex and (later) aggression drives in creative, constructive activity would eliminate conflict between the id and the superego. As long as the creative work was socially acceptible, the superego would not condemn it. This meant no sin, no guilt, and no neurosis. Instead, a veritable orgy of creative work could be attacked with gusto every day.

Note that sublimation is omitted from the glossary of defense mechanisms listed in the Diagnostic and Statistical Manual of Mental Disorders (DSM-III-R). Based on post-Freudian theorizing about a basic drive towards constructive activity, sublimation is no longer viewed as a transformation of the sex drive.[20]

However, Freud hit on something important in his conceptualization of work as defensive. For one thing, i) work can be a distraction from all the vegetative appetites. However, its most critical defensive goal is ii) salvation.

i) Distraction

One way to avoid sin is to tire oneself out. Moreover, work can be a distraction from thought and feeling, particularly from existential foreboding. It is a considerably less dysfunctional way to escape pain than many others.

ii) Salvation by works

The mistaken belief in salvation through good works is very much alive in every false religion. As an alternative or adjunct to "undoing," it offers "doing" as a way to strive for connection with God. It becomes compulsive, a constant scrambling to make a payment that cannot be paid.

Freud did not see the terrible life/death struggle the so-called sublimation process was aiming to resolve. Works can never be sufficient according to the standard of perfection. Never can enough be done, never is the quality good enough. The Bible describes all human efforts that are offered to God to try to buy ourselves back from Satan's clutches as "filthy rags" (Isaiah 64:6). It is ludicrous to hold out a few good works to God when the price for sin is death.

The workaholic knows, deep inside, that he can never achieve enough to save himself, and he is utterly miserable about it. Under the gun, there is no true creativity. Lacking the freedom to risk failure, he is forced to cling to the tried and true formula. There can be elements of sensual pleasure in it; it can feel "sexy" in a limited way, and to that extent it offers intrinsic gratification. But when the larger context is fear, creativity is constrained.

It is interesting that Freud placed such emphasis on sublimation as a solution. It is undoubted that he, too, unconsciously saw work as a form of salvation. According to the liberal Judaism in Freud's background, a person's offspring and works are the only form of after-life he can aspire to. In theory, a person can die content by leaving behind a legacy of good deeds, having made the world a better place than it was when he came into it.

There are four problems with this. One is that a person would have to delude himself in order to believe he is leaving the world a better place. Another is that the idea of contentedly going into extinction contradicts the aggressive drive for life that was so apparent to Freud in his patients. The third is that there is no immortality in works. Books go out of print and buildings get bulldozed. The last, and most important, is that it denies the reality of hell.

When we know we are saved by grace, not works, work takes on a different quality. It stops being compulsive. We are free to create because we want to, in whatever way we choose.

Self-forgiveness

Self-forgiveness is a concept adopted in recent years by the mental health establishment from Eastern religions. Since the establishment fails to consider the existential basis of guilt, this blasphemy is treated as a valid therapeutic option. Because only God can provide the forgiveness that produces mental health, self-forgiveness belongs among the Satanic lies, a superficial cover.

Although self-forgiveness has some similarities to rationalization, its dynamics are different. Both types of defense allow the perception of sin to enter conscious awareness, but they deny guilt in different ways. Rationalization excuses sin by transforming it into permissible behavior; self-forgiveness says sin is sin, but claims to pardon it internally.

Prophets of self-forgiveness claim it can heal. However, deep down, we humans know we do not have the power of existential forgiveness. Our guilt and shame are based on the fact that the price for sin is death, and humans cannot reprieve their own death sentence.

We are not gods, and our capacity for forgiveness is limited. If we need proof of this, all we have to do is look at how little forgiveness we have for other human beings.

DEFLECTORS

Deflectors get rid of threat through an unconscious deflecting or reversing function. Thie group includes displacement, reaction formation, projection, and identification. They are bizarre gyrations of a mind desperately twisting away from the doom in God's law. It simply makes no sense that our minds would distort so much just to protect us from being abandoned by our human support system.

In a curious way, however, the deflectors underscore biblical truth: that God has deflected our punishment away from us and put it on Jesus. Many people find the idea of that ridiculous. Yet these same individuals are undoubtedly using unconscious defense mechanisms to try to put their guilt on some external source.

Displacement

Displacement shifts a threatening feeling or impulse, often an angry one, from its true object. It vents anger on an object that is not guilt-provoking. The anger will be acceptable in this new situation, unrecognized for what it is. Smashing an inanimate object causes a lot less disruption, and triggers less guilt than smashing someone's head. Yet even that "someone" is not the true source of the emotion. Satan is responsible for all the misery and suffering in the world, and deserves all our anger. Yet our anger gets displaced on every object except the appropriate one.

Passive aggression is a form of displacement. Comission is replaced by the less threatening omission. Instead of acting on an urge to attack somebody who engenders anger, users of the passive-aggressive approach forget an appointment with them, procrastinate, become inefficient.

They are not consciously aware of this pattern. Consequently, when the other person confronts them about it, they are indignant. They were not being annoying on purpose. The illusion of innocence is maintained in front of others, the most important of whom is God.

Underneath a passive-aggressive attitude towards life is rage and a sense of powerlessness. The rage is towards the existential position from which humans are are powerless to extricate themselves.

Projection

Because it is essential for us to think we are never at fault, we unconsciously assign blame to whatever outside force we possibly can. Instead of seeing my sin in me, I project it on you. Everything my own conscience accuses me of is yours, not mine.

To avoid confronting the truth about my nature, I stick it on you. In fact, I make believe you are anything I want you to be to suit the situation. I justify my exploitation of you by deceiving myself that you like to be treated this way.

The story of the rape of David's daughter, Tamar, by her brother, Amnon, gives us a vivid example of not only projection, but also of the way idealization quickly turns to devaluation. The unconscious projection of sin is seen in the fact that after he violated Tamar, Amnon's obsession with her turned to contempt, as if she, rather than he, were the guilty party (II Samuel 13).

Paranoid projection

Paranoid projection allows me to maintain that it is not my own sin that dooms me. No, there is someone out there who wants to harm me despite my innocence. I must be constantly on my guard to avoid being foiled by that someone who plots against me endlessly.

This psychological defense must be differentiated, of course, from a realistic sense that Satan and his minions really are out to destroy me. As the old joke says: just because I'm paranoid, it doesn't mean nobody's out to get me.

Reaction formation

A reaction formation is a kind of whitewashing, turning the scarlet sin as white as snow. A guilt-arousing feeling, action, or thought is repressed and replaced by a conscious one that is the very opposite. A child who has a new baby brother will display exaggerated affection towards the infant. Underneath this are the homicidal impulses of acute sibling rivalry. Likewise, under the guise of "taking care of" the other person, a dependant person is actually gratifying a selfish need to be needed.

In the short run, this hypocrisy has some practical value. Not only can it keep us believing we are not sinners, but it can superficially smooth our interpersonal relationships. But sooner or later the true colors will show in an inadvertent way, through an act of unconscious malevolence.

Abused individuals often treat their abusers with excessive affection, not just to keep the peace and avoid abandonment, but to defend against feelings of rage they believe they cannot be forgiven for. They later become abusers and/or victims of the effects of repressed guilt and rage, resulting in psychopathology and physical illness.

The whiting of the sepulchre can produce no true peace because underneath it lies the unresolved terror. We cannot escape the sense of God watching us, knowing our deepest thoughts. But until we know that confessing the truth will not cause utter abandonment by God, we are too fearful to allow ourselves to exercise authenticity. This self-deception is one of the processes involved in development of a personality facade, or "persona," to be discussed next.

Identification

The final defense here is identification (or introjection), the reverse of projection. Identification is a process of assimilating some facet or facets of another person. In a sense, we "become" that other person. This happens through imitation and, probably, something else more subtle and intuitive. We acquire defense mechanisms, skills and knowledge of all kinds resulting in an amalgam of different identities that acts as a shield, a facade. The facade interfaces between us and our external and internal worlds. When we think of ourself, we avoid seeing the real us and look, instead, at the facade.

Jung called this facade the "persona."[21]   He classed it archetypical because of its apparent universality. However, a facade is only essential when we dare not risk confronting the nature that dooms us.

Chapter Five described Freud's hypothesis that the superego is acquired through identification. But that conflicts with the Bible's teaching of the innate origin of the moral code. Even if the little boy does go through a process of identification with his father during the so-called Oedipus period, the primary reason is to escape a death sentence his psyche already knows of. He has no desire for his father's damning moral code; he already has one of his own. What he wants to assimilate is his father's method of apparently evading the sentence.

The parent seems omnipotent and immortal to the child. Like a god, he has conquered death in the child's eyes; he is the child's rock, his source of supply. This is why gurus are so important. So-called adults identify with the seemingly perfect guru to escape eternal punishment.

Both psychosis and some misguided notions of Christianity treat Jesus in this manner. Salvation is to attained by becoming a perfect copy of him (or literally believing we are him in the case of psychosis). But whatever progress we make towards identication with Jesus, we can be sure we will miss the mark. We are stuck with our sin nature. The only way out is to claim his perfection as a cover for our many flaws.

THE ONLY GENUINE DEFENSE

This brings us to the only defense that has true worth. The only place we can attain lasting peace of mind, our only genuine hiding place from Satan, is behind Christ. He is our everlasting shield, the true atoner who deflects punishment away from us, our valid cover-up. God has given him to us; all we have to do is claim him as ours. This frees us from the abyss. Therefore it also frees us from the bondage of the psychological defense armour that twists and distorts us.

The ultimate stage of mature Christianity is to know this fact all the way down to our toenails. This is a stage that few, if anyone, reaches. So to some extent we are all forced to use the self-deceptive system of lights and mirrors so beautifully described by Freud and his followers.

EGO CONTROL AND THE FRUITS OF THE SPIRIT

Whether or not we have Christ as our defense, we humans have many wild impulses and tendencies that need to be dealt with. To be sure, God's eternal forgiveness eliminates the root conflict. However, our rebellious nature does not disappear. It continues to want to run amok.

This presents a different kind of task for the ego, separate from its defensive role. The task is what Freud called ego control. Ego control does not distort or conceal. Instead, it tames the nature. This is a more conscious controlling task, a synthetic or adaptive function of the ego. It resolves the ongoing conflicts between the id and the law by "pruning" the id. Moreover, ego control implies a process of confrontation rather than avoidance. It requires conscious admission of the law-breaking impulses.

Ego control: possible outside the Gospel?

Heinz Hartman[22] and David Rapaport[23] have focused on this adaptive task of the ego from a psychodynamic perspective. The problem with any non-Gospel-based attempt to gain such mastery is that the id cannot afford to reveal itself when it faces a death sentence every which way it turns. Without the Gospel, ego control is a practical impossibility. The id must lie hidden behind ego defenses, tied up like a wild animal, cut off from any taming influence. Taming the beast requires letting him out, but that would mean exposure to the threat of falling into the dark abyss. Unaffordable.

Obviously, we humans must acknowledge the presence of the beast to attain psychological integrity. But despite the Freudian claim that manipulation of our minds can enable us to accept our dark nature, that is not so. It is an option contingent upon knowing of God's complete mercy. Otherwise the fear is overwhelming. Unbelievers cannot let themselves see the utter, damning depravity of the id. All they have open to them is the juggling, distortion, and wriggling away from the horrible reality that the ego fruitlessly tries to accomplish, all the while creeping further and further down the path to insanity.

So the secular ego control theorists are talking about something that is simply unattainable through psychodynamic therapy. Admittedly these theorists aim to restrain the beast rather than transform him, i.e., check negative qualities rather than promote good ones. For them, ego control consists of resisting impulses, postponing gratification, and tolerating unpleasant states such as anxiety, tensions, and disappointment. The biblical terms would be patience and forbearance, to be gained through weak human will-power.

Ego control for a believer

The Bible believer is in a different situation. His ego, or whatever we call the part of us that makes conscious choices, is not alone. The Holy Spirit is available at each point along the way. This means there is the potential for not only restraint but actual transformation.

The defensive network gradually dissolves; the beast can be known. The sense of grace permits conscious experience of "bad" id impulses without fear. They will not sent us to hell, for all is forgiven when we claim Christ. The doorway is open for confession and repentance.

Nevertheless, part of ego control is knowing when to keep our mouths shut. Jesus said: "Behold, I send you forth as sheep in the midst of wolves: be ye therefore wise as serpents, and harmless as doves" (Matthew 10:16). He was addressing his apostles, who had the task of preaching the kingdom of heaven in a hostile climate. But this precaution applies to all of us. Solomon tells us, "A prudent man concealeth knowledge" (Proverbs 12:23). If we want to be sure of our safety, God is the only one we completely open up to. If we display our true colors to humans, we can be rejected or persecuted by unbelievers or legalistic, hypocritical "Christians. They will judge us for our iniquity so as to deny their own.

Among humans, the ones with whom we have the most freedom are other believers, real believers who face their own depravity with humility. Yet even the freest believer has at least one blind spot, a remaining defense towards a flaw of his own that makes him judgmental towards others. The Holy Spirit never stops working on us. He is a loving invader, carrying a bright light into an endless dark cave. Only he has the power to destroy the defensive walls of Jericho; psychological justification cannot do this.

Paul's picture goes far beyond the reduction of tension that was the best the Freudians could muster. States Paul: "But the fruit of the Spirit is love, joy, peace, longsuffering, gentleness, goodness, faith, meekness, temperance: against such there is no law" (Galations 6:22-23). Elsewhere he exhorts: "...follow after righteousness, godliness, faith, love, patience, meekness" (I Timothy 6:11).

Paul warns us not to expect ego control to come easily: "...tribulation worketh patience, and patience, experience; and experience, hope: And hope maketh not ashamed (disappointed); because the love of God is shed abroad in our hearts by the Holy Ghost which is given unto us" (Romans 5:3-5).

Only when we know God loves us are we able to go beyond, at best, tolerating life in this world. Only then can good come out of us. Then we can love others, experience joy, and feel truly at peace. Jesus said "I am come that they might have life, and that they might have it more abundantly." (John 10:10).

About one thing Paul is very clear, though. Good qualities may be gained, but we do not lose our corrupt nature. We are stuck with being sinners, riddled with depravity, until we die: "For I know that in me (that is, in my flesh,) dwelleth no good thing: for to will is present with me; but how to perform that which is good I find not." (Romans 7:18). While secular theory offers us only our very limited human will-power, God can transform our will and our performance.

SUMMARY AND CONCLUSIONS

The concern of this chapter has been ego defense and control. Ego defenses, the psychological fig leaves, have been the main focus. Outside of grace, these lies are essential to hide or contain the ravaging wolf of our desperate predicament. If ignorant of the Gospel, humans would be completely incapacitated without such self-deceit. Things are bad enough even with these defenses. They solve nothing and lead deeper into guilt and insanity.

Our defense equipment takes up a large part of our psychic budget. Lying is consuming and its cost is our psychological integrity. The depth, variety, pervasiveness and dysfunctionality of our defensive flight implies a formidable foe: the sense of being doomed to spend eternity in hell.

The defense network is amazingly varied and cunning, ranging from the primitive types to the more sophisticated ones. Primitive types include the eliminators (suppression, denial and repression), regression, acting out, and delusions. Sophisticated ones include the compartmentalizers, the analyzers, the pseudo-atoners and the deflectors.

The control of basic id drives, understood biblically as tempering the sin nature, cannot be achieved except in a fractured way until the basic conflict is resolved. After that, the Holy Spirit can tame our wild, selfish impulses and make us bear fruit.

Notes

1. Vaillant, G. E. (1986). Empirical studies of ego mechanisms of defense. Washington, D.C.: American Psychiatric Pess.

2. Ihilevich, D. and Gleser, G. C. (1991). Defenses in Psychotherapy. Owosso, Michigan: DMI Associates.

3. Laing, R. D. (1969). The Divided Self. New York, New York: Pantheon Books.

4. For example: Cohen, Frances and Farrell, D. (1984). "Models of the Mind." In Goldman, H., H. Review of General Psychiatry. Los Altos, California: Lange Medical Publications, p. 27

5. Kiley, Dan (1983). <u>The Peter Pan syndrome: men who have never grown up.</u> New York, New York: Dodd and Mead Publishers.

6. Gorsuch, Scott E. (1990). "Shame and acting out in psychotherapy." <u>Psychotherapy</u>, <u>27</u>, 4, pp. 585-590.

7. Brown, G. L. and Goodwin, F. K. (1986). "Human Aggression: A biological perspective." In W. H. Reid, D. Dorr, J. I. Walker, and J. W. Bonner III (Eds.), <u>Unmasking the psychopath.</u> New York, New York: W.W. Norton, pp. 132-155

8. Magid, K. and McKelvey, C. A. (1987). <u>High Risk</u>. Golden, Colorado: M & M Publishing. p. 182a.

9. Some Christians consider hypnosis inherently occultic. They reject it on that basis, little realizing that many Christian practises are trance-inducing. The parable method of teaching, with its use of visualization and metaphor, falls within what are considered today to be hypnotic techniques. The parable technique is used in Ericksonian hypnosis, named after Milton Erickson, who specialized in indirect, allegorical methods.

10. Freud, Anna (1946). <u>The Ego and the Mechanisms of Defense</u>. New York, New York: International Universities Press, Inc.

11. Bradford, D. T. (1990). "Early Christian martyrdom and the psychology of depression, suicide, and bodily mutilation." <u>Psychotherapy</u>, <u>27</u>, 1, pp. 30-41.

12. Beard, G.M. (1881). <u>American Nervousness</u>. Wyoming: G. P. Putnam's Sons.

13. American Psychiatric Association (1987). <u>Diagnostic and Statistical Manual of Mental Disorders, Third Edition, Revised</u>. Washington, DC: American Psychiatric Association, p. 373.

14. Nurnberger, J. I. and Gershon, E. S. (1982) "Genetics." In Paykel, E. (Ed.) <u>Handbook of Affective Disorders</u>. New York: The Guilford Press, pp. 126-145

15. Wolowitz, H. M. (1972).   "Hysterical character and feminine identity."   In J. M. Bardwick (Ed.) <u>Readings in the Psychology of Women</u>.   New York, New York: Harper, 1972.

16. Littlewood, R. and Lipsedge, M. (1987).   "The butterfly and the serpent."   <u>Culture, Medicine and Psychiatry</u>, <u>11</u>, pp. 289-355.

17. Fodor, I. G. (1974).   "The Phobic Syndrome in Women." In V. Frank and V. Burke (Eds.) <u>Women in Therapy</u>.   New York, New York: Brunner/Mazel.

18. Shoenfeld, Yehuda (1989).   <u>The mosaic of autoimmunity: the factors associated with auto-immune disease.</u>   New York, New York: Elsevier Science Publishing Company.

19. Freud, Sigmund (1953).   <u>The Future of an Illusion</u>.   New York, New York: Liveright.

20. White, R. (1959).   "Motivation Reconsidered: The Concept of Competence."   <u>Psychological Review</u>, <u>66</u>, 297-333.

21. Jung, Carl (1935).   "The Relations Between the Ego and the Unconscious." In <u>Collected Works</u>, <u>7</u> (2nd Ed.), 1966, pp. 121-241.

22. Hartman, Heinz (1958).   <u>Ego psychology and the problem of adaptation</u>.   International University Press.

23. Rapaport, David (1959).   "The structure of psychoanalytic theory: A systematizing attempt."   <u>Psychological Issues</u>, <u>6</u>.

Chapter Seven

SCHIZOPHRENIA, PSYCHOTIC

DELUSIONS, AND GOD

The mental health establishment defines psychosis as a break with reality. Not entirely true. In a significant way, it is a break with *unreality*. Psychosis is a window to the collective unconscious. The psychotic disruption of structured, conventional thinking reveals aspects of our existential dilemma we humans are generally not aware of in our supposed "normal" state.

HISTORY OF PSYCHOSIS AS A SPIRITUAL OPENING

Freud[1] and Jung[2] were aware that archetypical material surfaced in psychosis. William James saw the "neurotic temperament" as furnishing the condition for receptivity to divine knowledge and religious truth.[3] Anton Boisen (1876-1965), a minister who regarded himself as a recovered schizophrenic, viewed mental illness as an existential crisis of a spiritual nature.[4] Since then, this position has been taken by other American social scientists.[5] There is, in fact, a growing trend in the United States to treat psychosis as a spiritual opening.[6] Thus it is no surprise that spiritual approaches to mental health treatment are gaining acceptance even in the traditionally anti-godly psychiatric profession.[7] Up to now, however, no theorist has seen psychosis as an opening to specific biblical truth.

Focusing particularly on schizophrenia, this chapter shows that psychosis gives us glimpses of our universal innate awareness of impending doom. The psychotic disruption of the ego's defensive wall of protection permits such a revelation.

Terrifying inborn knowledge comes seeping through chinks in the wall.

The common themes of the false ideas known as delusions, a defining characteristic of psychosis, are particularly revealing. Delusions point to our sense of Satan's power over us.

WHAT IS SCHIZOPHRENIA ?

First, what is schizophrenia? Schizophrenia is a formal thought disorder involving an impairment in rational, logical thinking. Its features, which vary in degree over time, include a flattening of affect; mismatch between verbal expression and affect; loosening of associations; tangential thinking; inability to focus; delusions; hallucinations and other perceptual abnormalities; lack of insight; and a regressive withdrawal from reality into a private world, or autism. Schizophrenics (and, often, their family members) are commonly hypersensitive to hearing, sight, taste, smell, and touch. The disorder may or may not be accompanied by paranoia, that pervasive sense that someone or something is out to harm one.

This mental illness, more than any other, can involve devastating cognitive, affective and behavioral impairment. A high percentage of schizophrenics become incapable of taking care of themselves. Even when stabilized by medication, they usually need much outside help.

PERCEPTION AND THE SUPERNATURAL

Research has demonstrated that human perception is selective. What we see is influenced by our expectations, which, in turn, are structured by our belief system.[8] As a result of cultural learning, the "normal" present day scientific non-supernaturally-inclined mind has no way to integrate information from the spiritual realm. This mind either bypasses supernatural phenomena or attributes them to some non-supernatural agent. This point has been driven home by Castaneda in his books about an American anthropologist in the world of Mexican sorcery.[9]

A Bible-rejecting belief system acts as a defensive barrier to a perception of this other "unscientific" and highly threatening reality. It blocks archetypical material from coming up from inside and information of a supernatural order coming in from outside.

However, existential reality can present itself in such a way that the mind is forced to accommodate to it and form a new framework.[10] This is particularly likely to happen when the defense walls are weakened, as in a pre-psychotic or psychotic state. A breakdown must occur before a new structure can be built, and psychosis is one type of breakdown. In a sense, the lid comes off Pandora's box, a box filled with archetypical knowledge of a terrible dilemma. The agony of this knowledge has its cure in the message of the Gospel.

SCHIZOPHRENIA AND REVELATION

Let us look more closely at two aspects of schizophrenia that lead us to think of this illness as revelatory of our deepest conflict. These aspects are a. form and b. content.

REVELATION AND FORM

The formal aspect is the breakdown of the conscious thinking process caused by the various chemical and physical changes which take place in the schizophrenic brain. These changes impact the very process of thinking. They disrupt the psychological defense network, dissolving the boundaries between conscious and unconscious thought.

Nevertheless, the schizophrenic is never entirely without psychological defense mechanisms, but at the best of times they tend to be the primitive, global kind which snap under pressure: thought blocking, massive repression, affective splitting, incoherence of ideas, autistic withdrawal, and projection. Meanwhile, his hypersensitivity and telepathic ability can give him 1. a strong and pervasive sense of his vulnerability to Satan, and 2. strong intimations of doom, particularly in the case of the paranoid schizophrenic.

This is reflected in Minnesota Multiphasic Personality Inventory profiles of individuals with psychotic disorders. Their profiles include extremely low values on the scales targeting normal defensiveness and high values on the scales concerning a wide variety of bizarre thoughts and sensations, including spiritual ones.[11]

The truth cannot be escaped. All of us must cope with it in some way. For the schizophrenic, it keeps flooding into consciousness. Psychosis is itself an attempt to flee this, but it provides no refuge. Turning the head away from the storm only exposes the psychotic to a worse storm coming from the other direction.   Unsurprisingly, the suicide rate for schizophrenics is very high.[12]

REVELATION AND CONTENT
The second aspect of schizophrenic thought indicating existential revelatoriness is its pervasive psychic content. This includes telepathy and the "religiosity" theme common to delusions and hallucinations.

A. Telepathy
Telepathy is the ability of the mind to receive information from the mind of another, unseen individual. It may be an innate ability, something all intelligent life forms have to some degree that is drowned out by reason, perhaps, in that analytical being, the human. Dogs appear to display it; often they can sense fear or hostility in a stranger long before their owner does.

The available evidence, particularly the research carried out in Russia,[13] suggests that telepathy is no myth. However, this ability is unpredictable, apparently affected by situational factors such as fatigue. For this reason, it is difficult to work with experimentally.

In spite of their general inability to see themselves objectively or empathize with others, schizophrenics often display telepathy. Therapists who work with them can experience the disquiet of finding that the client appears to be reading their mind. For example, more than once a schizophrenic client has called to reschedule an appointment at the same moment I am realizing that I need to change my schedule.

Counselors at a humanistically-oriented residential treatment facility for violent schizophrenic adolescent boys, where physical restraints are minimal, find it dangerous to have telepathic clients. Any fear on the part of counselors is sensed and used by these boys. This has led to a constant fear of fear, making counselors subject to frequent, sudden, unprovoked physical attacks.[14] We must note that the humanistic orientation of the environment provides friendly turf to possessing demons.

In both "normals" and schizophrenics, emotional relatedness facilitates telepathy. One schizophrenic I know had an accident at work. A sharp piece of metal flew into his eye, causing a piercing pain but no serious injury. He later received a phone call from his mother, who lives four hundred miles away, asking him if he had been hurt. She had experienced a shooting pain in her eye at the time it was happening to him.

In addition to telepathy, sometimes other psychic abilities are found among schizophrenics. One is pre-cognition. Several schizophrenic clients in my practise have reported pre-cognitive dreams of specific major world disasters.

According to one school of thought, such phenomena are indicative of demonic possession; in certain instances they probably are. But if God can read our minds and knows the future as well as the past, it is not surprising that humans, made in the image of God, sometimes find themselves doing these things. The problem is that it is tempting for the recognizeably telepathic person to go further. Intrigued by this ability, he may pass the barrier to occultism--seeking information from the spirit world of demons posing as angels of light. Through this route telepathy can lead to possession.

B. Delusions

Delusions, or beliefs that contradict reality and the tenets common to society, are considered a diagnostic feature of psychosis. However, as compared to the standard psychiatric position, a biblical view of the psyche casts a very different light on what we call delusions.

According to the Bible, Satan has numerous evil angels, or demons, at his disposal (II Peter 2:4; Jude 6; Matthew 25:41). This means that there are countless invisible dark forces in our presence, spirit beings who wish to gain possession of a live body. So a psychotic's obsession with strange, evil "forces" is hardly unrealistic. A person experiencing what he refers to as "ghosts in the synapses of my brain" is a lot closer to reality than the psychiatrist who maintains this is a complete fiction.

Overt and covert religiosity

Most, if not all, delusions are either overtly or covertly religious. Overtly religious ones contain references to God, Satan, hell, angels, demons, and the like. Superficially, there may be a strong element of culture-boundness in the overtly religious delusion: individuals in Christian environments talk

about Jesus, whereas Moslems talk about Mohammed.[15]
However, the underlying themes are not culture-bound.
Unsurprising from a biblical perspective, one item of content
found in the religious delusions of all cultures is the concept of
evil spirits.[16] Psychosis makes a person keenly aware of the
power of Satan and his dark angels.

The covert form of religiosity makes more indirect
reference to the supernatural realm. A common feature is the
concept of an evil, controlling force of some type.

Unfamiliar with the workings of the Satanic realm, the
mental health profession does not realize how widespread
religiosity is, recognizing only the overt type. However, overt
religiosity alone is very common. Among delusional
schizophrenic and manic patients, over half of the delusions
had obviously religious content.[17] Undoubtedly the proportion
would be even higher if it included all the delusions of control
and persecution to be discussed later in this chapter.

The point is that underlying the obvious superficial
distortion of reality in the most common types of delusions,
there is truth. Just like dreams and myths, psychotic delusions
point to a deeper reality. They embody an accurate perception
of a world that "normal" people do not consciously see.

God warned us that our rejecting him would lead to such
craziness: "I also will choose their delusions, and will bring
their fears upon them; because when I called, none did answer;
when I spake, they did not hear: but they did evil before
mine eyes, and chose that in which I delighted not" (Isaiah
66:4).

Four major categories of delusions are discussed below:
1) control, 2) persecution, 3) other depressive delusions, and 4)
grandiosity. All can take either the overt or covert form of
religiosity. Like blind men all touching different parts of the
same elephant, different psychoses tend to be associated with
specific types of delusions. All stem stem from the same
existential crisis.

Research has shown that manic and schizophrenic patients
are equally likely to display delusional thinking. However,
manics display grandiose delusions; schizophrenics have
delusions of control.[18] Both types of delusion speak of Satan.
The first reflects his promise of godhood; the second, his
ability to use mind control.

Delusions of control

Delusions of control have a general theme of telepathic mind manipulation. These are the major varieties:-

Ideas of reference. One common type of delusion is called the "idea of reference," a belief that everything in the person's environment is focused on that person; the world revolves around him. When the radio plays a song, it is played especially for him; when people are having a conversation in a restaurant, he is the subject.

Beyond the godlike egocentricity in this type of delusion, it does suggest a sense of a supernatural force at work, reaching out at the person through whatever media are available. It is true that God tries to reach us, and he will use "synchronous" events that have this "especially for you" quality to bring us to attention. But we must be mindful that the devil and his demons also try to reach us through cunning juxtapositions. Not without reason is Satan called "the prince of the power of the air" (Ephesians 2:2).

Thought broadcasting. The phenomenon of "thought broadcasting," involves a belief that a person's thoughts can be heard by others. Thought broadcasting can be expressed in either active or passive modes. When a person uses the active mode, as in "I can beam my thoughts so people can hear them," it has the quality of a godly self-attribution of supernatural power. This is a close cousin to the currently popular New Age (Satanic) theme that thoughts can produce material transformation. But a person can send his thoughts to God through Christ in the form of prayer, and God will bring about material transformation if he so chooses.

The passive form, as in "other people can hear my thoughts," conveys a sense of a supernatural listening presence who hears what is happening inside a person. In truth, God does listen. But demons also have listening ability, albeit on a limited scale. Attending "aura" readings in the past, I was struck by the amount of detailed personal information spirit channelers appear to receive from the dark realm of demons posing as angels of light.

The Bible, shows us, however, that demonic mind-reading is limited. Only Daniel, through God's power, was able to tell Nebuchadnezzar the content of his disturbing prophetic dream. None of Nebuchnezzar's magicians had been able to do so (Daniel 2:27).

Thought insertion. "Thought insertion" involves a belief
that some alien force is able to put thoughts in a person's
mind and control his thinking. Allowing for the reality of the
supernatural realm, this perception makes all the sense in the
world. The devil's role as an intrusive evil thought planter has
been apparent from the time of Eden. But more important is
the Holy Spirit's power of thought insertion. When we pray
for help, it can come in the form of an idea, a fresh
perspective. The Holy Spirit is the one who changes a
person's mind and softens the heart.

Of course, claiming that a thought comes from an outside
agent such as a demon can play a defensive role. Freud went
to the extreme of claiming that the only reality to spirits and
demons was in the form of the projection of primitive
emotional impulses.[19] This projection would dissociate a person
from a threatening thought so as to deny responsibility for sin.

A schizophrenic client of mine who was a member of a
pseudo-Christian cult enjoyed the attention he received
obtaining "deliverance" through prayer ministries at his church.
He found it amusing, this phony release from the numerous
"spirits" which put thoughts of lust, anger, laziness and larceny
into his mind.

True, these thoughts may come from a possessing demon,
but they are also part of our nature. Our sense that this
nature dooms us is what makes us need to lie about it until
we are sure of God's forgiveness.

Other types of insertion delusion. There are other types
of insertion delusion: insertion of sensations, insertion of
feelings, insertion of impulses, and insertion of an outside will.
These certainly look more like possession phenomena than
psychological defenses, but both could be true.

A demon might capitalize on a psychological defense by
taking up residence in the "unlit" area it shields from
consciousness. But once the light of God's forgiveness shines
in, the demon is forced to vacate.

Thought withdrawal. Thought withdrawal involves a
sense that some force has removed a person's thoughts.
The schizophrenic will often claim that part of his
consciousness was lost or "sucked out" on a certain occasion.

This may be a perception of the fragmenting role of
psychological defenses. On the other hand, it may be truly the
work of Satan. However, God is ultimately in charge of

delusions; he can give and remove all the obsessions, fears, covetings, etc.   One client reported that he had experienced the same nightmare--of being chased by "aliens" which emerged from his closet--every night since childhood.   He left one therapy session resolving to ask God to remove this nightmare and keep him safe from any alien presence.   In the next session he reported that the nightmare had not recurred since the first night he had prayed about it.

Persecutory delusions

God said: "Ye shall flee when none pursueth."   This is one of the curses for disobedience (Leviticus 26:17).   Such flight is true of the psychological defense process in general, and of persecutory delusions in particular.

The underlying truth is that Satan *is* lurking out there, waiting to trap us.   However, persecutory delusions may stem from both a genuine perception of the demonic and a denial of the person's own dark side.   Through dissociation and projection, our mind bestows the sin nature that puts us under the death sentence on the outside world, mentally adding it to the legion of dark forces.

Persecutory delusions are found in several psychotic conditions.   Depending on the disorder, they are given differing explanations by those experiencing them.[20]   In schizophrenia and paranoid disorders, they are seen as jealousy of the persecutor.   In depression, they are due to moral failure, i.e., sin.   In mania, they are due to misunderstanding by the persecutor.   Only in organic disorders is no motive seen; the person expresses bewilderment at his "persecutors."

The depressive is closest to the truth.   Sin separates us from God and exposes us to the persecution of the devil.   But there is validity to the other interpretations.   Persecution *is* motivated by jealousy and misunderstanding on Satan's part.   Satan is not only jealous, but also envious of God.   Misunderstanding the nature of God's power, he is trying to destroy the most remarkable part of the creation: humans.

Other depressive delusions.   A variety of other types of delusion are common to people with psychotic depression and, to some extent, schizophrenia.   Like persecutory delusions, they are true statements of man's state outside of God's grace.   Delusions of guilt, poverty, nihilism, death, putrefaction, and illness are all based on a valid perception of the human condition and expectations if God had not bailed us out.

The following truths are written in our psyche: we deserve punishment; nothing truly belongs to us; we are worthless in terms of our ability to earn salvation; all our good works are like filthy rags; life is meaningless without God; death stalks us; and there is something profoundly ill and rotten about us. A hopeless state without our rescuer! However, the downward pull of these thoughts reverses when we perceive God's grace.

Grandiose delusions

There is widespread agreement in the mental health profession about the defensive role of grandiose delusions, common in Bipolar disorder with its alternating manic and depressive phases.[21]

Claiming godly qualities aims to escape hell. Nowhere do we see more clearly the attempt to identify with God than in the various types of common grandiose delusion: delusions of entitlement, of messianic abilities, of wealth, of power and giftedness, and of indestructible health and eternal life. Satan's lies at their loudest! Yet through Christ, the most important of these things, eternal life, becomes ours, and many of the others follow, not through our own grandiosity but through humility before God.

"Problem-solving" psychosis?

It has been noted that just after a certain type of brief psychotic-cum-mystical experience, people appear more sane.[22,23] Consequently, this has led to a belief in psychosis as an experience that is inherently problem-solving.[24] It has been described as positive disintegration,[25] creative illness,[26] and spiritual emergence.[27] Closely paralleling the Jungian archetypes mentioned in Chapter Four, the following eight themes have been found in the "delusions" of non-Christians having such psychotic episodes:

1. Death: being dead, meeting the dead.
2. Rebirth: new identity, new name, becoming a god.
3. Journey: sense of being on a journey or mission.
4. Encounters with spirits: "good" or evil.
5. Magical powers: telepathy, clairvoyance, telekinesis.

6. Cosmic conflict: good versus evil.
7. New society: change in society, religion, world peace.
8. Union with God.[28]

Judging by the content of the delusions, these psychotic episodes are not truly problem-solving. They appear to reflect openings to two sources: a) threatening internal archetypical knowledge; and b) the Satanic lies of demons posing as angels. They provide a deeper sense of reality but offer false reassurance about it.

C. Hallucinations
Hallucinations are another feature of psychosis, particularly schizophrenia. The mental health profession calls them distortions in perception but it is likely that there is more to them than that. One possible indication of their supernatural origin is that family members of psychotic individuals find that the dog leaves the room when the hallucinations start.[29] Moreover, a substantial minority of otherwise normal individuals report hallucinatory experiences.[30]

Auditory hallucinations
Auditory hallucinations are common in schizophrenia. They are frequently in the form of voices that comment on the person or give orders. Voices rarely say anything kind or constructive; persecution is nearly always their mode.

Auditory hallucinations have been linked to abnormalities in the temporal lobes[31] and basal ganglia.[32] Non-schizophrenic neurological patients report hearing hazy voices when their right temporal lobes are stimulated electrically.[33]

This does not mean that the voices do not stem from a supernatural source. An alteration in the brain means less effectiveness in screening out spiritual reality. The voices that Joan of Arc claimed to hear guided her to lead France in battle, establishing the Dauphin as king. When the Dauphin skeptically asked Joan why the voices did not come to him, Joan replied that they did, but he did not hear them.[34]

Joan's voices possibly had a godly source, but what are we to make of the evil voices heard in psychosis? The psychological explanation is that they are dissociated parts of the self, externalized guilt, represented as distinct persons. The biblical explanation identifies them as demons. Perhaps

both are true.   Satan can take any form in his roles of
deceiver and accuser.   The command type of hallucination,
which, in the most extreme case, tells a person he is so
worthless he ought to go and kill himself, appears most
Satanic.

Visual hallucinations

Visual hallucinations are more likely to take on obvious
religious themes than auditory ones, and tend to be more
archetypical.   Visions of raging fires, angels, demons, and the
like are common.   We must note that such experiences are not
peculiar to psychosis; they have been reported by "normal"
people who engage in spiritual practises.[35]

Claims of seeing demons certainly can be valid according
to the Bible.   However, the validity of claims to seeing or
conversing with God, Jesus, angels, or the Virgin Mary is
questionable.   One test is the fruit: Jesus said the tree is
known by its fruit (Matthew 12:33).   That is, what was
communicated during the vision?   If any element of it
contradicts the Bible, the apparition is demonic.   A specific
criterion is proposed by the apostle John (I John 4:3):   "And
every spirit that confesseth not that Jesus Christ is come in the
flesh is not of God."

For example, a client of mine claims to have had a
vision of a brilliant, shining light which was accompanied by a
spoken "revelation from God."   He was told that God had
never put animal sacrifices into the law, that the killing of
animals was forbidden.   There is a good reason to consider
this demonic.   Rejecting a God who asks for the shedding of
blood will lead us to reject the shed blood of Jesus, the free
pardon God gave us.   Paul, incidentally, mentions the rejection
of meat-eating in connection with demonic seduction in the
"latter times" (I Timothy 4:3)

There are other reasons to doubt the identity of a
"divine" apparition.   Visions of God?   The Bible tells us no
human can see God: "Thou canst not see my face: for there
shall no man see me, and live" (Exodus 33:20).   Visions of
Jesus?   Until his second coming, Jesus told us not to expect
any further signs of him after his resurrection, described as the
"sign of Jonah," a reemergence after three days in the fishes'
belly, a type of death and resurrection (Luke 11:29).   Although
he later appeared to Paul on the road to Damascus, this was

in the form of blinding light. Visions of Mary? The deification of the Virgin Mary is not biblical, so her "godly" apparition can only be demonic.

CREATIVITY AND PSYCHOSIS

We may wonder why God would allow such a thing as psychosis in our genes. Could it ever work for good? It certainly appears so. Some of the very same biochemical and physiological abnormalities that are associated with psychosis are also associated with creativity. Under the right circumstances, psychotic detachment from reality can be a blessing.[36]

During the energetic, less than full-blown, manic phase of a Bipolar disorder, many great works of art are produced. The composers Handel, Berlioz, and Schumann all suffered from manic-depressive psychosis. Periods of feverish productivity were followed by bouts of deep, incapacitating gloom.[37] However, mania becomes debilitating if the restlessness and distractibility associated with it go beyond a certain point.

The interesting thing about paranoid schizophrenics is that they are often highly intelligent,[38] gifted human beings in whom the breakdown in associative thinking can be an asset, facilitating creativity. However, this is when these fragile individuals are in a relatively non-psychotic state. In the loosening of associations of schizophrenia, there is the potential for breaking creative ground, making new connections. That is, until the illness becomes acute and the person loses the ability to focus on anything. Edgar Allan Poe was one writer who clearly had first hand experience with schizophrenia;[39] so were James Joyce, Anne Sexton, Virginia Woolf, John Berryman and Hart Crane.[40]

Taken as a whole, these findings suggest a U-shaped relationship between psychosis and creativity: a moderate level of eccentric thinking and feeling enhances creativity; too little or too much inhibits it. This is further supported by research showing high creativity in family members of individuals who are incapacitated by certain psychotic disorders; shared genetic abnormalities are probably responsible.[41]

The biggest gift of the schizophrenic may be his inability to stop being aware of the supernatural world. This means those who truly hear the Gospel will share it, and feed the sheep. We find schizophrenic characteristics in certain of the prophets. Ezekiel, for instance, displayed an isolating tendency and affective detachment. However, he had no symptoms of disturbed thinking process. His visions and dramatic, symbolic actions could be written off as hallucinations and bizarre behavior if it were not for the fact that they concerned accurate prophesies. Prophets had to be like Ezekiel, able to stand alone, with an overarching sense of God that made them unafraid of the consequences of what God made them utter.

Socrates said: "Our greatest blessings come to us by way of madness, provided the madness is given us by divine gift."[42] He saw that the psychotic's creativity cannot come to fruition unless it is God-centered.

SUMMARY AND CONCLUSIONS

Using schizophrenia as a showcase, this chapter argued that psychotic disorders reveal biblical archetypes universally present in the collective unconscious.

The secular psychiatric profession tends to regard the "religiosity" of the schizophrenic as delusional in toto. However, the underlying religious themes found in all types of delusions are too consistent with the existential dilemma depicted in Genesis to be dismissed as mere symptoms of mental illness. The truth revealed in psychotic "delusions" shows where the real delusions are: the goals of secular psychotherapy (see Chapter Nine).

However, despite the religiosity, the truth of the Gospel seems to be missing from the vocabulary of the person who is actively psychotic. Sensing that only supernatural power will save him, he deludes himself he is God or Jesus. He does not know God loves him and Jesus is his Savior.

This is not to say that psychotic spiritual experiences are always disturbing. A schizophrenic in a catatonic state may later describe having had a profound, oceanic, mystical experience.[43] This is also common in the brief, so-called "problem-solving" psychosis and in the "pro-dromal" period before a full-blown psychosis takes over. But it is not an opening to God. Without Christ, the mystical euphoria soon gives way to phenomena that are anything but comforting. As the walls to the unconscious break down further and the person goes deeper into psychosis, the truth about Satan's role and the desperate existential predicament become a consuming preoccupation.

Notes

1. Freud, Sigmund (1939). "Moses and Monotheism: Three Essays." In <u>Standard Edition, Vol 22</u>, 1964, pp. 1-82.

2. Jung, Carl Gustave (1951). "The Psychology of the Child Archetype." In <u>Collected Works, Vol 9</u>, Part 1 (2nd ed.), 1968, pp. 149-181.

3. James, William (1958) <u>The Varieties of Religious Experience</u>. New York: The New American Library,

4. Boisen, A. T. (1936). <u>The exploration of the Inner World: A study of Mental Disorder and religious Experience</u>. New York, New York: Harper Brothers.

5. Strunk, Orlo (1959). <u>Readings in the Psychology of Religion</u>. Nashville: Abingdon Press.

6. Spiritual Emergence Network, Institute of Transpersonal Psychology, 250 Oak Grove Avenue, Menlo Park, California, 94025. The organization is directed by Stanislaus and Christina Grof.

7. Rosen, Irving (1991). "The Spiritual Dimension of Cognitive Therapy." <u>Journal of Religion and Health</u>, <u>30</u>, 2, pp. 93-99

8. Ball-Rokeach, S. J., Rokeach, M., and Grube, J. W. (1984). <u>The Great American Values Test.</u> New York: Free Press. See also Harvey, O. J., Hunt, D. E., and Schroder, H. M. (1961) <u>Conceptual systems and personality organization.</u> New York: John Wiley and Sons

9. Castaneda, Carlos (1976). <u>Tales of Power</u>. New York, New York: Pocket Books.

10. Piaget, Jean (1923). <u>Language and Thought in the Child</u>. See Piaget's work for an explanation of the processes of assimilation and accomodation. Accomodation is a process by which a new cognitive structure is formed.

11.   Lachar, David (1974).   The MMPI: Clinical Assessment
and Automated Interpretation.   Los Angeles, CA: Western
Psychological Services, p.3.

12. Reynolds, David K. and Farberow, N. L. (1981).   The
family shadow: Sources of suicide and schizophrenia.   Berkeley,
CA: University of California Press.

13. Ostrander, S. and Schroeder, L. (1970).   Psychic Discoveries
Behind the Iron Curtain.   Englewood Cliffs, New Jersey:
Prentice-Hall, Inc.

14. Personal observation from a day spent at a Berkeley facility
with a Jungian orientation, January 8, 1983.

15. Jimens, L., Oritiz-de-Zorate, A., and Antonio, P. (1979).
"Brain delusions and myths."   Revista Psiquiatria Psicologia
Medica, 14, 113-122

16. Westermeyer, J.   (1988).   "Some Cross-Cultural Aspects of
Delusions."   In Oltmanns, T. F. and B. A. Maher (Eds.)
Delusional Beliefs.   New York: Wiley, 212-239

17. Cothran, M.C. and Harvey, P. D. (1986).   "Delusional
thinking in psychotics: correlates of religious content."
Psychological Reports, 58, pp. 191-199.

18. Cothran, M. C. and Harvey, P. D. (1986)   "Delusional
thinking in psychotics: correlates of religious content."
Psychological Reports, 58, pp. 191-199

19. Freud, Sigmund (1938).   The basic writings of Sigmund
Freud (A. A. Brill, Ed. and Trans.).   New York, New York:
Modern Library.

20. Othmer, Ekkehard, and Othmer, Sieglinde C. (1989).   The
Clinical Interview Using DSM-III-R.   American Psychiatric
Press, Inc., Table 4.4, p. 142

21. Neale, J. M. (1988).   "Defensive Functions of Manic
Episodes."   In T. F. Oltmanns and B.A. Maher (Eds.)
Delusional Beliefs, pp. 138-156

22. Perry, J. (1974). The far side of madness. Englewood Cliffs, New Jersey: Prentice-Hall.

23. Laing, R. D. (1972). "Metanoia: Some experiences at Kingsley Hall, London." In H. M. Ruitenbeck (Ed.), Going Crazy. New York, New York: Bantam, pp. 11-21.

24. Boisen, A. T. (1962). The exploration of the inner world. New York, New York: Harper and Brothers.

25. Dabrowski, K. (1964). Positive disintegration. Boston, Massachusetts: Little Brown.

26. Ellenberger, H. (1970). The discovery of the unconscious. New York, New York: Basic Books.

27. Grof, S. and Grof, C. (1985). "Forms of spiritual emergency." The Spiritual Emergency Network Newsletter, Menlo Park, CA: California Institute for Transpersonal Psychology, pp. 1-2.

28. Lukoff, David (1985). "The diagnosis of mystical experiences with psychotic features." Journal of Transpersonal Psychology, 17, 2, 155-181.

29. Moller, M. D. (1992) "Understanding and communicating with a person who is hallucinating." Out of the Fog: San Francisco Alliance for the Mentally Ill, 7, 1, pp. 4-5.

30. Bentall, R. P. (1990). "The illusion of reality: A review and integration of psychological research on hallucinations." Psychological Bulletin, 107, 1, pp. 82-95.

31. Barta, P. E., Pearlson, G. D., Powers, R. E., Richards, S. S. et al. (1990). "Auditory hallucinations and smaller superior temporal gyral volume in schizophrenia." American Journal of Psychiatry, 147, 11, pp. 1457-1462.

32. Lauterbach, E. C. (1989). "Humming, auditory hallucinations and dystonia." Biological Psychiatry, 27, 8, pp. 934-935.

33. Penfield, W. (1975). The Mystery of the Mind: A Critical Study of Consciousness and the Human Brain. Princeton, New Jersey: Princeton University Press.

34. Deen, Edith (1959). Great Women of the Christian Faith. Westwood, New Jersey: Barbour and Company, Inc., p. 62.

35. Bentall, R. P., op. cit.

36. Wolman, B. B. (1967). "Creative art and psychopathology." American Imago, 24, 140-150.

37. Krieger, L. M. (1991, April 7). "Studying the best and the battiest." SanFrancisco Examiner, pp. 2,7.

38. Ogdon, Donald P. (1977). Psychodiagnostics and Personality Assessment: A Handbook, 2nd edition. Los Angeles, CA: Western Psychological Services, pp. 9-12

39. Torrey, E. Fuller (1983). Surviving Schizophrenia: A Family Manual. New York, New York: Harper and Row, p. 7.

40. Krieger, (1991), op. cit.

41. Gottesman, I. I. (1991). Schizophrenia Genesis. New York, New York: Freeman Publishers.

Krieger, L. M. (1991, April 7). "Studying the best and the battiest." San Francisco Examiner, p. 2. Cites research by Ruth Richards of Harvard University showing that family members of Bipolar patients were highly creative.

42. Dodds, E. R. (1951). The Greeks and the irrational. Berkeley, CA: University of California Press.

43. Alexander, F. (1931). "Buddhistic Training as an Artifical Catatonia (The Biological Meaning of Psychic Occurrences)." Psychoanalytic Review, 18, pp. 129-145.

Chapter Eight

IS PSYCHOTIC RELIGIOSITY INNATE?

Why is religiosity so pervasive a feature of psychosis? Scoffers will say that if this reveals anything, it is the influence of religious background. But the small amount of research that addresses this issue certainly does not suggest that religiosity is learned. It suggests the reverse. But before we look at this research, let us first explore the origin of psychosis, once more using schizophrenia as our example.

I. WHAT CAUSES SCHIZOPHRENIA ?
The last chapter made a strong case that 1. schizophrenia is a showcase for 2. the central thesis of this book--the existence of universal, innate knowledge of doom which is at the root of all mental illness. What support have these two assertions from empirical research on schizophrenia?

ORGANICITY
First, is schizophrenia merely a set of maladaptive reponses to stress, or is it an organic disease of the brain? If it is a brain disease, the religiosity phenomenon so clearly a part of it can hardly be superficial. To answer this question, we look at some of the research on functional and formal differences in schizophrenic brain functioning.

FUNCTIONAL DIFFERENCES
Among the functional abnormalities, glucose utilization studies show significantly low usage of the frontal lobes, particularly the pre-frontal area, and of the entire left hemisphere.[1] The pre-frontal area is concerned with insight and

planning; the left hemisphere is involved in linear, analytical thinking.

Abnormal electrical activity has been found in the important limbic system, gateway to incoming stimuli and regulator of emotion.[2] Also, lowered glucose metabolism has been found not only in the limbic system but also in the basal ganglia which control motor activity.[3]

STRUCTURAL DIFFERENCES

The functional abnormalities are accompanied by structural differences. When the brain of a schizophrenic twin is compared with that of his non-schizophrenic twin sibling through magnetic imaging resonance systems, certain specific defects are found in the schizophrenic one. The temporal and hippocampal lobes are abnormally small. These parts of the brain are involved with thinking, concentration, memory, and perception, all of which are typically impaired in schizophrenia. There is also enlargement of the fluid-filled spaces called ventricles.[4]

Brain chemistry is also affected. The drugs effective in reducing the symptoms of the disease block the neurotransmitter, dopamine. This suggests an excess of this chemical in the schizophrenic brain.[5] Dopamine is a protein in the class of catecholamines which transmit information between nerve cells. The excess dopamine could disrupt the limbic system's normal filtering function, causing the schizophrenic to be bombarded with stimuli which cannot be organized and integrated in any way. These findings are consistent with schizophrenic speech patterns that indicate impairment in focusing: digressiveness, tangentiality and circumstantiality.

In sum, the evidence gives clear indication of a brain disease involving drastic alteration in function and form. Its most important aspect for present purposes is the loss of control of the thinking process. A fragmented mind means a breakdown in psychological defenses, an opening through which archetypical material can upwell.

POSSIBLE CAUSAL AGENTS OF SCHIZOPHRENIA

What causes this disease? Genes and stress seem to play a role, but they do not tell the whole story.

GENES

Clearly, the breakdown of normal brain processes in schizophrenia has a genetic basis. There is considerable evidence for this, particularly from research studies on identical twins and other family members. However, there is an all-important "but." Even among identical twins, the concordance rate for schizophrenia is still only thirty to fifty percent, and common prenatal environment cannot be ruled out as a factor.[6]

Moreover, a constellation of abnormal features accompanying schizophrenia are not in themselves necessarily indicative of psychopathology. Other family members of schizophrenics who have never displayed any symptoms of mental illness may also display certain of these features, such as abnormal eye movements and photosensitivity.[7] We do not know why they do not develop schizophrenia. They may have genotype differences;[8] they may have acquired more adequate psychological defenses; or they may experience less strain on the defense equipment with which they function.

At any rate, the evidence on schizophrenics and their family members indicates that more than just genes are required to explain the development of the illness.

ENVIRONMENT

Many theories have been advanced to explain schizophrenia as a response to a pathological environment. However, no single environmental factor has been found to display a strong relationship with the disorder.

Physical environment

On the purely physical end, viruses or chemical exposure are under increasing consideration. For example, a higher incidence of schizophrenia has been found in the adult offspring of mothers who contracted Asian flu during the second trimester of pregnancy. This is a time in fetal development that is critical for neuronal cell migration to the cerebral cortex. Cell migration is known to be altered by enzymes produced by the influenza virus. In line with this, slides of brain tissue have shown disarrayed cells to be characteristic of schizophrenia.[9,10]

The family

On the social end, there is, of course, the family. Cold, controlling, "schizophrenegenic" mothers have been unfairly blamed for driving their children crazy. But in the extensive "maternal influence" literature, statistical relationships have often been weak or insignificant, and no attention has generally been paid to causal direction.[11] After all, if the mother is cold and controlling, it might be a result of her child's illness instead of its cause. Also insufficient attention is paid to possible genetic similarities or underlying environmental influences common to mother and child.

However, we do know that familial factors such as hypercriticality, hostility, or over-involvement are associated with the relapse rate in schizophrenic patients who are released home after psychiatric hospitalization.[12]

"Crazy" society

When R.D.Laing[13] and others point to a crazy society as a cause for schizophrenia, they have no evidence for that. We can just as easily say that crazy individuals will produce a crazy society.

On a national level, no particular type of social structure as can be described as schizophrenia-prone. In fact, the rate of schizophrenia in every country in the world is approximately one percent.[14]

However, it is true that some unexplained local variations in the rate of the disease are associated with ethnicity and socioeconomic status. Low socioeconomic status is generally associated with a higher incidence of all types of psychosis.[15] It is not clear why. The stress of poverty could cause the illness or vice versa.

Time spent in illness

The number and length of psychotic episodes seem to be related to recoverability from schizophrenia: with more episodes or longer ones, the prognosis for recovery is reduced.[16]

One explanation of this would be that individuals who have more bouts of psychosis have more genetic abnormality, so they are sicker from the beginning. Recent evidence does indicate that adult schizophrenics were also abnormal as children. However, we do not know if those who were more abnormal are sicker as adults.[17]

On the other hand, it is likely that the decrease in recoverability is due to the fact that the active psychotic state, with its associated changes in chemical balance in the brain, actually causes brain damage, the more so with each episode.

Demonic influence

A different type of environmental influence comes from the supernatural realm, to which the spiritual sensitivity of the schizophrenic makes him particularly vulnerable.

Demonic possession and its subtler cousin, demonic oppression, are two modes of spiritual attack that precipitate or perpetuate schizophrenia and other mental disorders.

Possession

Spirit possession is a phenomenon mentioned throughout the Bible (Judges 9:23; I Samuel 16:14; Luke 11:24; Acts 5:16). Satan and his demons are spirits, able to achieve embodiment only by entering a living being; such spirits are always described in the Bible as evil or unclean.

Is schizophrenia a form of possession? Buddhistic medicine and other types of non-traditional healing consider spirit possession to be the cause of all mental illness.[18] However, in Matthew's account of healings displayed by Jesus, insanity and possession are differentiated from one another (Matthew 4:24).

Differences in opinion exist about whether demon possession is possible for a true believer in Christ. There is one school of thought that the indwelling Holy Spirit keeps such dark spirit forces outside; they can whisper temptations but not invade. On the other hand there is growing documentation of demonic manifestations among professing Christians.[19]

Incidentally, the fact that some members of the Christian community consider schizophrenia to be nothing more than a possession state may be largely due to a widespread popular misunderstanding about the nature of the disorder. It still tends to be called "split personality" and gets confused with the highly demonic-appearing Multiple Personality disorder (MPD).[20]

Possession criteria. Possession and mental illness do have many of the same characteristics. Several attempts have been made to develop a reliable set of criteria that differentiate between them. The following criteria are based on Gospel accounts of possessed individuals.[21]   Each criterion is followed, in parentheses, with the mental disorder of which it is also characteristic.

Supernatural knowledge (psychotic disorders; hallucinations, delusions); supernatural strength (manic episodes, other psychotic conditions); going about naked (general deterioration of appearance and social conformity common in psychotic disorders); unable to hear or speak, seizures, blindness (conversion disorders, organic mental disorders); use of a "different" voice or presence of a distinct other personality (multiple personality disorder); bizarre behavior (psychotic behavior); fierce, violent behavior (antisocial personality disorder, organic mental disorders); unusual behavior/attitudes, e.g., vicious toward self (psychotic and personality disorders); feeling of overpowering evil; self-report of demonic influence.

But since Satan is the great deceiver who is able to appear in any form, a possessed person may not present as abnormal in any of the ways listed.   Perhaps part of Satan's deception is to make us believe so many phenomena are indicative of psychiatric illness rather than demonic possession. However, accounts of exorcisms suggest that demonic possession is often conspicuous.[22]   This is because Satan's intelligence is limited.   If this were no so, he would not attempt to defy God.

About the conversion symptoms: I have observed numerous physical ailments such as blindness, deafness, and other types of loss of function in schizophrenic and non-schizophrenic clients who fulfilled several of the possession criteria listed above.   God made some specific curses for disobedience (i.e., rejecting him) that look very much like these symptoms (Deuteronomy 28:28):   "The Lord shall smite thee with madness, and blindness, and astonishment of heart."

Oppression

Individuals with schizophrenic symptomatology lack barriers to the supernatural.   If not actually possessed by Satan's realm, they are typically oppressed by it.   Their defenselessness makes them "fair game" for the pressuring, guilt-tripping techniques used by Satan's minions.

During an internship in a psychiatric emergency ward, I had an opportunity to read the files of patients involuntarily committed to a locked ward for observation and treatment.

Among schizophrenic patients, I found myself being surprised at the frequency with which there was a background of heavy occultic involvement by the patient or other family members. This ran from witchcraft, astrology, and spirit channeling to the pseudo-Christian cults.

This impression has been confirmed in my practise. Nearly always have I found schizophrenics to be involved in some religious doctrine of Satanic origin, either on a private basis or as a cult member or ex-member.

Scientific research supports these personal observations. Either 1. schizophrenics avoid organized religion; or 2. they are associated with a cult, i.e., a highly legalistic religion dominated by the esoteric teachings of its human founder.[23]

In terms of the first pattern, an oft-repeated finding has been that self-reported participation in personal and organized religious activity decreases significantly as psychopathology increases.[24,25] More psychopathology tends to be found in individuals claiming solitary religious experiences and expressing independent religious ideas.[26] On the other hand, simple schizophrenia has been shown to be three times more likely to appear in Jehovah Winesses than in the general population, and paranoid schizophrenia is four times more likely among them.[27]

In one way or another, the psychotic schizophrenic is under the yoke of psychic bondage, separated from God and seeking him in the wrong places, putting himself at the mercy of demonic spirits. Several of my clients have been actively psychotic schizophrenics who, nevertheless, profess to be Christians. None of them was clear about salvation through grace alone. They all had some occult beliefs.

A BIBLICAL HYPOTHESIS ON THE ORIGIN OF SCHIZOPHRENIA

The "diathesis-stress" theory states that stress plus genes cause schizophrenia.[28] However, science has not been able to establish this. The reason is that genes and stress are just part of the story.

The following hypothesis is consistent with both the scientific findings and the Bible:

The root cause of schizophrenia is an innate sense of eternal damnation. Religiosity is a manifestation of this. Genes only explain why a person develops schizophrenia rather than some other type of mental disorder when stress triggers the deep archetypical fear.

Thus the two major times of life transition are associated with onset of the disease. In adolescence and the forties, a person is dealing with basic existential questions that are profoundly disturbing and cannot be answered satisfactorily if there is no God and no rescue from hell: Why am I here? What's missing? Beyond life, what? Why do I fear?

It is the terror of hell that sends the genetically-predisposed person into a psychotic flight associated with chemical imbalances and permanent structural impairment.

II. IS RELIGIOSITY INNATE?

This is the crucial question. Religiosity is found in all types of psychosis, not just schizophrenia. Is there evidence that this is anything other than archetypical in origin? The evidence is scant, but so far none of it says that religiosity is anything but innate.

ORGANICITY

Some argue that organic changes in the brain somehow fabricate spirituality. We know that people have spiritual experiences when they take psychedelic drugs. Like psychotics, they display preoccupations reflective of both existential reality and the Satanic lies about it. Preoccupations range from paranoia about evil forces to grandiose feelings of omnipotence and supernatural identification.[29]

In fact, "altered states" of all kinds--meditation, hypnosis, alcohol, drugs--are frequently accompanied by mystical experiences.[30] Moreover, psychotic imagery shares many characteristics with dream experiences,[31] hallucinogenic drug trips,[32] "near death" experiences,[33] and shamanic experiences.[34] Certain non-psychiatric organic disorders are also associated with altered states. One is temporal lobe epilepsy. Just before a seizure, the epileptic displays various symptoms suggestive of withdrawal of psychological defense or even demon possession. Not only can he be wildly aggressive and sexually uninhibited. He is also commonly preoccupied with religiosity, paranormal experiences and a sense of a "presence."[35,36]

However, altered states do not fabricate spiritual experiences. Rather, they lift the lid off the hitherto unconscious knowledge of existential reality. They push away psychological defenses in a fashion similar to psychosis.[37,38] This can be terrifying. Despite what the gurus tell us about the benefits of mystical experiences, they often take a catastrophic form, leading to neurosis and psychosis.[39]

RELIGIOUS BACKGROUND

Is there any evidence that religiosity is acquired through the human socialization process? No. One example from my practise is particularly striking.

A case study

This client was born into an intellectual, atheistic family of Jewish ancestry, his father being a well-known child psychiatrist. Throughout his life, he has heard his parents condemn all forms of religion; he had no religious instruction as a child.

His first psychotic episode occurred at the age of twenty. During this episode, he recalls the emergence of a strong religious preoccupation. "Voices" told him the devil was going to get him, he was doomed to go to hell, and that God was watching him. He has experienced similar phenomena during all of his subsequent episodes. Yet his only religious training has been in the eastern mystical practices he espoused as he strove for peace of mind after several psychotic episodes. This training utilizes neither a personal God nor a devil concept.

This case is not unusual. The striking aspect is the severity of the preoccupation with hell and the devil, which cannot be adequately explained by influences from the social environment.

Research literature

Scientific research paints a picture consistent with the case study above. Unsurprisingly, the findings on religiously-preoccupied psychotics are similar to those on the overlapping population of schizophrenics. A recent study shows more overtly religious delusions in individuals not connected with organized religion or religious practises. They reported high religious involvement but identified less with fundamental beliefs and expressed less support for organized religion.[40] In other words, they were idiosyncratically involved in false teachings of some kind. Moreover, a study of messianic delusions in hospitalized schizophrenic men found strong counter-cultural tendencies typically present in these patients.[41]

Another study shows two distinct patterns amongst patients with religious delusions: either involvement in mercilessly legalistic fundamentalism (see Chapter Ten for a discussion of this) or the avoidance of socialized religion.[42] Such patients could be divided into two groups: one which displayed hostile and rejecting attitudes towards organized religion and another that strongly identified with the dogmatic concepts of their religious group. Other studies similarly show that if the psychotic or religiously deluded individual is involved in organized religion at all, it is a cult which attracted him because of a previously-established religious preoccupation.[43,44]

In general these studies either contradict or do not support the idea that the religiosity phenomenon results from involvement in organized religion. They present, instead, a picture of the religiously-deluded, psychotic individual as a loner and rebel toward the God of the Bible. Like a sheep who has gone astray, he has "turned to his own way" (Isaiah 53:6).

GRACE AND SANITY

My experience has been that a sense of grace profoundly changes individuals diagnosed with a psychotic disorder. It brings them essential peace of mind. The constant feeling of being plagued by the invisible demonic world--what the mental health profession calls paranioa--abates. There is an underlying sanity in these individuals, although they do not seem to lose their particular susceptibility to spiritual attack. Nevertheless, they can function fully if they have a God-filled, calm, supportive environment. Their religiosity continues but it now works to their advantage as a healthy clinging to God.

All psychiatric and non-psychiatric symptoms associated with their illness do not disappear. Some symptoms become characterological, part of the personality. Since permanent changes in the structure and functioning of the brain can occur over time, medication may be a continuing necessity.

One client who was disturbed for many years by a vision of an open door with bright red flames flames surging out of it now reports that she sees a white light shining out of that door. She says she finds the white light a little alarming but it does not fill her with the terror she had when she saw the flames.

I have had the opportunity to observe a family member who has at one time clearly displayed all the acute symptoms of schizophrenia. Over the years since he began to lean on the God of the Bible, he has changed. Some of his symptoms have completely disappeared: the delusions and auditory hallucinations. Others have been tempered: the autism, impulsiveness and emotional lability. Another feature called "loosening of associations" is less extreme and actually benefits him. It helps him make interesting connections in the writing he is now able to focus on. He has learned to accept his boundaries and obeys a need for much quiet and aloneness. This is certainly a different person from the human being who, at times in the past, would stare out of the window, sitting in the same position from dawn to dusk.

But without the message of the Gospel, the need to flee from the terrible dilemma can produce a state of living hell for one who is genetically predisposed to psychosis.

PSYCHOTIC REALITY IS TRUE REALITY

Some will argue that since schizophrenia and other types of psychosis are sicknesses, psychotic reality is not universally applicable. Not true. Psychopathology is revelatory of the innate sin/death conflict for the following reasons:-

1. Religiosity is not fabricated. Psychosis involves loss of control of conscious thought. A thought-disordered person is far less able to consciously fabricate than one who is not.

2. The religious nature of psychotic thought is pervasive and universal.

3. If schizophrenia has a genetic factor, how can the religiosity that is almost synonymous with it not have one?

4. So far the research does not indicate that the religious content of schizophrenic and other psychotic thought is a product of socialization.

5.   It makes sense that the tumult of acute schizophrenic disorganization, with its disruption of psychological defenses, would allow material from deep in the psyche to come uncensored to the surface.

6.   The underlying themes of delusional thinking are independent of culture and consistent with biblical reality, particularly the common idea of malevolent control by a supernatural agent.

7.   The themes of so-called psychotic delusions are found in the non-psychotic population during meditation, chemically-altered states, dreams, and myths.   No matter how mild or severe the disorder, in no case has any client I have seen for psychotherapy denied a sense of impending doom.

SUMMARY AND CONCLUSIONS

No theory can better explain psychotic religiosity than the innate sin/death equation.   The psychotic's sensitive antennae pick up something terrifying in the spiritual realm.   He cannot get away from the sense of a malevolent spirit or "alien" world, not visible or knowable through the normal human channels.   He sees what most people are blind to.

In our quest to find the origin of religiosity, we looked at the source of psychosis itself, focusing on schizophrenia. Despite evidence for its genetic basis and its associations with some environmental factors, more is needed to explain the incidence of this disorder.   There is every reason to believe that environmental stress merely triggers the deep, innate terror of eternal darkness.   This terror leads to psychosis in the genetically-predisposed person.   Taken as a whole, scientific research so far supports this Bible-based interpretation.

There is no evidence that socialized religion makes psychotic people unable to stop talking about God, hell, sin, demons, and alien forces.   On the contrary, schizophrenic and psychotically-religious individuals tend to isolate.   Typically they are loners who are preoccupied with idiosyncratic religious beliefs.   In a small percentage of cases, they have some involvement in an anti-Christian or pseudo-Christian cult.   The likelihood is that psychotically-religious individuals seek formal religion as a result of a preoccupation that is already established. Even heavy cult involvement would not be a sufficient explanation of their extreme religious preoccupation.

So far, psychotic religiosity has every appearance of being innate. However, more needs to be known about it. For example, how prevalent are the biblical archetypes in psychotic thought content? Further, we should include the more covert religious delusions in our definition of religiosity instead of only the overt type. Religious cultural background does not affect religiosity *per se*, but it does influence the terminology and concepts used to describe universal spiritual experiences.[45] Individuals with a biblical backgound are more likely to talk about demons; individuals from a secular one talk about alien forces. Both are describing the same experience; one is overtly religious, the other covertly so. A very high proportion of delusions would be included in a definition of religiosity that inlcudes both types, making an even stronger case for psychosis as revelatory of our universal existential predicament.

It must be noted that none of the research provides reliable indices of the type, amount, and causal direction of religious influence. Moreover, none of it examines past influences. Most important, however, is that in no case has any attempt been made to differentiate grace from spurious forms of religiosity.

We need to know more about the relationship between false religion and psychosis, on one hand, and between the Gospel and mental health, on the other. My own experience suggests that psychotic episodes are rare or nonexistent for people who truly know the grace of God. Thus they would not have shown up in previous research, which generally uses actively psychotic hospitalized subjects.

Notes

1. Buchsbaum, M. S. (1977). "The Middle Evoked Reponse Component and Schizophrenia." <u>Schizophrenia Bulletin</u>, 3, pp. 93-104

2. Heath, R. G. (1958). "Correlation of Electrical Recordings from Cortical and Subcortical Regions of the Brain with Abnormal Behavior in Human Subjects." <u>Confina Neurologia</u>, <u>18</u>, pp. 305-315

3. Bower, B. (1991). "Schizophrenia, Depression Share Brain Clue." <u>Science News</u>, <u>138</u>.

4. Perlman, David (1990, Mar 22). "New Study, New Drug for Schizophrenia." <u>San Francisco Chronicle</u>, p. A17

5. Torrey, E. Fuller (1983). <u>Surviving Schizophrenia: A Family Manual</u>. New York, New York: Harper and Row, p. 85.

6. Torrey, op. cit., p. 83.

7. Clementz, B., A. and Sweeney, J. A. (1990). "Is eye movement dysfunction a biological marker for schizophrenia?" <u>Psychological Bulletin</u>, <u>108</u>, 1, pp. 77-92; see also Torrey, op. cit., p. 83.

8. McGue, M. and Gottesman, I. I. (1989). "A simple dominant gene still cannot account for the transmission of schizophrenia." <u>Archives of General Psychiatry</u>, <u>46</u>, 5, pp. 478-480.

9. Mednick, S. A. (1991). "Fetal neural development and adult schizophrenia." <u>The Journal of the California Alliance for the Mentally Ill</u>, <u>2</u>, 4, pp. 6-7.

10. Scheibel, A. B. (1991). "Schizophrenia--cells in disarray." <u>The Journal of the California Alliance for the Mentally Ill</u>, <u>2</u>, 4, pp. 9-10.

11. Torrey, op. cit., p. 91.

12. Kantner, J., Lamb, H. R. and Loeper, C (1987). "Expressed emotions in families: a critical review." <u>Hospital and Community Psychiatry</u>, <u>38</u>, pp. 374-380

13. Laing, R. D. (1969). <u>The Divided Self.</u> New York, New York: Pantheon Books.

14. Torrey, op. cit., p. 1.

15. Hollingshead, A. B. and Redlich, F. C. (1958). Social Class and Mental Illness. New York, New York: John Wiley and Sons.

16. Fuller, op. cit., p. 66.

17. Walker, E. and Lewine, R. J. (1990). "Prediction of adult-onset schizophrenia from childhood home movies of the patients." American Journal of Psychiatry, 147, 8, pp. 1052-1057; see also Torrey, op. cit., p. 63.

18. Epstein, M. and Topgay, S. (1982). "Mind and mental disorders in Tibetan medicine." Revision, 5, 1, 67-79.

19. Dickason, C. Fred (1987). Demon Possession and the Christian. Chicago, Illinois: Moody Bible Institute of Chicago.

20. Hammond, F. and I. M. (1973). Pigs in the Parlor. Kirkwood, Mo: Impact Books.

21. Rodger K. Bufford, "Demonic Influence and Mental Disorders." Journal of Psychology and Christianity, 8, 1, pp. 35-48.

22. Dickason, op. cit.

23. Mac Donald, C. B. and J. B. Luckett (1983). "Religious Affiliation and Psychiatric Diagnoses." Journal for the Scientific Study of Religion, 22, 1, pp. 15-37

24. Lindenthal, J. J. and Myers, J. K. (1970). "Mental status and religious behavior." Journal for the Scientific Study of Religion, 9, pp. 143-149.

25. Stark, Rodney (1971). "Psychopathology and Religious Commitment." Review of Religious Research, 12, pp. 165-176.

26. Beit-Hallahmi, B.J. and Argyle, M. (1977). "Religious ideas and psychiatric disorders." International Journal of Social Psychiatry, 23, pp. 26-30

27. Spencer, J. (1975). "The mental health of Jehovah Witnesses." British Journal of Psychiatry, 126, pp. 556-559

28. Torrey, op. cit., p. 97.

29. Smith, H. (1964). "Do Drugs Have Religious Import?" Journal of Philosophy, 61, pp. 517-530.

30. James, William (1958). "Mysticism." In The Varieties of Religious Experience. New York, New York: The New American Library, pp. 292-328.

31. Hall, J. A. (1977). Clinicaluses of dreams: Jungian interpretations and enactments. New York: Grune and Stratton.

32. Kleinman, J. E., Gillin, J. C. and Wyatt, R. J. (1977). "A comparison of the phenomenology of hallucinogens and schizophrenia from some autobiographical accounts." Schizophrenia Bulletin, 3, 4, pp. 560-586.

33. Grof, S. and Grof, C. (1980). Beyond Death. New York, New York: Thames and Hudson.

34. Halifax, J. (1979). Shamanic voices. New York, New York: Crossroads.

35. Dewhurst, K. and Beard, A. W. (1970). "Sudden Religious Conversions in Temporal Lobe Epilepsy." British Kournal of Psychiatry, 117, pp. 497-507.

36. Makarec, K. and Persinger, M. A. (1985). "Temporal Lobe Signs: Electroencephalic Validity and Enhanced Scores in Special Poulations." Perceptual and Motor Skills, 60, pp. 831-842.

37. Lachar, David (1974). The MMPI: Clinical Assessment and Automated Interpretation. Los Angeles, California: Western Psychological Services, p. 3.

38. Pahnke, W. N. (1966). "Drugs and mysticism." International Journal of Parapsychology, 8, pp. 295-314.

39. Neuman, E. (1964).   In <u>The Mystic vision.   Papers from the Eranos Yearbooks.</u> Princeton, New Jersey: Princetone Un8iversity Press, p. 397.

40. Cothran and Harvey, op. cit.

41. Levinson, P. (1973).   "Religious delusions in counter-culture patients." <u>American Journal of Psychiatry</u>, <u>130</u>, pp. 1265-1269.

42. Lowe, W. L. (1954).   "Group beliefs and socio-cultural factors in religious delusions." <u>Journal of Social Psychology</u>, <u>40</u>, pp. 267-274

43. Murphy, H. B., Wittkower, E. D., Fried, J., and Ellenberger, H. (1963).   "A cross-cultural survey of schizophrenic symptomatology." <u>International Journal of Social Psychiatry</u>, <u>9</u>, pp. 237-249.

44. Stark, Rodney (1971).   "Psychopathology and Religious Commitment." <u>Review of Religious Research</u>, <u>12</u>, 3, pp. 165-176.

45. Jimens, L., Oritiz-de-Zorate, A., and Antonio, P. (1979). "Brain delusions and myths." <u>Revista Psiquiatria Psicologia Medica</u>, <u>14</u>, pp. 113-122.

Part Two

GRACE AND SANITY

Part One of this book showed that mental illness stems from innate fear of hell. Therefore the assurance of escape from hell is essential to mental health. Is this assurance to be found anywhere other than the Gospel, with its message of grace? No. The following chapters of Part Two concern the empty promises found in secular psychotherapy, non-Biblical spirituality, and spiritual therapies. Even the Christian approaches to mental health miss the centrality of grace; this is also largely true of research on the psychology of religion...

Chapter Nine

HOW SECULAR APPROACHES TO

MENTAL HEALTH LEAD US ASTRAY

To be sure, all the major secular approaches to mental health contain truth. But in every case this is contaminated by the leaven of a false gospel, a point made by certain Christian writers such as the Bobgans,[1] and Dave Hunt.[2]

SECULAR MENTAL HEALTH FOR A CHRISTIAN NATION?

It hardly seems that the humanistic goals of the mental health profession in this country are congruent with its predominantly Bible-oriented population. Thirty one percent of all U. S. adults endorse the statement that "The Bible is the actual word of God and is to be taken literally, word for word." An additional twenty four percent agree that: "The Bible is the inspired word of God; it contains no errors, but some verses are to be taken symbolically rather than literally." Beyond this, another twenty-two percent agree that "The Bible is the inspired word of God, but it may contain historical and scientific errors."[3] In other words, seventy seven percent of our population basically accepts the Bible.

So why have humanism and other forms of ungodliness gone largely unchallenged as remedies for psychopathology in a Bible-based country?

One reason is that we give too much authority to people with degrees. Our great universities, founded for the teaching and study of God's Word, now exclude it. Even the Christian universities with counseling programs are strongly humanistic. "We don't do much God talk," explained a teaching staff member at one pastoral counseling program in the San Francisco Bay area.[4]

Moreover, psychological defenses keep humans from applying God's truths. That leaves us wide open to Satan. We are blind to the inherent contradiction between secular recipes for psychological health and God's recipe.

Another reason is that a significantly low proportion of psychologists and psychiatrists report a Judaeo-Christian religious affiliation: sixty five percent as compared to eighty seven percent of the general public. Among those, there is a considerably smaller proportion, twenty nine percent, who express a belief that religious matters are important for treatment with many or all clients.[5,6]

Moreover, secular therapists often automatically consider the religious beliefs of their clients to be harmful, urging them to let go of those beliefs.[7] This may be why most people suffering emotional distress prefer to seek help from clergy rather than mental health professionals.[8] Yet they do end up using the mental health profession.

SATANIC HUMANISM

Why is humanism Satanic? Humanists glorify humans as gods in control of their lives. This is what Satan wants us to believe. It is never explicitly stated by the secular establishment, of course. If it were made explicit, we would be more likely to reject it. Deep inside, we know we are incapable of the only transformation that will produce genuine mental health: resolution of our unconscious sin/hell equation, the quieting of the spirit. Only God can produce the "peace which passeth all understanding" (Phillipians 4:7).

There is no doubt that we can manipulate *some* changes in ourselves, either alone or with some outside help that is not God--chemical alteration or the direct and indirect effects of the therapeutic situation.

Obviously, not everyone who has not claimed Christ has symptoms sufficiently extreme to be classified as a mental disorder. Yet sooner or later the fear of hell and the underlying turmoil associated with it will catch up with everyone. It may be only when the person is close to death that it shows itself clearly. Looking back on that person's life we will see it has been driven by guilt, full of the secret desperation of an unmet need for atonement.

SECULAR "HEALTHY" DELUSIONS

Outside the Bible's message, the semblance of mental health is best produced by what we might call "healthy" delusions. These are false ideas about human power, optimism and goodness. We may understand how a psychotic person can spend a whole lifetime functioning under a grandiose delusion, such as a belief that he is the archangel Gabriel (overt religiosity) or Napoleon Bonaparte (covert religiosity). However, we do not generally realize that "normal" humans operate under more subtle delusions, often in collusion with each other.

Outside of grace, these lies of the devil are the best humans have to sustain them, and they work for a while. Optimism: "Ye shall not surely die" (Genesis 3:4). Human control and human goodness: "ye shall be as gods" (Genesis 3:5). The very opposite is true.

PERSONAL CONTROL

Many psychotherapeutic approaches aim to enhance a person's sense of being in control. Research has shown that a self-reported sense of personal control in adults is positively related to psychological adjustment.[9] In the immediate sense, this "do it yourself" approach can be beneficial, but it is a detour from the truth. Although we are made in the image of God, we humans are not the captains of our souls. The paradox is, we have responsibility for ourselves, but not the control which would enable us to fulfil that responsibility. We can depend only on God for that.

Some think that faith in God means passivity. Nothing can be further from the truth. Over and over, the Bible uses the word "walk" in connection with faith. Faith involves action.

Faith in the self can be a lifelong delusion. Hopefully it will snap before it is too late. Some of the world's greatest self-believers and critics of Christianity have repented in all honesty on their death beds and confessed their need for Christ. One of them was one of the founding fathers of America, Thomas Payne.[10] But far more of those critics have slipped off into eternal darkness.

OPTIMISM

Optimism, the expectation that things will work out for the good, is another delusion promoted by the secular mental health profession. Research has shown that optimists experience fewer negative physical symptoms,[11] display faster or better recoveries from certain physical illnesses,[12] and are more psychologically healthy.[13] Cognitive therapy, and to some extent other therapeutic approaches, have been found effective in superficially changing beliefs to produce more optimistic attitudes that enable people to cope better. However, the long-term benefits have not been established.[14]

For non-believers, optimism is a delusion. Only believers in the God of the Bible have a basis for hope. Paul said "All things work together for good to them that love God" (Romans 8:28). For everyone else, there is no foundation for such a belief. In a random world, there is no more basis for expecting good things to happen than there is for expecting bad things.

Humans have good reason for their existential dread.[15] Past programming does not explain this. We expect punishment because our underlying sense of existential guilt is always tugging at us. The only way this expectation can be truly changed is for us to know we are forgiven by God.

HUMAN GOODNESS

"We are good, we are good, we are good, we are good; deep down inside us we are good."[16] This is the secular humanist fallacy. The truth in it is that we have a conscience that tells us what goodness is, and we feel better when doing its bidding. But the baseness of human nature has been pointed out several times already in this book. Made in God's image we are, but with the contamination of the leaven of sin. "A little leaven leaveneth the whole lump" (I Corinthians 5:6).

MAJOR SECULAR PSYCHOTHERAPIES

The secular approaches to psychotherapy have goals that only the God of the Bible is capable of achieving. As we take a brief journey through some of the major ones, we will see why those approaches cannot achieve their stated goals, and why only the Gospel can. Our journey is organized, somewhat artifactually, into humanistic and non-humanistic categories, but first we look at the support/insight dimension.

SUPPORT VERSUS INSIGHT

There is a distinction in the mental health profession between supportive therapies and insight-oriented therapies. Supportive therapies have a goal of helping people to cope better as they recognize their strengths, so reinforcing self-esteem. This type of therapy does not go into the underlying reasons why people have problems. Consequently, its goal is often only short-term change. It fosters pride and ignores the dark in us.

Created in God's image, we humans certainly have beauty. But we cannot appreciate that until our darker aspect and its deadly consequence has been confronted. Supportive therapy is like paving over a landslide. Constant maintenence is needed to present even the vaguest appearance of soundness.

Insight-oriented therapies aim to help people go below the surface and understand why they feel bad about themselves. Then, in theory, the necessary corrective experience is provided in therapy, with a goal of long term change. But who will open Pandora's box without a guaranteed safeguard? If the essential support from God is missing only superficial insight is possible.

Freudian theory has led to many insight-oriented offshoots besides the lengthy traditional psychoanalysis. Transactional analysis, object relations therapy and ego psychology are some of the varieties. None of these models recognizes the innate Genetic existential dilemma as the cause of conflict, needless to say. All view socialization agents, particularly parents, as the culprits. None can heal.

HUMANISTIC APPROACHES TO PSYCHOTHERAPY

Several psychotherapeutic approaches embrace the humanist fallacy mentioned earlier. The French philosopher, Jacques Rousseau,[17] is an exemplar of this view of man, which has been the basis of many revolutionary movements.

Humanism espouses the mistaken belief that socialization is the spoiler, that man needs freedom from the blocking effects of environmental influences in order for his innate goodness to flourish.

Contrarily, the Biblical picture displays a preponderance of innate evil in humans. Our rebellious nature makes us want to disobey God's voice in our conscience. The innate corruption in man has quickly taken over the humanistic revolutions we have seen in history, and the personal growth in therapy.

Humanistic approaches to therapy are typically nondirective and evocative, aiming to foster the expression of inner strength and good by removing whatever blocks are in the way. Here we look at Rogerian, Gestalt, Existential and Maslowian psychotherapy as representatives of this school.

Rogerian therapy

According to the therapeutic approach founded by Carl Rogers,[18] unconditional love, or "unconditional positive regard," which is really the same thing, is the context in which healing takes place. This is hardly a surprising conclusion for one who switched from preparing for a career in the ministry to a career in psychotherapy. Rogers tried to take God out of unconditional love and came out with an illusion.

Humans may experience flashes of unconditional love for one another, but they are unable to sustain it. Some documentation of psychotherapy sessions with Carl Rogers showed that even the founder of this school of therapy displayed variability in his stance toward the client, becoming cold and distant in manner at times.[19] The prophet of unconditional love was unable to come even close to the mark himself.

The problem is, the therapist is just another human being, with his own set of biases, judgments, transference reactions, et cetera. No therapist can give us what we need for mental health: resolution of our deep fear and an ongoing, sustaining relationship with God. There is no comparison between human love and God's love. A therapist's love is conditional. One condition is a fee. The therapist comes to genuinely care for the client, yet sooner or later his time will not be available if a fee is not paid. But God is always available. He will not fail to listen. He too, requires a fee, but it is a fee that humans are unable to pay. So he paid for us.

Gestalt therapy

Fritz Perls[20] founded a "here and now" school of psychotherapy which deemphasizes the past. Its strong emphasis on self expression is based on the premise that there is a self-actualizing tendency within each human.

According to Gestalt theory, most disorders originate in childhood and involve interference with the process of what is termed "gestalt formation and destruction." A gestalt is a conceptual field, the entire set of a person's ideas, attitudes, beliefs, concepts, emotions, thoughts, etc. Problems arise when the gestalt is rigid and unresponsive to change.

Gestalt therapy involves much finger pointing. It fosters catharsis of present feelings towards the significant others who must have messed us up earlier in our lives. The goal is to break down the rigid, "outmoded" gestalt. In theory, expressive techniques such as the "empty chair" or psychodrama destroy the old gestalt and produce a new, flexible one.

However, we cling to these rigid "gestalts," or psychological defenses, for good reason. In reality, they have little to do with childhood experiences. The rigidity comes from the sin/death equation. Until we know Christ, they are not "outmoded," for they help us hide from our sense of doom.

In Gestalt therapy, we can role play a dialogue with that criticizing parent. We pin the blame on him for making us feel bad about ourselves. Our screams at him aim to catharsize the rage we feel, the cumulative anger he "deserves." But the defense wall will break only temporarily, if at all. Satan just loves the fact that we transfer his accusing role to our parents. He will encourage us to keep focusing on our self-righteous anger, continuing to repress the root problem so that we reject God's gift of salvation. As stated in Chapter Five, parents do have an impact, but we attribute far too great a role to them in our psychopathology. The basic dilemma has nothing to do with our parents.

In line with this, research shows that catharsis can hurt rather than help.[21] It only justifies and intensifies our blaming mechanisms. Here we are, one sinner venting spleen on another sinner, feeling helplessly enraged and hurt by him, wanting to hurt him back. We may call it justice but it is revenge. Our fellowship with God is broken by our judgment and vengeance. God said: "To me belongeth vengeance" (Deuteronomy 32:35).

We will drop that stance when we are hit by the impact of God's gift. Instead of roaring with rage we will sing songs

of praise.   However, in Gestalt therapy no account is made of
the inherent wickedness of our nature and the dilemma
resulting from it.   However, if--and this is a big "if"--Gestalt
techniques can be used within a Bible framework to help us
open up that Pandora's box of our own depravity and the
dilemma it puts us in, they are useful.   First we need to
experience the forgiving eyes of God on us as if beyond the
one-way mirror.   The more we see ourselves as forgiven
sinners, the more we appreciate God's grace.   "To whom little
is forgiven, the same loveth little" said Jesus (Luke 7:47).   To
the extent that we know we are loved and forgiven by God,
we can give love and forgiveness to others.

A Gestalt interpretation of the Fall of Man highlights its
basic disagreement with the biblical view.   It states of Adam
and Eve: "So, by the fruit of that tree they become as we
are, divorced from the union of awareness and expression, the
synaptic experience of spontaneous and integrated behavior."[22]
In other words, the "mythical" Fall forced humans to live in
the grip of rigid opinions, ideas, and judgments, insisting on
their own wisdom, unable to let go of control and allow
ourselves to respond with spontaneity.   The pre-Fall condition
was one of living completely in the moment, in an unconscious
state with no superimposition of abstractions.

Where the Gestaltists are right, it is for the wrong reasons.
We *are* divorced from spontaneity, but that is due to our
divorce from God.   Spontaneity is unaffordable when our
human qualities doom us.   Gestaltists are incorrect in assuming
that abstraction was in the fruit of the tree.   If Adam and
Eve could respond to the concepts like "good," "evil," and "die"
in the Satanic seduction, they were already able to abstract.
They did not eat abstraction; they ate God's law with its
message of doom.   It is our sense of condemnation, or
existential guilt, that causes the separation of consciousness and
unconsciousness.

Certainly the Gestalt focus on the "here and now" is
more useful than an endless preoccupation with the past, but it
still is not looking in the right place.   We have to take our
issues outside the present into eternity, fully acknowledging our
existential position and God's mercy.

Existential therapy

Existential therapy does go into the future, but leads us astray in a different way. It offers false solutions to conflicts over the larger issues of life, the vital questions about our existence: meaningfulness versus meaninglessness, life versus death, isolation versus separatedness, and freedom versus responsibility. Says Victor Frankl, founder of a form of existential psychotherapy he called "logotherapy,"[23] about healing of the human psyche: "The importance of the freedom of the human will is the ability to chose a stand on the meaning of life, which, when found, will produce mental health."

This means that existentialism actually takes a clear stand against the God of the Bible. According to its theory, there is no ultimate objective reality. Reality is whatever I decide it to be. The universe has no meaning or purpose other than what I personally create out of it in my imagination. There is no higher authority than me. Implied, of course, is that I am a god in the center of the universe I create.

Existential therapists may claim to be supportive towards a person's belief in the God of the Bible; they claim they will support whatever belief system the person has. However, the existentialist cannot support the Bible as truth, because the Bible discards every other belief system, existentialism included. Faith in the God of the Bible is likely to avoided as a topic in therapy, or subtly attacked.

The idea that I create my reality hardly gives me a sense of being safe from the "dark abyss," which the existential thinkers acknowledge to be a core problem. I cannot believe my definition of an alternate reality will keep me out of the abyss. Deep in my psyche a part of me knows I am bound for that abyss unless a power greater than myself pulls me out of it. Nevertheless existentialists treat hell as if were a state of mind I can control.

Existentialist therapy, with its "you're boss" solution, cannot heal the pain of isolation. This pain is not simply a sense of separation from other people. If it were, we would be in a real bind, because constant, intimate human contact is unattainable. But constant, intimate contact with God is attainable through Christ.

The existentialists are right on the mark in their definition of the basic issues which concern us, but they are way off track in their answers to them. The only way we attain a sense of true meaning is in a relationship with God as part of his intentional creation. The purpose of free will is not for us to define our own universe, but to make a decision about relationship with God. The choice is either to acknowledge the seed of knowledge God planted in us, or to fall into the abyss. Human life is so sordid, trivial and temporary that it is really only makes sense as a testing ground for faith. Otherwise, as Solomon said: "All is vanity and vexation of spirit" (Ecclesiastes 1:14).

Maslow's self-actualization

Abraham Maslow theorized that mental health was "self-actualization," attained by rising through a hierarchy of needs. The needs had to be satisfied from the ground up, i.e., from basic survival (worldly physiological and safety needs), through human belongingness and self-esteem to the pinnacle of self-actualization.[24]

He proposes the following characteristics of the healthy "self-actualized" mind: accurate perception of reality; acceptance of reality; spontaneity; problem centering rather than self centering; need for privacy; self-sufficiency; detachment; capacity for peak experiences and ability to attain transcendence; identification with humanity; capacity for feelings of intimacy with a few others; democratic character structure; a broad sense of humor; ability to distinguish means and ends; creativeness; a nonconformist personal style and resistance to enculturation; and ability to transcend dichotomies (see things other than in black and white).

But other than in a deluded form, none of the needs in his hierarchy can be met outside of grace. Maslow ignores the inherent sin in human nature which makes "self-actualization" a euphemism for "sin-actualization." However, if we substitute eternal survival for basic survival in Maslow's model, his hierarchy of needs superficially agrees with the biblical picture. He is right that higher values can be reached only after we know our basic survival need is met. From a biblical point of view, survival is escape from eternal darkness.

Once we feel assured of a God-given escape despite our depravity, we want to please God. We can open up and concern ourselves with higher values. Missing from Maslow's hierarchy is the need for our cup to overflow with God's love before love can flow out of us.

None of the self-actualization characteristics can be attained outside of grace. Furthermore, self-sufficiency and transcendence are characteristic only of a god. And where is the "accurate perception of reality" if the prospect of hell is not considered? The survival need is never satisfied by human means for it concerns eternal darkness. Without God, humans are stuck on the lowest rung of the ladder.

NON-HUMANISTIC THERAPIES

In contrast with the humanistic therapies, non-humanistic ones emphasize inculcation over revelation. They consider learning more important than exposing the inherent "good," and they focus on personal control and optimism, the other two delusions mentioned above. Consequently they are more directive in approach.

Cognitive therapies

Cognitive therapies focus on changing dysfunctional beliefs, or cognitions. The premise is that it is not the actual facts about our situation that cause us pain, but what we believe about them. Just as in existentialism, we find the claim that there is no ultimate truth beyond the present reality. Beliefs are flexible, and we can choose the way we feel because we can fix them. We must challenge the beliefs causing pathological emotions and behavior.

According to the cognitive school, mental disorder is the result of faulty programming, old tapes that keep playing. Such theorists as Albert Ellis[25] and Aaron Beck[26] define strategies for replacing dysfunctional beliefs with functional ones. Much of their work has focused on trying to cure depression, a disorder in which the person's negative thinking process is particularly accessible. The self-attacking beliefs are right out there on the surface. These are to be challenged and replaced by self-constructive beliefs.

One problematic belief humans have is that they must be perfect. The cognitivist solution is to reprogram with the message that we are really "O.K." as imperfect human beings. For a while this may seem to work. It can make us temporarily feel less bothered by that nagging sense of being doomed by our flaws. We believe that if we tell ourselves in the right way or often enough, the perfectionistic message will disappear. But the truth is that we can only accept our imperfection when we know God has rescued us from its consequence.

Cognitive therapy is a soft form of Zen Buddhism (see next Chapter for an elaboration of Buddhism). It does not allow for the fact that we have some basic, inflexible, inherent beliefs and emotions that are tied to immutable truth, and these beliefs just will not go away. Ellis stated that the "concept of sin is the direct and indirect cause of virtually all neurotic disturbance."[27] This is true. However, the concept of sin is based on the reality of sin. We cannot apply an eraser to the mind and rid it of this offensive concept.

It is true that certain problems in our lives can be alleviated without touching on the root dilemma. However, the change is not deep or lasting. On close inspection, all our neurotic beliefs are tied in some way to our existential crisis. Although cognitive therapies show some short-term effectiveness, in the long term, the effects wear off.[28] The depressed person's negative beliefs reflect truth. This truth will eventually crack apart the positive thinking installed by the cognitive approach.

Our self-defeating behaviors, fear of success, self-punishment, escape into addiction, and all the other defensive patterns mentioned in Chapter Six...these stem from the generally unconscious knowledge of being unworthy sinners in a terrible bind, needing atonement.

The value of cognitive therapy is its demonstration of the importance of beliefs for mental health. The most important belief is in the saving grace of the God of the Bible.

Behavioral therapy

Behavioral therapy focuses on changing behavior, not cognitions. On the supposition that humans are like their "ancestors," the lab rats on which much behavioral theory rests, they are expected to act on the basis of self interest, seeking pleasure and avoiding pain. Therefore their behavior can be "modified" through a system of reinforcements.

Desired behavior is to be promoted by the contingency of positive reinforcers in the form of rewards or punishments. A rat may run a maze either because there is food at the finish or to avoid an electric shock. Undesired behaviors are extinguished by punishments or lack of reinforcement. Past experience governs present and future expectations.

Although behaviorism focuses on the observable and quantifiable, behavioral theorists come in various shades. These range from the radical, "observable-behavior only" type, like B.F. Skinner,[29] to the moderates like Miller and Dollard,[30] who make some inferences about the motivation underlying observable behavior.

Existential issues are simply not addressed in the behavioral approach. Most of its theory is premised on the similarity between humans and "other" animals, an outgrowth of evolutionary thinking. Simple behaviorism has no way to explain complex phenomena such as self-punishment, which seems to seek pain rather than avoid it. Rats and pigeons just do not do that.

There is plenty of evidence that behavioral therapy is useful in controlling symptoms, particularly those of phobias and psychosomatic disorders. However, there is no evidence that it leads to peace of mind, i.e., mental health.[31] In many ways, its model is naively oversimplistic as far as humans are concerned, but it has some utility for our understanding of the Bible and its relationship to mental health. It explains why "the fear of the Lord is the beginning of knowledge" (Proverbs 1:7). Assuming that, unlike rats, humans are aware and concerned about more than just their next meal, the entrance to God is a form of aversive conditioning that appeals to our basic human instinct for survival: run for cover, hell is coming!

But spiritual hunger is subtle. Unlike the rat, we may not know we are hungry. We do not realize we are in a dilemma, starved of any resource to pay the price for sin, unless we pay attention to God's Word and see how it fits with our experience. The electric shock of this realization, when it finally does come to us, will send us running to the end of the maze. Not, initially, because we love God, not because we want our lives enhanced, but as our only refuge. Only after this is positive reinforcement effective. Grace is what shows us we are safe at the end of the maze, that we are running towards open, loving arms.

Social learning therapy

Social learning therapy, typified by Albert Bandura and his colleagues,[32] is an approach to change that brings in both behavioral and cognitive concepts. Instead of controlling behavior directly through reinforcement contingencies, it is controlled by vicarious reinforcement via observation, identification, and imitation of a role model.

One question social learning theorists have attempted to answer is whether aggression in humans is innate or learned. Further, if aggression is innate, is any particular mode of expressing it, such as physical violence, innate? Evidence for an innate aggressive urge has been found in the animals studied by ethologists such as Konrad Lorenz.[33] Animals have a propensity to attack one another without having had any apparent opportunities to learn this.

But these questions are actually impossible to answer in the case of humans. No human has ever lived in a controlled environment without an opportunity to learn an aggressive reponse of any kind since conception.

What research on children in a preschool situation has found is that instigation to physically violent aggression increases after such behavior is observed in a role model.[34] On the other hand, such behavior decreases after a role model displays non-violent behavior in the form of cooperation, verbal methods of settling disputes, and the like. But since children display aggressive behavior under both conditions, we do not know where the behavior comes from in the first place.

Despite the fact that Bandura found no evidence that social learning is solely responsible for producing aggression in humans, he concluded: "Since aggression is not an inevitable or unchangeable aspect of man but a product of aggression-promoting conditions operating within a society, man has the power to reduce his level of aggressiveness."[35]

So then, who were Adam and Eve imitating when they disobeyed God? It could not be God, himself. And then, who was Satan imitating? As far as we are informed, Satan's aggression towards God and humans came from nowhere but himself (Isaiah 14:12-20). Nothing in the Bandura group's research contradicts the idea that despite imitation of "good" parental models, a child could still become a vicious criminal.

The thing most important for parents to model is that they have found peace with God as sinners, and that they walk in faith leaning on God's word.

FAMILY THERAPY AND GOD'S FAMILY

Family therapy theories are all based on combinations of the preceding approaches. They, too, define healing processes that in reality can only be accomplished through faith in the God of the Bible.

Take, for example Murray Bowen's[36] definition of "enmeshment" versus "individuation" in the dysfunctional family. Enmeshment is a condition in which family members cannot differentiate their boundaries and are unable to recognize individual needs, i.e., individuate.

Bowen talks about anxiety as the cause of enmeshment. When people are anxious, they display pathological symptoms, one of them being an addiction to other people, often clinging to other family members. For Bowen the cure is to foster individuation in the family through alliances with individual members. This starts with the one who is most individuated already. Following this lead, family members gradually acquire the ability to distance themselves from one another.

The major hurdle is that the anxiety that produces the clinging also produces rigidity. In an anxiety state, clingy family members are less able to tolerate each other's differences than usual. This threatens the "oneness" they are seeking and interferes with individuation.

Bowen's recipe cannot produce lasting change, which only comes by bringing God into the picture. Family members can release the death-grip they have on one another when they can cling to God. Once they have that "oneness" with God, they can achieve individuation, flexibility, toleration for differences, and genuine support for one another.

DOES RESEARCH SUPPORT EVEN THE SHORT-TERM EFFICACY OF SECULAR THERAPY?

Research on the effectiveness of secular psychotherapy has presented a conflicting picture. Because of this, one meta-analysis pooled the results of many studies. Its finding was that in seventy five percent of the studies examined, psychotherapy was more effective than no therapy.[37] However, most of the differences were insignificant and there was no evidence for the superiority of any approach to psychotherapy.

However, the evidence does suggest that certain approaches are superior under limited circumstances. For example, a behavioral technique called "systematic desensitization" has become the treatment of choice for phobias.[38] However, no secular approach has been found to cure the anxiety underlying phobias.[39]

Research has shown the therapist to be the major variable in therapeutic outcome, and that the traits of the therapist are key.[40] For example, Steven Rothstein cites the following traits of the effective therapist: empathy, respect, genuineness, warmth, concreteness, confrontiveness, self-disclosure, immediacy, potency, and self-actualization.[41] These personal qualities are found to be independent of type and length of training or clinical orientation.

But given the nature of our deepest human fear, no therapist can have depth in any of these qualities unless he knows the God of the Bible. Being genuine means not being in hiding from oneself, which depends on feeling safe in front of God.

SUMMARY AND CONCLUSIONS

This chapter took a brief journey through the major secular approaches to psychotherapy. We saw that what they have to offer may quiet the surface, but cannot still the storm deep in the human psyche. All types of therapy can be of some short-term benefit in helping us adjust and cope more effectively with the harsh world we live in. However, this is pitted against the all-important long-term gain, lulling us into complacency, taking the focus away from the deep current of fear. In other words, secular therapy is dangerous. It masks the symptoms of the disease, taking us further away from God.

All of the major humanistic and non-humanistic approaches err in failing to include the sin/death conflict in the equation. Instead, they focus on worldly beliefs, expectations and relationships and posit human solutions to mental health. Consequently, in the long term, none of the goals of these therapeutic modes can be met.

This is supported by the fact that research on the effectiveness of psychotherapy has produced some mixed findings. Therapist traits, regardless of clinical orientation, appear to be the major determinant of outcome. Yet God forbid that the traits of the therapist should be key! The therapist is another imperfect human being. One sinner cannot save another sinner.

Regardless of therapist qualities, the client needs to take away the living water with him, so he will never again thirst. The only thing of lasting value the therapist has to offer is communication of the Gospel. It happens that the deeper the Gospel inside the therapist, the more he will display desirable traits. But never will he be able to provide the essential unconditional love, i.e., grace. His job is to point the client towards God for that.

Notes

1. Bobgan, Martin and Deirdre (1979). The psychological way/the spiritual way. Minneapolis, Minnesota: Bethany House Publishers.

Bobgan, Martin and Deirdre (1987). Psychoheresy: The psychological seduction of Christianity. Santa Barbara, California: Eastgate Publishers.

2. Hunt, Dave and McMahon, T. A. (1983). The Seduction of Christianity. Eugene, Oregon: Harvest House Publishers.

3. Princeton Religious Research Center. (1990). Religion in America. Princeton, NJ: Author.

4. Personal communication (1988, May 4). Orientation for new students, Counseling Department, Holy Names College, Oakland, CA.

5. Bergin, A. E. and Jensen, J. P. (1990). "Religiosity of psychotherapists; A national survey." Psychotherapy, 27, 1, pp. 3-7.

6. Marx, J. H. and Spray, S. L. (1969). "Religious biographies and professional characteristics of psychotherapists." Journal of Health and Social Behavior, 10, pp. 275-288.

7. Bergin, A. E., Stinchfield, R. D., Gaskin, T. A., Masters, K. S. and Sullivan, C. E. (1988). "Religious life styles and mental health: An exploratory study." Journal of Counseling Psychology, 35, pp. 91-98.

8. Veroff, J., Kulka, R. A. and Douvan, E. (1981). Mental Health in America. New York, New York: Basic Books.

9. Morganti, J. B., Hehrke, M. F., Hulicka, I. M. and Cataldo, J. F. (1988). "Life-span differences in life satisfaction, self-concept, and self-control." International Journal of Aging and Human Development, 26, 1, pp. 45-56.

10. Paine, T. (1794). The Age of Reason. New York, New York: The Thomas Paine Foundation.

11. Scheier, M.F. and Carver, C. S. (1985). "Optimism, coping, and health: Assessment and implications of generalized outcome expectancies." Health Psychology, 4, pp. 219-247.

12. Peterson, C., Seligman, M. E. P. and Vaillant, G. E. (1988). "Pessimistic explanatory style is a risk factor for physical illness: A thirty-five-year longitudinal study." Journal of Personality and Social Psychology, 55, pp. 23-27.

13. Scheier, M. F., Matthews, K. A., Owens, J. F. and Magovern, G. J. (1990). "Dispositional optimism and recovery from coronary artery bypass surgery: The beneficial effects on physical and psychollgical well-being." Journal of Personality and Social Psychology, 57, 6, pp. 1024-1040.

14. Blackburn, I. M. and Davidson, K. (1990). Cognitive therapy for depression and anxiety: a practitioner's guide. Boston: Blackwell.

15. Kierkegaard, Soren (1844) (1957). The Concept of Dread, 2nd edition. Princeton,New Jersey: Princeton University Press.

16. Sondheim, S. and Bernstein, L. (1961). "We are good." From the musical: West Side Story. Milwaukee, WI: International Publishing Company.

17. Rousseau, Jean Jacques (1898). "Emile." In T. Davidson (Ed.), Rousseau and Education.

18. Rogers, Carl R. (1951). Client-centered therapy: Its current practice, implications and theory. Boston, Massachusetts: Houghton Mifflin.

19. Truax, C.B. and Carkhuff, R. R. (1967). <u>Toward effective counseling and psychotherapy: Training and practice</u>. Chicago, Illinois: Aldine Publishers.

20. Perls, Fritz S. ((1969). <u>Gestalt Therapy Verbatim</u>. New York, New York: Real People Press.

21. Tavris, Carol (1982). <u>Anger, the misunderstood emotion.</u> New York, New York: Simon and Schuster.

22. Latner, Joel (1973). <u>The Gestalt Therapy Book.</u> New York, New York: Julian Press, Inc., p. 95.

23. Frankl, Victor (1988). <u>The Will to Meaning</u>. New York, New York: Penguin Books, Inc.

24. Maslow, A. H. (1968). <u>Towards a Psychology of Being, 2nd edition</u>. New York, New York: Van Nostrand.

25. Ellis, Albert (1962). <u>Reason and emotion in psychotherapy.</u> Secaucus, New Jersey: Lyle Stuart Publishers.

26. Beck, Aaron et al. (1979). <u>Cognitive therapy for depression</u>. New York, New York, Guilford Press.

27. Ellis, A., op. cit., p. 46

28. Blackburn, I. M. and Davidson, K. (1990). <u>Cognitive therapyfor depression and anxiety: a practitioner's guide</u>. Boston, Massachusetts: Blackwell Scientific Pulications.

29. Skinner, B.F. (1953). <u>Science and human behavior</u>. New York, New York: Macmillan Co.

30. Dollard, J., Doob, L. W., Miller,F. E., Mowrer, O.H., Sears, R. R., Ford, C. S., Hovland, C. I., and Sollenberger, R. T. (1939). <u>Frustration and Aggression</u>. New Haven, Conneticutt: Yale University Press.

31. Wolpe, J. (1980). "Behavioral therapy for psychosomatic disorders." <u>Psychosomatics,</u> <u>21</u>, 5, pp. 379-385.

32. Bandura, Albert (1973). <u>Aggression: a social learning analysis.</u> Englewood Cliffs, New Jersey: Prentice-Hall.

33. Lorenz, Konrad (1966). <u>On Aggression.</u> New York, New York; Harcourt Brace Janovitch Publishers, Inc.

34. Bandura,A., Ross, D., and Ross, S. A. (1961). "Transmission of aggression through imitation of aggressive models." <u>Journal of Abnormal and Social Psychology</u>, <u>63</u>, pp. 575-582.

35. Bandura, <u>Aggression</u>, p.323.

36. Bowen, Murray (1966). "The use of family therapy in clinical practice." <u>Comparative Psychiatry</u>, <u>7</u>, p. 345.

37. Smith, M. L., Glass, G. V., and Miller, T. I. (1980). <u>The benefits of psychotherapy.</u> Baltimore, Maryland: Johns Hopkins University Press.

38. Munby, M. and Johnston, D. W. (1980). "Agoraphobia: The long-term follow-up of behavioral treatment." <u>British Journal of Psychiatry</u>, <u>137</u>, pp. 418-427.

39. Ascher, L. M. (1987). <u>Anxiety and stress disorders: a cognitive-behavioral assessment and treatment.</u> New York, New York: The Guilford Press.

40. Smith, Glass and Miller (1980), op. cit.

41. Steven M. Rothstein (1989, November 18). "Being a more effective therapist: The Ten Traits that Make the Difference." Unpublished manuscript, Hypnotism Training Institute of Los Angeles, Glendale, CA, 91204.

Chapter Ten

LEGALISM AND INSANITY;

GRACE AND SANITY

PARSIMONY AND SCHEMA

A religious belief system is a cognitive schema, or a model of reality in the human mind.[1] All of us operate with some set of assumptions about reality, of course. Unfortunately, most people are unaware of the nature of their assumptions. Their beliefs remain unconscious and unexamined. This is extremely dangerous, as this chapter will point out.

Research shows that a person's schema of existential reality can affect every aspect of behavior. The deeper the root of a schema, the more areas of life it applies to and the more aspects of human functioning it influences. According to Ball-Rokeach et al., it can give rise to "selective remembering and forgetting, information processing, decision-making, conflict resolution, ego defense, denial, withdrawal, judging, intending, trying, praising and condemning, exhorting, and persuading-- and doing."[2]

Now, the theme of this book is that humans possess an innate schema of existential reality. This means they cannot adopt a religious belief system unless it agrees with what is already there. To be fully accepted and integrated, a schema acquired through learning must resonate with a person's inherent, internal programming. It can augment and amplify; it can add any missing piece of the puzzle; it cannot disagree.

It must also be parsimonious. According to the Gestalt perceptual laws introduced in Chapter Two, parsimony is a standard by which humans judge incoming information, either consciously or unconsciously. When we examine religious belief systems in terms of their underlying premises, we see that they vary in their parsimoniousness, i.e., their inclusiveness, elegance, and closure.

THE DOCTRINE OF PERFECTION

Mental health is peace of mind, or spiritual closure. Humans are archetypically programmed with both a sinful nature and an innate sense that the price for sin is death. This means that no religion based on the doctrine of perfection, or salvation through works, or self-purification, can provide spiritual closure. Humans are innately aware that they cannot meet the standard of total flawlessness, nor come even close to it.

Therefore, such religion presents a "bad," non-parsimonious schema that will stick in the craw. It cannot and will not be fully accepted for it does not address the underlying dilemma; it is not sufficiently inclusive; it cannot provide spiritual closure. Its adherents cannot be sound of mind.

However, all non-Biblical doctrines and religions are based on the doctrine of perfection. This doctrine says that humans can attain perfection and unite with God through their own effort. The "fine print" or underlying premises of all spiritual belief systems need to be scrutinized for this bad schema. Underneath what might superficially appear closure-producing can lurk merciless, damning legalism. Only grace offers closure, and grace cannot be found anywhere but in the God of the Bible.

Jesus said that "Strait is the gate, and narrow is the way, which leadeth unto life, and few there be that find it" (Matthew 7:14). He was referring to the fact that in no other spiritual belief system than the message of the Gospel are we given a way to connect with God and, thus, to avoid hell. In other words, nowhere else do we find God stepping in to heal the breach between himself and humans, making a gift of the essential payment for sin.

Yet all creeds implicitly acknowledge that sin, or human imperfection, separates humans from God. This fact indicates that humans are innately aware of their predicament. If there were no dire consequence for being separated from God, there would be no need for any of these creeds. Their presence implies humans are driven by a universal need for reconciliation with God.

The purpose of this chapter is to show that all other religions beside the Gospel keep humans separated from God, now and forever, by requiring the impossible: that man remove his own sin, i.e., make himself perfect. Their deceptive creeds foster the illusion that the impossible is possible; they sound superficially plausible. But they superficially deceive humans and deepen the underlying insanity.

Two pathways are offered. One is external. It is based on actions, the performance of good deeds and right living. The other is internal. It involves controlling the mind through meditation to establish separation from the baser aspects of being human, i.e., eliminating sin from thoughts.

ABOUT MEDITATION

As a practise, meditation is common to all spiritual doctrines, except that its goals and form vary. In the Eastern religions, there is a futile attempt to achieve detachment from human corruption and live in a state of perpetual transcendence above the personal ego (unlike the Freudian ego this refers to the sin nature).

The so-called "moment of surrender" which the Eastern schools claim to be the equivalent of going to God through Christ is, in fact, in no way comparable to it. It is a moment of dissociation, a loss of ego boundaries, when a person experiences a sense of identification with the creation. Since the Eastern schools identify the Creator with the creation, this loss of ego feels like a state of connection with God.

But the Bible shows us the Creator and the creation are separate. And this moment of surrender is just that: a moment. It gives a mystical sense of God's presence, but it is not connection with God.

Unlike the Bible believer's sense of a continuous walk in this world with God, the experience of ethereal connectedness in Eastern meditation depends on removal of attention from the world. As soon as practitioners get up from meditation and go about their daily business, the mystical sense of connectedness is broken. The high does not last. Living in the world requires stressful interactions with ungodly things. The anger felt over getting stuck in a traffic jam on the way home from the meditation center soon brings them down.

We can maintain that our worldly existence is just an illusion for only so long. Maybe stomach cramps due to hunger are also an illusion, or death due to starvation. The mind's lack of control over objective reality is clearest in the matter of aging and death. No amount of telling ourselves these things are just an illusion will truly convince us.

Eastern meditation is *not* the doorway to God and it is highly dangerous. It is an opening to demonic possession. The mantras used in the supposedly innocent Transcendental Meditation are the names of "deities," i.e., demons. Generally unknown to the practitioner, use of the mantra invites demons to take up residence.

NON-BIBLICAL MAJOR WORLD RELIGIONS
We will see, in what follows, how only the Bible enables humans to connect with God. All the non-Biblical major world religions are based on the Satanic doctrine of perfection.

HINDUISM AND THE LAW OF KARMA
Anyone who consider Hinduism more assimilable than the Bible's message just does not know enough. Two essential aspects of Hinduism are the law of karma and reincarnation. The law of karma, the cosmic score-card for good and bad deeds, implies that humans can control their own destiny. Its partner, the theory of reincarnation, attempts to remove the fear of hell, and, thus, the fear of God. Reincarnation proposes a series of lifetimes in which humans can work their way closer and closer to perfection. With each lifetime of striving to do what is right, it is possible to come out ahead in the karmic score and enter higher ground in the next lifetime, continually moving up the ladder.

The idea of karma supports a caste system. A persons's station in this world results from past lifetimes and cannot change. We must learn to accept a miserable existence if that is what we are born into.

If we miss out on attaining perfection, or even getting ahead this time around, no problem. If we wind up with a bigger karmic debt, also no problem. At worst, we spend the next lifetime in a bearable hell. Many think this lifetime is one of the bearable hells, with inevitably something better to look forward to next time around.

The false belief is that unlike Sisyphus, who endlessly pushed the rock up the mountain only to have it fall just before it reached the top, we will eventually make it all the way. Finally we will have no negative karma, or debt for wrongdoing, to pay off. The belief is that we humans can make ourselves flawless, perfect in thought, word, and deed. Then we can then unite with God and live happily ever after.

What underscores this is the belief in human godliness. For example, the central teaching of the Vedanta branch of Hinduism is: "In truth I am the Supreme Brahman." The fact that we do not find around us anyone who appears to even be close to perfection, despite the avowals made by certain gurus, is a big problem for Hinduism. It is dealt with in some sects by postulating that beyond a certain point, there are incarnations on other levels of existence outside this world.

Hinduism assumes a degree of self-control that humans do not possess. Unconsciously, they know this, and their spirit groans beneath the futile striving. Sisyphus is a perfect metaphor for not only Hinduism but for all non-Biblical creeds. The illusion of progress relies heavily upon psychological defense mechanisms to enable a person to avoid seeing the extent of his inherent depravity. One day the defenses snap and the illusion is blown.

The karma/reincarnation concept denies the finality of this lifetime for those who do not claim God's provision to cover sin. It does not address the universal existential anxiety. Somewhere inside, we know the price for the slightest departure from perfection, or sin, is death. What is the karmic price for a wicked thought, such as wanting something nasty to happen to the boss after he has refused that raise? To truly acknowledge our depravity would tell us we have no hope under this law; we are continually creating more bad karma.

Some equate the law of karma with the talionic principle "an eye for an eye" that we find in the law God gave to Moses. But the talionic law only applies to human relationships. God's law pertaining to our eternal destiny is actually both much tougher and much easier. It is tough when it comes to the price for sin, any sin whatsoever, being eternal darkness after only one incarnation. One false step is all it takes. We cannot lose an eye or do a penance and go merrily on our way.

The easy part is that God offers a completely unearned reprieve from our sentence, the only requirement being our willingness to believe it.

TRADITIONAL BUDDHISM

Buddha stated that desire was the cause of suffering. This is really not so different from the Miller and Dollard theory that frustration causes aggression.[3] Both implicate expectations as culprit. "Don't expect anything, then you won't be frustrated, angered, or disappointed." The Buddhist assumption is that expectation is not the fabric of which we are woven. But eliminating expectation is about as easy as chopping off our own heads.

Suppose we trained ourselves not to count on the sun "rising" tomorrow, or our heart to continue beating beyond the next second? Obviously we do not live every day or moment as if it were our last. Our lives are filled with covert expectations.

It is true that many of our expectations are completely unreasonable. They should be challenged because they cause unnecessary suffering when they inevitably are not fulfilled. For example, it makes us less resistant to challenge when we expect life to be difficult rather than easy.

Rather then eliminating expectations, we need to acquire some new expectations, the most important one being the prospect of an escape from eternal darkness. This expectation makes an inestimable difference in our ability to weather the storms of this world.

However, Buddhism is not just concerned with getting rid of unreasonable expectations. Its goal is to reach a state of no expectations and no desires. Bliss is to be the outcome of this. No goals, no plans, totally living in the now. No initiating, no executing, no ego. An internal "yes" to everything. But, of course, saying that "yes" must involve no effort, because effort is based on desire. The dog begins to chase his own tail. How are we to get rid of desire without desiring to do so? Here is the catch, the double-talk of the "bad" schema. The futile attempt to get rid of desire has enormous frustration potential.

Even if it were possible, would elimination of desire lead to bliss, or just complete numbness? For example, if I burn my finger, I must feel no pain, because pain will make me desire to remove my finger from the fire. Yet if I become numb, unfeeling, how can I feel bliss?

The grain of truth in it is that it is good to accentuate the positive, our acceptance of what is. But this can happen only if we have the sense that we live in an orderly world with God at the helm, rather than a meaningless, random world.

So Buddhism is a merciless legalistic system, focusing on the control of thought and action. The "four noble truths" of Buddhism incorporate a combination of different types of external and internal change. Suffering is universal, suffering is caused by desire (which is caused by ignorance), desire can be overcome, and the way is the eightfold path.

The impossible eightfold path. The eightfold path of right understanding, right thinking, right speech, right conduct, right livelihood, right endeavour, right mindfulness, and right meditation...has no Day of Atonement for lawbreakers, no provision for sin. It is absolutely despotic.

A misconception in Buddhism, the other eastern religions, and the ancient Gnosticism is that by knowing enough, we can avoid suffering...the "knowledge is power" idea. But look what happened when Adam and Eve ate of the Tree of the Knowledge of Good and Evil. Knowledge only increases sorrow, it does not alleviate suffering. The very attempt to make ourselves all-knowing shows us we are under a death sentence that we cannot escape through our own means. Only God is all-knowing.

However, Buddhism emphasizes truth rather than God, thus breaking the greatest of God's commandments. Its practises involve meditation and chanting rather than prayer. It relies on self-power not God's power. Of course, prayer is impossible when the sin/separation issue has not been dealt with. Besides, in Buddhism there is no concept of anyone to pray to. Thoughts and spoken words are believed to have the power to alter reality, i.e., implicitly humans are gods imbued with supernatural power.

Buddhism concerns itself with enlightenment rather than salvation, as if there were no hell. Enlightenment, or nirvana, is actually conceptualized as a state of extinction. The flame of desire is to be finally extinguished, freeing the self to achieve unity with the cosmos in death. Here we see a parallel with Freud's idea of a masochistic drive, a drive towards extinction (see Chapter Five). What a cunning plot of Satan, to make us believe there is something good about ceasing to exist as an individual! Satan sells us, in Buddhism, the idea of universal life rather than the individual soul. But this runs counter to our human desire to continue. It denies the reality of eternal darkness.

In Buddhism, heaven and hell are conditions of life created by us here and now, not places after death. Godlike, we can choose not to "create" hell. Yet humans never fully buy this idea. The part of us that experiences the terror of the abyss remains unconvinced.

If there is no God, then who established the eightfold path? Who has come back from death to report there is no heaven or hell? And where is the evidence that anyone has reached that fabled state of enlightenment? There are individuals who have claimed to do so, Buddha included. But Buddha reputedly died after stuffing himself with pork[4], which hardly sounds "right" for an enlightened one.

In the traditional Buddhist and Hinduistic schools, sin is classified as not real, just an illusion. This leads to denial, repression and dissociation from sinful ("negative") feelings and thoughts. All thoughts must be subject to the censor's scrutiny. This fractures the psyche, eliminates spontaneity and deepens insanity.

Says the Dalai Lama, "Is it possible to get rid of the afflictive emotions completely or is it possible only to suppress them? From the Buddhist point of view, the conventional nature of the mind is clear light, and thus defilements do not reside in the very nature of the mind; defilements are adventitious, temporary, and can be removed. From the ultimate point of view the nature of the mind is its emptiness of inherent existence.

"If afflictive emotions, such as hatred, were in the very nature of the mind, then from its inception the mind would always have to be hateful, for instance, since that would be its nature."[5]

No such thing as a dirty mind! The Dalai Lama's faulty logic can lead us to the very opposite conclusion: if the mind were clear light, then it would have to be so all the time, since that would be its nature. But the more we know ourselves, the more we see the dark inside.

ZEN BUDDHISM

In contrast with traditional Buddhism, Zen Buddhism says there is no right or wrong. Its elimination of absolutes does away with any such notion as the eightfold pathway of righteousness. Traditional Buddhism treats sin as illusory; Zen goes a step further and tells us that the very concept of sin is illusory. Through meditation, the Buddha-mind, which is our mind, will be seen as a void in which there is no good or bad, no right or wrong. All is one and God is the void. Therefore connection with God is attained by detaching the mind from feelings, evaluations and worldly attachments in meditation.

One branch of Zen functions somewhat differently. It conceptualizes all aspects of human experience, such as feelings, evaluations, and ignorance, to be part of the Buddha-mind, not separate from it. Thus the Buddha-mind is more than just a void. The meditation of this branch is then a process of letting the mind take its own course without actively responding to it, rather than attempting to void it.

This, too, is a practical impossibility. The Zen exhortation to "go with the flow" means never standing up against evil. For example, the rage that we feel about being exploited cannot lead us to resist exploitation, because resisting cuts us off from that "life force." In theory we "accept" the exploitation, but in practise we do ourselves the psychological damage of burying the rage. Much of that buried, festering rage is towards the very "life force" for the constriction this produces.

Zen tells us to acknowledge anger without acting on it, to be a container that is larger than the anger. But there is an inherent contradiction in this. I cannot fully experience the anger if I cannot go to the next step of resolving it in some fashion. The adrenalin released during an anger outburst prepares me for action of some kind; it will poison my system if I do nothing. I can dissociate from it, but it will not go away, nor will it fail to result in guilt.

Jesus told us to turn the other cheek, for vengeance belongs to God (Matthew 5:39). This may sound like Zen, but it comes from a diametrically opposite perspective. He was providing a point of comparison for our instinctual vindictiveness. The point he was making during the Sermon on the Mount is that God's law is a mirror for our sinful selves. This mirror forces us to conclude we need a Savior.

Who can turn the other cheek, on any level, every time someone hurts us? Our awareness of our failure to do this shows us we cannot avoid sin and guilt. Our only recourse is the forgiveness of God.

One symptom of psychosis is split-off affect. The way to insanity is paved by dissociation. Emotions are part of the human apparatus that is necessary to inform and guide action. The pain felt in touching the fire tells us to move away from it. Repressed emotions do not just go away. They are not just an illusion. We cannot accept or forgive them unless we know God has done so.

ISLAM

The legalistic Koran, written around 600 A.D., can in no way be equated with the Bible. Mohammed based his religion on God's law in the Pentateuch. He removed forgiveness for sin and added a few of his own non-divinely inspired ideas and a bit of flotsam and jetsam from other religions, including Zoroastrianism.

The most important aspect of Islam for present purposes is that Allah, though supposedly loving and compassionate, provides no dispensation for lawbreakers. This means Islam breeds insecurity and insanity just like all other legalistic creeds.

Five duties are essential to the Moslem: repeating the Moslem creed daily, prayer five times a day facing Mecca, almsgiving, fasting every day during the "holy" month of Ramadan, and one pilgrimage to Mecca during a person's lifetime. Perfection is not required to keep humans out of the permanent hell described in the Koran, but good deeds have to outweigh bad deeds.

The ratio concept of good deeds versus bad deeds may sound superficially easier than Buddhism or Hinduism. However, not only is it impossible for us to become perfect, we cannot even come out ahead. We are desperately wicked. The more we try to be good, the more we see how bad we are. Even in the process of doing a "good deed" there will be transgressions, perhaps even ones we commit knowingly. When the prophet, who claims Allah's authority, promises instant martyrdom if we go and die in a war he is waging, we might find ourselves justifying rape and robbery of the enemy.

True good deeds are actions performed selflessly out of love in accordance with God, not in obedience to the whimsy of the "prophet," nor for a selfish motive. The promise of instant martyrdom appeals to the totally selfish motive of avoiding hell. If Allah is judging intention, the selfish motive completely negates our "good work." Offering our life to save our own soul is no sacrifice.

Actually, nothing motivates us to do good more than knowing that God does not require good deeds to keep us out of hell; we want to do good when we know how freely and extensively God gave of himself. Some psychological research illustrates how we rebellious humans stop wanting to perform well when the voluntary element of our actions is interfered with. A study on elementary school children suggests that extrinsic reward can destroy intrinsic motivation. When the children were offered material rewards for constructive activities they had formerly chosen for intrinsic reasons, they stopped performing those activities.[6]

JUDAEO-CHRISTIAN RELIGIONS

Hinduism, Buddhism and Islam--the other major world religions besides the Judaeo-Christian ones--do not resolve mankind's archetypical fear of hell. Their schemata promote the internal splitting that leads to mental illness. However, because of misinterpretation of the Bible, the Judaeo-Christian religions have not done much better.

JUDAISM

Judaism is based on the Torah, the law God gave to Moses, and the the man-made Talmud, an interpretative procedural manual based on the Torah. In different ways, both orthodox Judaism and liberal Judaism emphasize human works rather than God's great work of atonement. They neither have Christ, nor do they follow the blood sacrifice contract for God's forgiveness laid out in the Torah.

CHRISTIANITY

As we move away from the Bible as a nation, false doctrines move in on us. Among these are counterfeit forms of Christianity. These fall into two basic groups: liberalism and legalism.

Liberalism and legalism

Liberalism, which says humans need no blood sacrifice, is gaining ground. It ignores hell and focuses on the goodness of humans made in God's image. This serves to foster superficial pride and complacency. Under this facade, the fear and guilt remain, along with a general sense of lostness. There is blindness to the essentialness of Christ, blindness to the deadly juggernaut.

On the other hand, legalism says human works must cause or maintain salvation rather being the voluntary result of it. Usually the salvation is worldly rather than being salvation from hell. This runs formally or informally through Roman Catholicism and many branches of Protestantism, not to mention the cults like the Seventh Day Adventists and Jehovah Witnesses. Each is saying that grace. i.e., the gift of Christ, is not sufficient. Some human effort is essential. Good works and penances for sin; glossolalia; abstention from alcohol and nicotine; door-to-door evangelizing; begging and pleading for forgiveness--actions such as these are required beyond what God did for us. Under such a legalistic system, a person can never be sure if he has done enough. No peace of mind is possible. This is another form of the Satanic doctrine of perfection.

But as we stated in Chapter One, legalistic teaching is not the cause of the terrible sense of guilt and condemnation that people feel. Such teaching only brings this up to consciousness. It does exacerbate it, though. Each pseudo-Bible-based denomination or cult that departs from the true Gospel is a "bad" schema that not only does not bring closure to our inner conflict but increases it.

These are wolves in sheep's clothing that foster the delusion that humans can attain perfection or that they already are perfect. On the other hand, true, grace-revealing biblical fundamentalism is the bread of life to us, nourishing the "psyche," the Greek word for soul. The counterfeits miss the central importance of grace, i.e., God's gift of Christ as the essential and complete payment for sin.

False prophets

How can we know who is telling the truth? In the first epistle of John (I John 4:1-3), we are advised to test the spirits "because many false prophets are gone out in the world. Hereby know ye the Spirit of God: Every spirit that confesseth that Jesus Christ is come in the flesh is of God: And every spirit the confesseth not that Jesus Christ is come in the flesh is not of God:"

This confession, a kind of password, does not come in a vacuum. It presupposes adherence to the five elements of what we call Christian fundamentalism: inerrancy of the Bible, the Virgin birth, the death and resurrection of Christ, his substitutionary work of atonement for us, and his imminent second coming.[7] Of incomparable importance is the fact that Christ alone did the work of atonement that saves humans.

Anti-fundamentalist bias
Satanic deception has led Biblical fundamentalism to have a bad name. Its precepts are a source of ridicule in our "liberal" society. Hell is archaic; a personification of evil is ridiculous; and a loving God would never let us fall away into a black hole. The preachers of hell fire and brimstone are treated as a joke.

Fundamentalism has been given an undeserved negative stereotype by the media and the supposedly impartial social science community. Adorno devised a measure of "authoritarianism," the famous F scale which taps cognitive inflexibility and personality rigidity.[8] Without any basis in reality, it is popularly assumed that Christian fundamentalism has a strong positive relationship with authoritarianism. Research using the F-scale has found the reverse to be true.[9]

Further, as compared to more liberal Protestant denominations, members of congregations affiliated with conservative denominations expressed higher levels of social concern, autonomy, openness to change,[10] faith maturity, and horizontal or "other-directed" religiousness.[11]

It has also been assumed that Biblical fundamentalists are politically conservative, but other than on issues such as abortion where God gives a clear mandate, research has shown that to be untrue.[12,13]

Moreover, fundamentalism is typically described only in negative terms, as if it had no scientific basis and were not "for" anything. Take, for example: "Fundamentalism is...a mood of militant opposition to secular culture, liberal theology, and scientific views that challenge literal Biblical interpretations."[14]

Fundamentalism, sin, and grace
Biblical fundamentalist preaching is rejected for its "damaging" emphasis on our pervasive sinfulness. Certainly

psychologists like Albert Ellis support that view. Ellis states
that the "concept of sin is the direct and indirect cause of
virtually all neurotic disturbance."[15]   But Ellis has no belief in
a higher law, in moral absolutes, or in an innately sinful
nature.

The anti-fundamentalists have missed the point of the
Bible.   The Bible does not cause guilt and fear.   It explains
the pain we already have, then offers complete relief.   If we
reject the predicament, we reject the remedy.   Yet all forms of
Christian fundamentalism are under attack.

It is true that if God's Word did not contain the news
about his provision of a free pardon for all of us, biblical
fundamentalist teaching would be pernicious.   When the spectre
of guilt over missing the mark is raised without the assurance
of God's forgiveness, it cause havoc.

There is a some research evidence for this.   If empty of
grace, fundamentalism can shatter faith and drive a person
away from God, leading to severe depression.[16,17]   But in a
series of studies on the relationship between guilt and
psychological functioning, the effects of guilt were found to
vary with the person's perception of grace.   For Pentecostal
Christians who scored higher on a measure tapping the
experience of grace, guilt was associated with positive
psychological functioning; for members of other religious
denominations scoring lower on the grace measure, the opposite
was true.[18]

Denomination and truth

This suggests some religious denominations are closer to
the truth than others.   Curiously enough, research has shown
that denomination itself tells us little about a person's sense of
the Gospel.   A number of studies have noted the lack of
reliability and validity in "denominational affiliation" measures.[19]
Further, there is much within-denomination variation in belief
as there is between denominations.[20]

Nevertheless, in addition to the study on Pentecostals,
there is evidence showing denominational affiliation to have
some overall associations with a person's relationship to God.
One study on the many dimensions of religiosity discovered a
"salvation by works" factor in the religious beliefs of Catholics
and unorthodox Protestants.   This factor was not present for
orthodox Protestants.[21]

What makes for within-denomination variability in religious belief system? We do not know if it is due to variation in preachers within those denominations, or to individual members of congregations. One thing we do know: those who search the Scriptures will find grace.

THE FUTURE: ONE WORLD RELIGION
Biblical prophesy foretells one world religion involving a leader imbued with Satanic supernatural power, a rejection of the God of the Bible, and persecution of Christians (II Thessalonians 2:3-4, 8-9; Revelations 13:7-8).

All around us we see the signs of this. One is the pluralistic ecumenical church movement in the United States, a banding together of all religions. Another is the widespread rise of Satanic cults that promote human godliness or usurpation of supernatural ppower: Gnosticism, paganism, witchcraft, Christian Science, Unity, and on and on.[22]

One world religion will be achieved by seeking the common ground and rejecting the divergent aspects of religion. It means a creed including a higher power, some form of prayer, and the equation of Jesus with Mohammed, Buddha, Mary and the "other" prophets. Left by the wayside will be the essentials: hell, the dilemma due to sin and Jesus as son of God and Savior. This will be Satan's last seduction.

CHARACTERISTICS OF FALSE RELIGIONS
One, they are based on the doctrine of perfection or "good works", instead of the doctrine of grace. They correctly acknowledge that sin, or human imperfection separates humans from God. However, they handle this problem by calling sin an illusion, or by advocating self-control to purge sin, or by at least trying to make good deeds come out ahead of bad deeds. Since truly none of these things could be done without supernatural power, each approach makes an implicit claim to godliness, thus evoking Satan's seduction in the Garden. In practise, perfectionism leads to massive defensiveness. The denial of the sin nature places it squarely in Satan's hands.

Two, God is seen as merciless, having made no provision for human imperfection.

Three, since perfection, attained by humans only by assuming the mantle of Christ, is required before connection can be made with God, these belief systems offer no way to experience an ongoing, personal relationship with God.   Either God is above me, far removed, or inside me but separate from my human foibles.   If God is inside me, I view him as "it," an impersonal force that I am part of.   Either way, there is no experience of a person to pray to, nor of forgiveness.

Four, this tends to perpetuate the status quo.   There is no basis for acting in faith.

Five, a human leader is frequently deified.   He is free to set the price for salvation and uses this for corrupt ends.   He may, for example, offer instant martyrdom for dying in his wars.

Six, in most cases no concept of a permanent state of darkness, or hell, is adhered to.   This is the other part of Satan's seduction: "Ye shalt not surely die:" (Genesis 3:4).

Seven, no peace of mind is possible.   The unconscious undertow of the fear of hell is not resolved.

All in all, the doctrine of perfection is a "bad" schema that the human psyche cannot digest.   It may be acceptable on a conscious level if taken with a large gulp of self-deceit.   The cost is mental health.

SUMMARY AND CONCLUSIONS

This chapter has shown that all non-Biblical religions only perpetuate and foster guilt and terror about our existential crisis.   They offer pathways that may seem superficially appealing but never give us a sense of closure.   The Satanic seduction is apparent in these "bad" schemas when the underlying premises are scrutinized.

All false religions, including spurious, liberal or legalistic Bible-based ones, operate according to the doctrine of perfection or "works":   that in some fashion, man can heal the breach due to human imperfection.   Of course, the double-talk changes from creed to creed.   Perfection is to be humanly attained by: merely recognizing it is already there; laying sin aside; getting rid of the personal ego; working off karma; compensating for bad deeds by good deeds; redefining sin;" or learning to accept our dark side and forgive ourselves for it, as if the price is not death.   Pagan religions that are regaining poularity even go as far as futile human sacrifice.

Inside us, we know we cannot make it according to any of these ideas.   We know we are sinners, that the price for sin is death, and that we cannot change ourselves sufficiently to avoid the penalty.

Nevertheless there are truths in all these belief systems. "Right action," or obeying God's Law, does make it easier for us to live with ourselves. However, this will be pathologically defensive unless it springs from the heart, preceded by the knowledge of God's saving grace.

All forms of meditation can give us a sense of a deeper and more important reality than the worldly concerns that can easily take up all of our consciousness. As Solomon, who had a chance to sample all the best the world has to offer, concluded: "All is vanity and vexation of spirit" (Ecclesiastes 1:14). But meditation without Christ leads humans astray and opens them to the demonic realm. This is why meditation is completely rejected as a practise by certain Christian fundamentalists.[23] Nevertheless it is, in fact, mentioned throughout the Bible as a form of worship (e.g., Genesis 24:63). Christian meditation has power unlike any mentioned in this chapter. Focusing on God's law and gift of forgiveness (i.e., Christ) leading to everlasting life, it truly does produce the peace which passes all understanding.[24]

Notes

1. McIntosh, Daniel N. (1991). "Religion as schema: Implications for the relation between religion and coping." Paper presented at annual meeting of American Psychological Association, San Francisco, CA, August, 1991.

2. Ball-Rokeach, S. J., Rokeach, M., and Grube, J. W. (1984). The Great American Values Test. New York, New York: Free Press, p. 27.

3. Dollard, J., Doob,L. W., Miller, F. E., Mowrer, O. H., Sears, R. R., Ford, C. S., Hovland, C. I. and Sollenberger, R. T. (1939). Frustration and Aggression. New Haven: Yale University Press.

4. Ferm, Vergilius (Ed.) (1984). The Encyclopaedia of Religion. Secaucus, New Jersey: Poplar Books, p. 94.

5. Dalai Lama (Fall, 1989). "The luminous nature of the mind," in The Snow Lion Newsletter and Catalog, p. 1

6. Deci, E. L. (1975). Intrinsic motivation. New York, New York,: Plenum.

7. Ferm, op. cit., p. 291.

8. Ellis, A. (1962). Reason and emotion in psychotherapy. Secaucus, New Jersey: Lyle Stuart.

9. Moyers, J. C. (1990). "Issues in the psychotherapy of former fundamentalists." Psychotherapy, 27, 1, p. 8.

10. Vitz, P. C. and Gartner, J. (1984). "Christianity and psychoanalysis, Part 2: Jesus the transformer of the super-ego." Journal of Psychologyand Theology, 12, pp. 82-90.

11. Yao, R. (1987). Addiction and the Fundamentalist Experience. New York: Fundamentalists Anonymous.

12. Watson, P. J., Morris, R. J. and Hood, R. W. (1988). "Sin and Self-Functioning, Part 1: Grace, Guilt, and Self-Consciousness." Journal of Psychology and Theology, 16, 3, pp. 254-269.
--"Sin and Self-Functioning, Part 2: Grace, Guilt, and Psychological Adjustment." Journal of Psychology and Theology, 16, 3, pp. 270-281.

13. Campbell, C., and Coles, R. W. (1973). "Religiosity, religious affiliation, and religious belief: The exploration of a typology." Review of Religious Research, 14, 151-158; Finner, S. L. (1970). "Religious membership and religious preference: Equal indicators of religiosity?" Journal for the Scientific Study of Religion, 9, 173-179; Lazerwitz, B. and Harrison, M. (1980). "A comparison of denominational identification and membership." Journal for the Scientific Study of Religion, 19, 361-367.

14. Brinkerhoff, M. B. and MacKie, M. M. (1984). "Religious denominations' impact upon gender attitudes: Some methodological implications." Review of Religious Research, 25, pp. 365-378

15. Stark, R. and Glock, C. Y. (1968). <u>American Piety: The nature of religious commitment.</u> Berkeley: University of California Press.

16. Adorno, T. W., Else Frenkle-Brunswik, Daniel J. Levinson and R. Nevitt Sanford (1950). <u>The Authoritarian Personality</u>. New York: Harpers.

17. Stark Rodney (1971) "Psychopathology and religious commitment." <u>Review of Religious Research</u>, 12, pp. 165-176.

18. Pargament, K. I., Echemendia, R. J., Johnson, S., Cook, P., McGrath, C., Myers, J. G., and Brannick, M. (1987). The conservative church: Psychosocial advantages and disadvantages. <u>American Journal of Commuity Psychology</u>, **15, pp. 269-286.**

19. Benson, P. L. and Eklin, C. H. (1990). <u>Effective Christian education: A national study of Protestant congregations - A summary report on faith, loyalty, and acongregational life.</u> Minneapolis, MN: Search Institute.

20. Benson and Eklin, op. cit.

21. Hood, Ralph E., Jr., Morris, Ronald J. (1985). "Boundary maintenance, social-political views, and presidential preference among high and low fundamentalists." <u>Review of Religious Research</u>, 27, pp. 134-145.

22. For example: Hunt, Dave and McMahon, T. A. (1985). <u>The Seduction of Christianity.</u> Eugene, Oregon: Harvest House.

23. Hunt and McMahon, op. cit.

24. Ray, D. (1977). <u>The Art of Christian Meditation</u>. Wheaton, Illinois: Tynedale House Publishers.

Chapter Eleven

DANGEROUS SPIRITUAL THERAPIES

Non-Biblical spiritual therapy is on the rise. It is always based on the Satanic lies. Some of its various forms are built around one specific theory or theorist, others are a mishmash. In Chapter Four we looked at Jungian therapy, a major force in the spiritual mental health movement. Our first visits in this chapter are to two Jungian offshoots, i.e., Psychosynthesis and the more eclectic Transpersonal psychotherapy. Then we move on to the sinking sand of the popular Twelve Step program of recovery with its generic concept of God.

PSYCHOSYNTHESIS

Psychosynthesis is a therapeutic form incorporating Jungian and Gnostic assertions of the divinity of man and the central role of knowledge. Its founder, Roberto Assagioli,[1] proposed an egg-shaped model of the psyche. The "egg" has three concentrically-ordered elements. Coming from the center outwards, these consist of 1. a conscious self or ego; 2. three areas of the unconscious, i.e., the middle unconscious in which the conscious is initially centered, and at the extremes, the lower unconscious and the spiritually aware higher unconscious or superconscious with a "higher self" at its apex; and 3. surrounding all this, a species-aware collective unconscious.

The path to healing begins with knowing the various sub-personalities which may be in conflict. Then the sub-personalities must be controlled or tamed by ego mechanisms. Third, the ego has to migrate from the middle unconscious to the true or "higher" self, the unifying center around which the fourth step of forming a new, harmonious personality can be formed.

Clearly this is one more way of saying humans are divine. No payment for sin is necessary. Healing comes from connecting with the god inside and organizing all other elements of the personality around it.

THE TRANSPERSONAL LIE

In the last twenty years, psychotic religiosity (see Chapters Seven and Eight) has been the focus of the non-traditional world of "healers." There is a growing school called "Transpersonal" psychology, typified by the Spiritual Emergence Network,[2] which views mental illness as a psychic process, a spiritual awakening...an awakening, that is, to everything but the Gospel. It is curious that, as interested in spirituality as the members of this group seem to be and as scholarly in approach as many of them are, they also appear to be unversed in the true message of the Bible.

According to Transpersonalists, psychosis is itself a healing process. A person in a psychotic state is regarded as experiencing a spiritual opening. So far the Transpersonal and Bible-based views agree. However, when the Transpersonalists state that this is a spiritual opening to a divine self, their view is anti-biblical, and so is their method of treatment.

The Transpersonal approach advocates passively providing a climate for the spiritual force supposedly residing inside the person to take over. Contrarily, the Bible-based approach states that without Christ, a spiritual "opening" is demonic. Spiritual healing comes only through the God of the Bible. It must be accompanied by Christ's blood as payment for sin, a fact of which humans are innately aware. But there is no immediate fee for the demons posing as angels of light who wish to possess a living human. Sin separates us from God but not from demons. And a spiritual opening to demons has a terrible cost: Gospel-blinding control and deeper insanity.

The truly Bible-based approach is necessarily directive and didactic. It prescribes soaking up the Gospel as the antidote to spiritually-induced psychosis. Satan's influence is written all over the Transpersonal school. It says: you are god, there is no Satan, and there is nothing to fear in the spiritual realm. The shamanic practises currently popular with this group make spirit contact central; they foster the worship of the creation, not the Creator. The popular "shamanic journeying" attempts to create rebirth through visualization of a voyage through the underworld and out into the light, encountering human and animal spirit guides along the way. The innate human sense of the danger in this encounter with "familiar" spirits (demons) is denied. Adherents may have no conscious sense of playing with fire until it is too late.

In fact, the therapeutic practises advocated by this group include most of those forbidden by God (Deuteronomy 18). What else is the coiled snake of the so-called "kundalini" energy but a representation of Satan?   Asking this "energy" to enter oneself through one of the supposed "chakras" at the base of the spine is merely inviting demonic penetration.

No genuine healing takes place among these practises. At best, only temporary relief occurs.   At worst, there is an intensification of symptomatology of all kinds.

A friend of mine who was deeply involved in Eastern mytical practices and sorcery several years ago claims to have been temporarily blinded during a kundalini experience.   The retinas of both his eyes were partially burned.   He regained his sight afterwards, but, unsurprisingly, decided to discontinue his psychic exploration.

Some research suggests that the Transpersonal approach is dangerous to its own practitioners.   A study compared psychiatry residents with community-based "alternative" (i.e., Transpersonal) healers.   Although the "alternative" healers displayed no more obvious psychopathology than the others, they reported more dissociative experiences; more of the major symptoms of schizophrenia, such as hearing voices and seeing visions; more ESP experiences; and more of the symptoms of multiple personality disorder.[3]

What will they look like further down the road?   Since I used to place therapy advertisements in a New Age newspaper, several clients I have seen have been heavily involved in occultism, some of them previously earning a living as spirit channelers.   These individuals are now physically and/or psychiatrically disabled.   Some present with the full set of criteria for demonic possession outlined in Chapter Eight. Others present with depression, paranoia, panic attacks, bulimia, conversion disorder and physical illness.   The practitioners attribute these problems to "becoming ungrounded."   A necessary feature of their spiritual work is supposedly going out of body, leaving themselves wide open to demonic attack. Ungrounded they certainly are until they build their home on the true rock, Jesus Christ.

Some have been receptive to the Gospel.   It is rare, but it does happen when they are desperate enough to see through the lies that have brought them only misery.

TWELVE STEP RECOVERY VERSUS THE BIBLE

The Twelve Step program for recovery from addiction has caught on like wildfire in the United States. This self-help group movement began with the formulation of Alcoholics Anonymous ("AA") in 1935 by a stockbroker and a physician. The movement has spread into a variety of areas of human weakness besides alcoholism. Although originally Christian, it has sidestepped Christ in favor of a generic god. Supposedly in the interest of being non-discriminatory, the most fundamental tenets of the Bible are omitted. These are: human separation from God due to sin; the fact that humans are therefore doomed to go to hell; and Christ as the payment for sin necessary before humans can freely approach God.

Twelve steppers usurp God's sovereignty as they, themselves, decide who God is: a "Power greater than ourselves" or "God as we understand him" (GAWUH). Although twelve-steppers call God "him," they are in no way limited by thise. For many of them God might well be an impersonal brick or their Teddy bear.

A BIBLICAL TRANSLATION OF THE TWELVE STEPS

The problem is, there is no way to achieve the third of the twelve steps without Jesus Christ. See for yourself:

The first three of the twelve steps

1. We admitted we were powerless over alcohol, that our lives had become unmanageable.
2. Came to believe that a Power greater than ourselves could restore us to sanity.
3. Made a decision to turn our will and lives over to the care of GAWUH.

The biblical theme essential for step three

1. We saw that the price for sin is death. We admitted that we were lost sinners, powerless over our separation from God. We were in Satan's clutches, doomed to go to hell.
2. Came to believe that God provided a rescue for us as a gift in the form of the subsitute death of his only son Jesus. We could claim the perfection of Jesus Christ as the essential shield for our own endless flaws, our bridge to God.
3. Claimed that unearned gift and experienced our total freedom to have an ongoing relationship with God as forgiven

sinners. Although remaining sinners all our lives, we found ourselves increasingly willing to do what God wants us to do out of our gratitude to him for his gift of a rescue from hell.

The point is, the first three steps of the Twelve Step recovery program cannot be achieved before the three steps immediately above. Step three is the crux. There is no way to approach God without the payment for sin, i.e., Jesus. God is not "GAWUH," he is the God of Abraham, Isaac and Jacob who reveals himself in the Bible. Step three is impossible without Christ. Only with this entrance fee can we come in front of God and turn our lives over to him. If we say we need no entrance fee, we are implicitly saying we have equality with God, i.e., we are gods. Satan must be smiling.

The remainder of the Twelve Steps deal with a process of recognition of sin; confession to God, oneself, and another human being; and a process of making amends to all those one has harmed...a sham if a sense of God's existential mercy is lacking. The steps finish with a commitment to seek conscious contact with "GAWUH" through prayer and meditation, and to spread the word among other addicts. The gospel of AA to be spread with such diligence has nothing to do with our existential dilemma and the free rescue. This is a false gospel which does not touch the true basis for addiction, i.e., knowing we face eternal darkness. There is no mention of Christ as our only means of atonement with God.

It has been my experience that many people who try to follow the steps in a feeling and conscientious way reach a state of frustration with them that can open the way to the true Gospel. However, most get led astray by the Twelve Step movement. Either the movement itself becomes "GAWUH" as a clinging to social support, or the generic deity concept opens the door to Eastern spirituality and demon possession.

RESEARCH ON SPIRITUAL CURES FOR ADDICTION

The Twelve Step movement has rapidly produced converts and led many to quit addictions of various types. However, research on just how and why the program is effective has been conducted only on a very small scale, and has not addressed the specifics.[4,5,6]

Project Match, a large-scale study funded by the federal government, plans to investigate the effects of different treatments for addictions in eight treatment centers. The

research design includes the Twelve Step approach and its
demonic "GAWUH." We must beware of its conclusions.
Such research is likely to attribute the inexplicable, sudden
cures found in "spiritual" programs to a generic god who is
accessed without going through the blood of Christ.

Abrupt, dramatic cures for alcoholism and other
addictions can and do occur outside of a true relationship with
God. This can happen through a sudden insight that provokes
an awakening, a shift in beliefs and attitudes leading to an
immediate change in behavior. Research has shown that
instant cures of cigarette smoking can occur in response to an
experience of humiliation.[7] Such a thing can be explained by a
term taken from Gestalt psychology: "perceptual shifting," a
secular type of repentance. The change following it has
nothing to do with faith in God.[8]

SUMMARY AND CONCLUSIONS

The recent emergence of spiritual psychotherapy is not
good news. This chapter reviewed three major non-biblical
spiritual approaches to therapy: Psychosynthesis, Transpersonal
therapy, and the Twelve Step approach. All embody the
Satanic "you-are-god" deception.

Psychosynthesis and Transpersonalism explicitly locate god
in the self. The Twelve Step approach does so implicitly: it
lets the person define divinity. The proponents of all three
approaches purport to be open to Bible believers. In practice
they omit or even forbid mention of Christ as the only
acceptable payment for sin. At best, these approaches give an
illusion of recovery. At worst, they lead to a worsening of
symptoms and open the door to demon possession. In all
cases, they foster blindness to God's saving grace.

Watch out! In the future, we can expect to find more
information on the effectiveness of the Twelve Step approach.
If positive changes were attributed to a generic spiritual power,
actually a demonic "god" who can be attained without Christ,
this would further blind people to the truth in the Bible.

Notes

1. Assagioli, Roberto (1971). <u>Psychosynthesis.</u> New York,
New York: The Viking Press, Inc.

2. Spiritual Emergence Network, Institute of Transpersonal Psychology, 250 Oak Grove Avenue, Menlo Park, California, 94025. This organization is directed by Stanislav and Christina Grof.

3. Hever, A. S., Fleisher, W. P., Ross, C. A., and Stanwick, R. S. (1989). "Dissociation in alternative hers and traditional therapists." (1989). <u>American Journal of Psychotherapy</u>, <u>43</u>, 4, pp. 562-574.

4. Brandsma, J. M., Maultsky, M. C., and Welsh, R. J. (1980). <u>Outpatient treatment of alcoholism: A review and comparative study.</u> Baltimore, MD: University Park Press.

5. Emrick, C. D. (1989). "Alcoholics Anonymous: Membership characteristics and effectiveness as treatment." In M. Galanter (Ed.), <u>Recent developments in alcoholism</u>, <u>7</u>, pp. 37-54.

6. Miller, W. R. and Hester, R. K. (1986). "The effectiveness of alcoholism treatment: What research reveals." In W. R. Miller and N. Heather (Eds.) <u>Treating addictive behaviors: Processes of change</u>. New York: Plenum Press, pp. 121-174.

7. Premack, D. (1970). "Mechanisms of self-control." In W. A. Hunt (Ed.) <u>Learning mechanisms in smoking</u>. Chcago: Aldine, pp. 107-123

8. McMullin, R. E. (1986). "Perceptual Shifting." In <u>Handbook of cognitive therapy techniques</u>. New York: W. W. Norton, pp. 73-157.

Chapter Twelve

FATAL FLAWS IN CHRISTIAN

APPROACHES TO PSYCHOTHERAPY

Do the popular theories and approaches to Christian counseling center on the essentialness of Christ's blood? No. The two common pitfalls are legalistic perfectionism and liberalism. The narrow path of grace lies between them. Merciless legalism preaches against the sin that causes existential guilt rather than opening the door to grace, God's payment of the penalty for sin. Liberalism is a version of humanism in Christian clothes. It says since we are made in God's image, we simply need to realize how wonderful we are to regain sanity. Both imply godhood. They embody the Satanic doctrine of perfection which says that humans are able to connect with God through the perfection that they can attain or see in themselves. The truth is, sin is the fabric of which we are woven, so we must rely on God's grace to cover us. God made a law for our defense not our prosecution.

This chapter explores the major Christian approaches to mental health. They contain truth but they are contaminated by the little bit of leaven that spoils the whole lump.

JAY ADAMS AND THE MISLEADING "SIN" CONNECTION

An approach typified by the widely-read Jay Adams[1] attributes mental illness to guilt concerning specific sins, not existential guilt. Like many other Christian psychologists, Adams bases his approach on the work of O. Hobart Mowrer.[2] Mowrer advocated a psychotherapeutic approach that blamed patients in a guilt-arousing atmosphere. In theory, they would then reject the sinful behavior that caused guilt and sent them to "hell." Note that for Mowrer, not a Christian, hell was neurosis or psychosis.

SPECIFIC SINS

For Adams, too, the cure is getting rid of sin...as if that were possible. This is one more version of the Satanic doctrine of perfection. Paul expresses the difference between intention and human ability: "For that which I do I allow not: for what I would, that do I not; but what I hate, that do I." (Romans 7:15).

The more we look at the sin in our lives, the more we find we have no control over it. God will not necessarily remove it, either. Three times Paul asked for God to remove an unnamed "thorn in the flesh," (II Corinthians 12:7) and three times God told him grace would have to suffice, suggesting this thorn was a sin. Without the feeling of those thorns sticking in us, we might delude ourselves we have finally made it to that perfect state where we have no need of God's payment for sin.

Outside of an unearned relationship with God through Christ, we are in a double bind. We carry the full burden of the consequence for sin but do not have the control to stop it.

It is true that quitting a trespass may reduce guilt and make us saner. The conscious and unconscious ramifications of the guilt and fear resulting from it will disappear. However, that sin may have had a psychologically defensive function. If a genuine sense of God's forgiveness is absent, it may actually makes us more crazy to quit. This is especially so if the sin has been a central subterfuge in our life. Stopping drinking or lying denies us an escape from the terrifying reality that led us to do these things in the first place.

For many, getting rid of a sin through personal efforts will be accompanied by self-congratulation, a swelling of pride, probably a worse sin than the one eliminated.

And what if our feelings towards stopping the sin are ambivalent? Aware that we ought to stop, we may not be at all sure that we want to. We feel enslaved by it.

The first step in the cure is to know God accepts us as sinners, that he paid the price for the sin which doomed us. Then we can begin to look at our corruptness. The assurance of his complete forgiveness and the remorse and thankfulness we feel towards him for his rescue from our sinking ship...this will motivate us to want to please him. Only this will open our hearts and make us want to change. Our ambivalence will fade. We will be inspired to ask God to *make* us want to do his will. "For it is God which worketh in you both to will and to do of his good pleasure." (Phillipians 2:13).

THE SIN NATURE PROBLEM

The worst aspect of the "specific sin" approach is that it completely skirts over the real issue: man's sinful nature, and the impossibility of eradicating it. The Adams approach only adds another layer to the guilt, fear, rage, and other dark emotions that are the reaction to our knowledge that we are doomed. It does not reach the true source of mental illness.

There is a wild goose chase to hunt down the specific sin theoretically causing the anxiety, depression, or other symptoms. In the process we feel that we must be a worse sinner than the other people around us who do not seem to suffer from a mental disorder. Others treat us accordingly. As the illness persists we are blamed for stubbornly holding on to some secret sin.

If we could get rid of the sin nature, certainly that would heal us. It would get us out of our predicament. But that is not an option. Even if all the specific sins could be eliminated from our life, our sin nature would still be in the way. It will always fall short, disconnecting us from God and giving rise to existential guilt. As we saw in the discussion of the Twelve Step program in the previous chapter, until we are assured of grace, we cannot turn any aspect of our lives over to God. That can only happen when we know we have free access to God through Christ. The only cure is to know that by killing Christ, God has paid the price for our sin nature and every sin we commit. Adams fails to tell us this.

JOHN WHITE:
GRACE IS IMPORTANT BUT NOT ESSENTIAL

John White, a Christian psychiatrist who has written several books, looks at two ways in which sin is connected to mental illness.[3] The first is the "specific sin" route that we discussed in relation to Jay Adams.

The second sees the Fall and the entry of sin in the human race as causing the loss of God's protection. The loss of protection gives rise to various types of debilitation in man: physical illness, mental illness, decay and death. So much is true. However, like Adams and, as we will see, all the other major Christian psychologists, White does not see mental illness arising from our attempts to flee from our conscious or unconscious awareness of being doomed.[4] Consequently, he does not judge the firm knowledge of God's grace to be absolutely essential to mental health.

In line with other members of the psychiatric profession, he leans heavily on drug therapy as the best cure for depression. But it is well known that drugs help only with the symptoms. This raises a chicken/egg problem: which comes first, depressive thinking or chemical changes in the brain? A biblical perspective leads to the conclusion that depressive thinking causes the chemical imbalance. Dark thoughts about eternal damnation affect the brain's neurotransmitter secretion (see Chapter Fourteen for a discussion of depression).

Due to the blinding influence of Satan, we are all at risk for depression. This most common disorder is clearly a disease of the spirit. My experience has been that depression sufferers become decreasingly subject to dark, hopeless periods as the strength of their attachment to God grows.

M. SCOTT PECK'S LIBERALISM

Although M. Scott Peck has written some best-sellers ubiquitous on the shelves of liberal pastors and psychotherapists, his notion of spirituality is Gnostic[5] rather than Christian. It embraces inner wisdom and leans on human solutions rather than godly ones.

Peck's idiosyncratic interpretation of the Bible has led him to some false conclusions. For example, he equates original sin with laziness[6], to be cured--or eliminated--by the upward movement of grace. In other words, he does not see human depravity, particularly what he calls "evil," to be innate. Nor does he pay attention to the sin/death equation.

Peck equates God with grace as an inanimate force. Hindu-fashion, grace causes the spiritual evolution of man, making each generation more godly than the last. He does not see grace as God's provision of a free pardon waiting to be claimed by humans who recognize there is no other way out. Besides, the Bible shows us that man's basic depravity quotient is not reduced from generation to generation. The manifestations of our depravity change only ontogenetically (over the individual life span), not phylogenetically (over the span of human existence), and only as a function of faith in God.

In truth grace does produce spiritual growth, but by removing the barrier between man and God due to human sin. Peck does not see this barrier. Since he regards the story of Adam and Eve as a myth, he is able to see an open door to God through human perception. There is no need for the payment for sin; Christ is inessential.

Says Peck "When we truly know what we are doing, we are participating in the omniscience of God."[7] This is arrogant nonsense, Gnosticism's Satanic lure of knowledge. It is humanly impossible to truly know what we are doing, because we do not have God's vantage point. Our perspective is extremely limited. And we certainly cannot even begin to see our true selves until demolition of the psychological defense walls is triggered by a sense of God's forgiveness.

Even more presumptuous is Peck's advice that we question God about his motives.[8]

In spite of all Peck has to say about the transforming power of grace, he shows his true humanistic colors when he talks about the transformation of evil: "The healing of evil--scientifically or otherwise--can be accomplished only by the love of individuals."[9] Where's God in it?

Here is even more confusion: "When one has purified oneself, by the Grace of God, to the point where one can truly love one's enemies, a beautiful thing happens. It is as if the boundaries of the soul become transparent, and a unique light then shines forth from the individual." So rather than assuming the mantle of Christ, we purify ourselves, do we? And whose light shines forth from us, ours or God's?

The fact is, when we explore ourselves honestly, the truest love we find for our enemies is our desire that they not go to hell. There is nothing pure or lovey-dovey about it. Dark emotions may accompany this desire. We may continue to detest their behavior. Yet when all is said and done, we do not want them to fall into the never-ending abyss. This love for our enemies springs from knowing how much undeserved mercy God extended to us. Jesus put it this way: "To whom little is forgiven, the same loveth little" (Luke 7:47).

PAUL TOURNIER: FALSE GUILT?

Paul Tournier, a Swiss doctor who has written extensively on the relationship between the spirit, the psyche, guilt and physical healing, is popular in Christian psychotherapy circles.

Tournier differentiates between two kinds of guilt.[10]   One is "false guilt," consisting of other people's judgments of us and our perception of our inferiority according to false standards. He uses the example of our own illnesses. We do not usually cause our illnesses, yet we feel guilty about them.

It is true that there is misplaced guilt, but this does not deserve the place of distinction Tournier gives it. The author misses the true reason why our sense of our inferiority plagues us so. It comes from our knowledge of the existential consequence of falling short, i.e., sin, or our inferiority in relation to God's law. Our sense of missing the mark produces the awareness of deserving eternal punishment.

Hence what Tournier calls "false guilt" is actually based on the true, existential guilt that cannot be explained outside of God's law. Other people, with their distorted moral code, can provoke false guilt but it has a deeper underpinning. The reason why it is so easy for others to engender guilt in us is that we know, unconsciously, that missing the mark is deadly. The slightest reminder of our human failure to attain total adherence to God's law arouses deadly existential guilt. Fortunately, however, God's law spells out a God-given reprieve, a pardon for sin.

One of Tournier's examples of false guilt is the woman who is guilty about a less than perfectly clean home. Despite what Tournier states, this does not just arise out of distorted, superficial human standards. It becomes an obsession with her because it is a manifestation of her own sense of uncleanness. Her dirty house is an unaffordable reminder of the dire consequence for sin.

For Tournier, "true guilt" is "the failure to dare to be oneself" rather a sense of eternal condemnation. By not seeing that what underlies this failure is the fear that our true nature dooms us, he misses the point. We cannot be ourselves unless we know God has given us the key to his door, a key with no strings attached.

Neurosis is not, as Tournier says, a conflict between the true and the false. The task of psychotherapy is therefore not one of weeding out the false guilt. Neurosis is based on the guilt of missing the mark. Unlike Tournier's idea of true guilt, this true guilt is resistant to confession because of its consequence. It takes much hearing of the Word of God for us to believe that as long as we claim the mantle of Jesus Christ, we humans are under no condemnation (Romans 8:1).

Moreover, repentance from sin is not the door to grace as Tournier says it is. He has it backwards. Grace has to precede repentance from sin. Prior to my perceiving grace, I still believe I am under the death sentence. Thus I am unable to see myself for the sinner I truly am. Only under grace can I dare to approach God or see myself. Only then I will find myself inspired to love God, wanting to confess and repent sin.

Tournier describes the "happy guilt" of the Christian who "begs" for grace. Well, the Christian is in a happy position and guilt has lost its sting. But grace is not something we need to beg for. It is the free pardon, already given to us, waiting to be collected. Through grace we are freed to see ourselves as we really are--sinners. Grace is the solid rock, the defense which permits us to drop all our other defenses.

First we have to see is that one chink in our armour ... that one place where we know there is no way we can be perfect according to the law. When we seize on grace as our only hope, guilt will no longer cause psychological problems. However, Tournier preaches against the sin of lacking the courage to be ourselves rather than opening the door to the grace of God that frees us to do this.

THE MINIRTH-MEIER CLINIC

Frank Minirth and his associates at the Minirth-Meier clinic are Christian psychiatrists who have written extensively on the relationship between Christianity and psychiatry.[11]

While they point to the God of the Bible as a provider of mental health, they do not see him as its sole provider. This is because they fail to see that mental illness is caused by God's damning law, born into all humans.

In Minirth's basic text, he states peace of mind comes from Christ's removal of sin from the soul (mind, emotion, will), rather than a sense of forgiveness.[12]   But Satan uses the false expectation of the cleansing of sin from our nature to make us fall away from Christianity.   God can, and does, overcome certain sins in our life yet the voice of our sin nature will continue to shout.

In Minirth and Meier's book on "codependency," a term for addiction to another person, they point out the need to replace this with an addiction to Christ.   But they do not say that this is the only cure: "The most effective means for overcoming codependent relationships is to establish a relationship with Christ himself.   This is done merely by realizing that "all have sinned and fall short of the glory of God"; that there is a penalty for sin, yet sin's penalty has been paid through Christ's death in our place.   Because of this, we can receive forgiveness, meaning in life, enablement to overcome sin and even addictions, and a home in heaven forever merely by trusting Christ."[13]

All this is true.   But Minirth and company miss the core cause of codependency: existential guilt.   Humans innately know they are doomed sinners.   Codependency is both a bid to pay for sin and a desperate clinging to another person in place of God.   It offers a temporary hiding place from the death sentence and provides several ways to psychologically defend against it.   These include displacement, whereby attention is focused on the other's problems; and pseudo-atonement, whereby suffering, martyrdom, and rescuing strive to pay for sin (see Chapter Six on pseudo-atonement).

The only way out of codependency is through resolution of the existential dilemma.   Therefore Christ is not just the best solution, he is the only solution.

THE INNER HEALING MOVEMENT

The "Inner Healing" movement is promoted through the writings of the Linn brothers and Agnes Sanford.[14,15]   Some Christian writers have accused this movement of occultism, and there is some truth to this.[16]   Inner Healing focuses on the freedom attained through the healing of past hurts.   It involves mentally reliving painful experiences by visualizing an indwelling Jesus who comforts, consoles and heals the pain of an abused childhood.

This is definitely a questionable practise, but it may not be inherently occultic.   God gave us the ability to visualize, but the question is how to use this tool. Jesus is not the genie of the lamp who will do whatever we want him to do, or give us permission to do what we like ourselves, even if it is only in our imagination. To treat Christ this way *is* blasphemous. To say that we have a god inside that does our bidding is tantamount to putting ourselves above God.

The general goal of the Inner Healing movement--healing past hurts--has an occultic thrust. Healing past hurts aims to eliminate the flaws in our personality that lead us to sin. Parents and other socializing agents are blamed for the wounds which produce these flaws. The goal is to heal the wounds and become sinless, meeting the mark of perfection. Yes, here is that Satanic doctrine of perfection. This approach actually keeps us stuck in the past, trying to attain the impossible just like the Freudian approaches do.

A problem with the Inner Healing approach is that it inevitably leads to the question: if Jesus, or God, was there while I was being abused, why didn't he stop it? In all probability, Jesus was not there; Satan was. It is likely that many parents and others who abuse children are demonized.[17] The demons use parental abusiveness to gain a stronghold in the child, so fulfilling the prophesy: "The sins of the parents shall be visited on the children unto the the third and fourth generation" (Exodus 34:7).

The real problem with the movement is its failure to look at the only form of healing of any real importance, which is the healing of the spirit. It blinds us to the real importance of Christ: the payment for sin. We are distracted from the central issue--guilt over our own corrupt nature and what this implies about our place in eternity. It fails to emphasize that God has provided us safe passage from hell by sacrificing his only son, thereby quieting our deepest unrest. This knowledge preempts the need to erase sin or inject comfort into those painful old memories by hypnotically reliving them in the company of a visualized Jesus.

We do need to see that Jesus is real, that God has always been present up to now in our lives. Could we have made it all the way to today without him? Nevertheless, our focus needs to be on now and the future. Paul talks of "forgetting those things which are behind, and reaching forth into those things which are before" (Philippians 3:13). That does not mean sweeping the past under a rug, however. It means regarding the past from a new vantage point, a context of God's infinite forgiveness and mercy.

Visualization itself is not inherently occultic. On the contrary, the Bible capitalizes on our power to visualize. It is filled with healing pictures of God's presence in the lives of humans just like us. The appropriate approach is to use text from the Bible. For example, we can see ourselves in the parable of the prodigal son, at first afraid to approach God after rejecting him and going our own way, *knowing ourselves to be fit only for the pig-pen,* then joyous about the way our heavenly father welcomes us home to his house.

Fear of hell is our sore. Our anticipation of the future makes us mentally ill. Knowing God has taken care of it for free will heal us. In the process, pain from the past will be forgotten.

SUMMARY AND CONCLUSIONS

This chapter shows that despite all the truth in some of the major Christian counseling literature, its theorists miss the mark in a profound way. They invariably fail to connect mental illness with our inherent human knowledge of a terrifying existential dilemma. This leads them to espouse the Satanic doctrine of perfection. They are so close, yet so far, from the mark. The twin pitfalls are legalism and liberalism, both of which only deepen the inner conflict. Neither open the door to grace.

Notes

1. Jay Adams (1970). <u>Competent to Counsel.</u> Grand Rapids, Michigan: Baker Book House.

2. Mowrer, O. Hobart (1960). "Sin, the Lesser of Two Evils." <u>American Psychologist,</u> <u>15,</u> pp. 301-314.

3. White, John (1982). <u>The Masks of Melancholy.</u> Downer's Grove, illinois: Intervarsity Press.

4. To the author's knowledge, no other Christian psychologist has theorized that mental illness is caused by the archetypical knowledge of eternal damnation.

5. Gnosticism is pre-Christian oriental mysticism. It holds that humans come from the light, are temporarily associated with darkness, and return to the light. This process occurs not only over the individual life span but also over the life span of the human race. Confirmatory knowledge about this situation comes from within the person. This human-as-god theme, of which a so-called Christian version makes Christ merely a role model for humans to emulate, embodies the Satanic lie.

6. Peck, M. Scott (1978). The Road Less Travelled. New York, New York: Simon and Schuster, p. 273.

7. Peck, (1978), op. cit., p. 286.

8. Peck, (1978), op. cit., p.274.

9. Peck, M. Scott (1983). The People of the Lie. New York, New York: Simon and Schuster, Inc., p.269.

10. Paul Tournier (1962). Guilt and Grace. New York, New York: Harper and Row Publishers, Inc.

11. Minirth, Frank B. (1977). Christian Psychiatry. Old Tappan, New Jersey: Fleming H. Revell.

12. Minirth, op. cit., p. 70.

13. Hemfelt, R., Minirth, F., and Meier, P. (1989). Love is a Choice: Recovery for codependant relationships. Nashville, Tennessee: Thomas Nelson Publishers, p. 277.

14. Linn, Dennis and Linn, Matthew (1978). Healing Life's Hurts. Paulist Press.

15. Sanford, Agnes (1982). The Healing Gifts of the Spirit. Old Tappan, New Jersey: Fleming Revell Publishers, Inc.

16. Hunt, Dave and McMahon, T. A. (1985). The Seduction of Christianity. Eugene, Oregon: Harvest House Publishers.

17. Dickason, C. Fred (1987). Demon possession and the Christian. Westchester, Illinois: Crossway Books.

Chapter Thirteen

RESEARCH ON RELIGION AND

WELL-BEING: WHERE'S GRACE?

Grace is God's unmerited favor, the existential pardon in the blood of Christ. As the single means of reconciliation with God so as to escape eternal condemnation, grace is the only cure for existential guilt. It is therefore the foundation of mental health and all human well-being.

God promised well-being: "Seek ye first the kingdom of God, and his righteousness; and all these things shall be added unto you" (Matthew 6:33). "His righteousness" is imputed to us through Christ; "these things" include mental and physical health.

So far this book has provided strong biblical, theoretical, deductive and anecdotal backing for Christ's blood as the key to mental health. Many autobiographical testimonials also attest to this.[1] Now we consider large-scale scientific research. We will see that while much of this research does not single out grace as *the* important variable, it backs our thesis when it does so.

A word of caution ... Most of the research has been done in the United States, a nation that appears very religious. The 1985 Gallup poll shows a large majority of Americans say they have a religious affiliation (95 percent), go to services, pray and believe in God. In a 1987 Detroit study, 95 percent stated they believed in God and 77 percent reported attending religious services.[2] Moreover, in a 1991 telephone poll of 600 adults for a television show, faith in God was the highest ranked aspect of life.[3] Forty percent stated that faith in God was the most important thing in their lives, whereas only 29 percent ranked good health highest.

However, these figures say nothing about the perception of grace. Research shows that even in the major Bible-based

denominations, our nation fails to value salvation from hell.[4]
As we saw in Chapter Two, only 31 percent of Americans
agree that "The Bible is the actual word of God and is to be
taken literally, word for word." Most miss the critical facts
about their existential predicament and Christ's atoning blood.
The awareness of God's gift of a pardon is the all-important
factor that is, nevertheless, missing in most of the research.

BACKGROUND TO THE STUDY OF RELIGIOSITY

What does science say about the psychology of religion?
It is not a new area of investigation. Before this century
began, two men were performing introspective studies on the
phenomenology of religious experience: William James in the
United States[5] and Wilhelm Wundt[6] in Germany. But between
that time and the 1970s, there was a lull in scientific
investigation of this topic.

Several textbooks on the psychology of religion have been
published in recent years.[7] The first ones employed scientific
studies of the Christian population but often treated religion as
if it were monolithic. Indeed, relatively few attempts have
been made to investigate the effects of any specific doctrine.
The most recent and comprehensive text claims to be "non
Christo-centric." It is less monolithic about religion than
previous texts but it ignores grace and displays a tendency to
favor non-Christian spiritual practises.[8]

Despite the lack of empirical evidence, for many years the
mental health community assumed that all religiosity was "bad."
The frequently-cited "proof" was psychotic religiosity.
Apparently the prevalence of the psychotic's spiritual
preoccupation never led scientists to perceive its universal,
innate source. However, as Chapter Eight shows, psychotic
religiosity reveals a real spiritual dilemma common to all
humans.

Freud sought to enlighten us all by defining religion as
infantile, terming it "regression in the service of the ego."[9]
Cognitive and humanistic theorists maintain that religion--
particularly the Christian variety--is harmful for mental health
for a different reason: its conceptualization of sin.[10] Needless
to say, these theorists do not consider the humanistic self-
empowerment that they preach to be a dangerous. Nor do
they regard it as the religion it certainly is. Yet the American

Humanist Society has been chartered as a tax exempt religious organization.[11]

The results of a large-scale 1983 study of patients in a psychiatric clinic fly in the face of the "religion is bad" proponents: the clinic patients were less likely to report a religious affiliation than the general population.[12] Similar findings had been produced in earlier studies.[13,14]

MEASUREMENT OF RELIGIOSITY

Early research on religiosity (not to be confused with psychotic religiosity) studied differences associated with 1) denominational affiliation; 2) single aspects of religious behavior such as frequency of church attendance; and 3) the degree of religiousness people say they have. It produced some interesting findings despite the fact that first type was blind to the individual, the other types often paid no attention to the nature of the religion, and none of it focused on grace.

DENOMINATION AND PSYCHIATRIC PATIENTS

Although members of a religious denomination vary widely in their sense of grace and its impact of their psychological adjustment, some denominational differences have been found to be related to the psychiatric diagnosis among mental health patients.

In the 1983 study mentioned above, a breakdown was made of psychiatric diagnoses according to general denomination. While the "No religious preference" and "Unknown denomination" patients were high on substance abuse and psychosis, patients belonging to "Sects" (Christian Scientists, Jehovah Witnesses, Mormons and Adventists) had the highest incidence of psychosis. The less severe neurotic and adjustment disorders belonged to the more orthodox groups: Non-Mainline Protestants had more adjustment disorders of childhood and depression; Catholics had more obsessive compulsive disorder and hysterical neurosis; and marital maladjustment and hysterical personality were associated with Mainline Protestants. Though members of specific denominations are less likely to become mentally ill than those claiming no religious affiliation, when they do become ill they do it in ways possibly explainable by denomination-specific misinterpretations in doctrine.

We would expect a "salvation-by-works" ethic to operate more strongly in Catholicism and Mainline Protestantism. This could explain the repression of existential guilt and its resurfacing in the distorted form of hysteria and obsessive behavior rather than the more overt form of guilt found in the depression of the Non-Mainline Protestants. Note: we would expect "grace aware" members of these denominations not to become sufficiently dysfunctional to show up in such a study.

The finding for psychotics is consistent with research mentioned in Chapter Eight. There we saw that their general tendency is to avoid organized religion, particularly mainstream Christianity, yet they do display some involvement in cults.

Regarding cults, a number of studies have found higher rates of schizophrenia in the Catholic population than in other religious groupings.[15,16,17] Though we cannot rule out a genetic basis for this, such findings are interesting in view of the fact that Catholicism has been shown to fulfil all the criteria for a cult[18] defined by experts such as Walter Martin, late founder of the Christian Research Institute.[19]

All in all, the further we get from the Bible, the more insanity there is. Are there grace-filled denominations? Probably not. The problem is that the major denominations have their little bit of leaven taking them away from God's Word. Some are more biblically sound than others. And within the sounder ones, pastors vary as do congregation members. Individual Bible study is essential.

SINGLE BEHAVIORAL MEASURES: ATTENDANCE

Research on single, behavioral measures of religiosity has produced more consistent associations with mental health than denomination or self-reports of religiosity. Church attendance has been the most fruitful single measure.

Much evidence shows that church attendees are more physically healthy and live longer.[20] They are also less likely to commit suicide,[21] be delinquents,[22] or report marital dissatisfaction.[23] Church attendance has been found to correlate with duration of marriage, satisfaction with family life, and commitment to the institution of marriage.[24] One research review finds considerable evidence that church attendees are more likely to report general well-being.[25] On the other hand, attendees consistently report less psychological distress;[26] and schizophrenic church attendees have lower rates of rehospitalization.[27]

However, we do not know if this pretty picture of church attendees comes from a true relationship with God or from behaviors typically associated with church membership: lower rates of drinking, drug-use, and smoking; and opportunities for social support. Moreover, sick people are less likely to go to church. Many of the apparent benefits of church attendance disappear when these confounding factors are controlled. Such intervening behavioral variables explain why cult members, who clearly have no personal relationship with God, report lower levels of psychological distress both immediately after conversion[28] and four years later.[29]

All in all, these findings make it impossible to say that religion is harmful. However, because correlational research prohibits causal inferences, we also cannot say that it is beneficial. Besides, the appearance of well-being can be deceptive. Outside of grace, the best that religion provides is false sense of security, a defense system that blocks the truth that will save us...but more of this later.

GLOBAL RELIGIOSITY

A global assessment of religiosity has often been obtained in the research by asking people how religious they are. Self-reports indicate that religiosity has a profound effect on the management of life crises and stress.[30] Religious persons display lower blood pressure,[31] better adjustment and happiness,[32] lower morbidity when recovering from coronary bypass surgery,[33] and an improved recovery rate from burns.[34]

In a longitudinal study of 1,650 men and women in their early fifties, religiosity was positively related to the overall well-being of both sexes and the job satisfaction of men.[35]

In terms of the family, religious students have been found to view their families as more happy, warm, and accepting than non-religious students.[36] Religiosity in married couples is associated with better marital adjustment, happiness, and satisfaction.[37] In fact, this global measure has been found to be the factor explaining most of the variance in husbands' and wives' marital satisfaction.[38]

Moreover, destroying the popular myth of religion as sexually repressive is the fact that very religious women report greater happiness and satisfaction with marital sex as compared

with moderately religious and non-religious women. The very
religious group claim more freqent orgasms and more
satisfaction with the frequency of their sexual activity.[39]

Religiosity is also generally a negative predictor of serious
self-destructive behavior. Over and over in the research, drug
abuse and suicide have displayed negative relationships with
measures of religiosity.[40,41,42,43]

RELIGION: GOOD OR BAD?

Despite the positive associations between religiosity and
well-being reported above, the overall trend of this research has
not been so clear. Although religiosity measures have shown
consistent positive relations with physical health,[44] some
conflicting findings have been reported in its relations with
mental health.

However, one overview of twenty four such studies found
that religion had more positive than negative associations with
mental health.[45] Another even more comprehensive analysis of
one hundred and sixteen studies produced a similar finding.[46]
This seems to generally disprove that religion is harmful.

THE WRONG DEPENDANT MEASURES

But wait a minute. The false doctrine of perfection is
basic to every religion besides the Gospel. It also lurks in the
legalistic and liberal interpretations of the Bible which have
pervaded organized religion. Is it possible for its adherents to
appear mentally healthy? The answer is "yes," given a limited
definition of mental health as improved ego defense and
control. Many of the measures of healthy functioning used in
research on the psychology of religion are based on a model of
mental health which conflicts with the biblical one.

For example, humanistic psychology promotes the
assertion of individual rights and self-esteem. In contrast, the
God of the Bible advocates concern for others and points to
man's inherent weakness and sinfulness. Therefore valiant
Christian soldiers who are prayer warriors and walk in faith
may be low scorers on traditional personality measures defining
assertiveness and self-esteem.[47]

It so happens that most of the studies that have linked
religious commitment with psychological dysfunctionality have
used personality tests with secular definitions of mental health.
On the other hand, most of the research linking religiosity to

positive mental health has used real life measures, i.e., how people actually behave.[48]

It is true that adherents to the false gospels based on the doctrine of perfection can give a superficial appearance of well-being. This is because the internalization of a religious belief system can bolster and upgrade the ego's repertoire in many ways. The ego can acquire superficially comforting ideas about reality, a sense of meaning, coping skills, moral attitudes, and much more. Religion offers ways to hide and atone that may be more functional than the ones previously employed. For example, a "nice guy" facade is a lot more socially acceptable than psychosomatic illness or passive-aggressive behavior.

But the underlying fear will only be buried unless a sense of grace has penetrated. There will also be much "secret sin" that is out of control. Religion that contains no grace will be, in a sense, one massive defense mechanism which will eventually fall apart. It is a "bad" schema that cannot be fully assimilated.

INTRINSIC/EXTRINSIC RELIGIOSITY

For several years the scientific community has recognized that some forms of religiosity may be beneficial and others harmful. Attempts have been made to define what is "good" versus "bad," still failing to look at the blood of Christ.

One well-researched distinction lies between the "good" active or intrinsic religiosity (i.e., living one's faith, religion as an end in itself) and the "bad" passive or extrinsic kind (i.e., attending church but participating without conviction, religion as a means to other ends). Gordon Allport's self-report measure is generally used to define the intrinsic-extrinsic styles, which are not defined by any particular religion.[49]

Among adult subjects, intrinsic religiosity has been found to be associated with decreased symptoms of mental illness, whereas the extrinsic kind has been found to be associated with not only increased symptoms of mental illness,[50] but also with lower levels of psychosocial competence.[51]

For student subjects, significant positive correlations have been found between intrinsic religiosity and the following: personal responsibility, an internal locus of control (i.e., perceiving oneself rather than external agents to control one's life), intrinsic motivational traits, and grade point average. Extrinsic religiosity, on the other hand, displayed significant positive correlations with dogmatism and authoritarianism; and negative correlations with personal responsibility, internal locus of control, intrinsic motivation, and grade point average.[52]

Another study controlled for church attendance and background characteristics. The intrinsic qualities of religiosity defined by reportedly feeling close to God or some generic spiritual force and praying were associated with increased happiness and satisfaction.[53]

INTRINSIC EXTRINSICS AND GRACE

However, the same research also shows that some individuals are high on both extrinsic and intrinsic religiosity. How can that be? The problem lies in the fact that outside of Christ's blood, all religiosity is extrinsic, a means to an end.

True intrinsicness involves voluntarism, unselfishness, religion as an end rather than a means. This can happen only *after* humans know their selfish but desperate need for salvation has been met by a gift from God. No longer under the gun, they are inspired to praise God and please him.

When the religious belief system involves merciless legalism, religiosity cannot be an end in itself. No matter how inspired the person appears, the entire motivation is means, not end. The goal is to escape hell; "compulsion" not "want to."

This may be why Mormon students, particularly returning missionaries, displayed higher intrinsic religiosity scores than students in non-Mormon campuses.[54] Mormonism is a highly works-oriented religion promising godhood in eternity for those who stick to the rules; those who do not stick to the rules not only lose godhood and salvation but also acceptance in the Mormon community. For those living in Salt Lake City, the Mormon headquarters where the study was done, this means social ostracism, loss of a place to live, and loss of a job.

In line with this, belief in God and the practise of religion have been found to be unrelated for Mormon males.[55] Powerful social sanctions lead them to practise Mormonism whether they believe or not.

In the study of Mormon students, intrinsic religiosity was positively related to sociability, well-being, responsibility, self-control, tolerance, making a good impression, and achievement by conformance. The interpretation that this is a "pleaser" facade, a false front, is consistent with the strong relationship between intrinsic religiosity and social desirability in the group.

Religion provides a strong defense structure for these students. They lean on a belief that superficial adherence adherence to the law will save them.

It is likely that ultra-Orthodox Jews displayed less stress during the Palestinian uprising than secular Jews for the same reason.[56] There is no grace in Orthodox Judaism. Since the destruction of the temple in Jerusalem in 70 A.D., the Jews have not availed themselves of the God-given blood atonement for sin defined in the Torah (see Chapter One). Blind to their sin like the Pharisees at the time of Jesus, they expect their works to save them.

INTRINSICS AND DEATH

True intrinsicness is only possible through Christ. Thus non-Christians intrinsics do not have the same characteristics as Christian intrinsics. They can have no peace of mind about eternity. Some research on death-related attitudes points to this. Unsurprisingly, research has found intrinsic religiosity in a Bible-based population to be linked with positive attitudes towards death.[57] But when Christian intrinsics are compared with Buddhist ones, only the Christians see death in a positive light.[58] This is no surprise; nobody can have peace of mind about eternity under the merciless perfectionism of Buddhism.

FAITH IN THE SELF

Skeptics will say that the benefits that seem attributable to faith in God are just a result of positive thinking, an atheistic concept. Secular existentialist therapy says a strong belief in *any* philosophy will be beneficial: choose your delusion, do whatever works, you are the boss (see Chapter Nine). There is some truth to this. However, just any old philosophy will not deal with the existential guilt which underlies all psychpathology.

One study highlights the deficits of weak religious belief and lends support to the beneficiality of strong belief *per se*, specifically that in the short term faith in yourself can appear as beneficial as faith in God. However, the same study also suggests that the more the religious doctrine embodies salvation by grace, the more people appear to be psychologically adjusted.

A telephone survey investigated the relationship between degree of religious belief and psychological distress.[59] Among persons who stated they had a specific religious belief system, the stronger it was, the lower was the level of psychological distress that they reported.   However, there were some significant overall differences based on the type of mainstream religion--Protestantism, Catholicism, or Judaism.   Members of the most grace-oriented one, Protestantism, had the lowest level of distress.   Then followed "salvation by works-oriented" Catholics, then atonement-lacking Jews, and lastly, other groups.

However, individuals in these groups who reported only weak faith in God actually had higher levels of distress than a group that stated that they had no religion.   It appears there is an inverted U-shaped relationship between religiousness and distress; lukewarm is worse than hot or cold (Revelation 3:15).

But what does it mean to claim "no religion"?   It is likely that the so-called "no religion" group had a strong belief in the power of the self.   This is suggested by the fact that when the overall content of beliefs was examined in a multiple regression analysis, the strongest predictor, which was named "personal efficacy," displayed a highly significant negative relationship with psychological distress.   Personal efficacy, or faith in oneself, was a much stronger predictor than a "faith in God" variable, which also displayed a significant negative relationship with distress.

Faith in the self, or humanism, is a religion, often an unconscious one that is not seen as such.   Yet humanism is now a legitimate religion in this country.   The humanist notion of the godliness of man is the underlying Satanic theme of all false religions.   Even worse, it is often the true religion of members of the Christian church.   Many of those who think they are Christians place more faith in themselves than in God. For them, God is at best a co-pilot rather than the boss.

To be sure, self-empowerment has some short term benefits; selling one's soul to Satan can provide certain advantages in this world.   One is a false sense of security.

THE U-SHAPE

The paralyzing effect of lukewarmness explains why a U-shaped relationship between Christian religious faith and some aspect of positive functioning has appeared over and over in the research.   Lower levels of racial prejudice have been found for groups at the extremes of Christian religiosity.   This applies to cadets in the Salvation Army and members of the Young Humanist Association.[60], Very frequent church attenders and non-attenders have been found less prejudiced than occasional attenders.[61] Individuals in these two extremes have also been found less likely to administer severe electric shocks in experimental studies of compliance,[62] more likely to report having had mystical and religious experiences,[63] and to report both increased overall happiness and fewer pathological mental and physical health symptoms.[64]

So let us not assume that non-attenders or "no religion" claimers have no faith. Faith of some sort is essential for moral behavior, growth and action. If faith is not in God, it is, in some fashion, in the self.

Those who trust in themselves are not awake to the danger they are in. They live in the illusion they are not subject to the death sentence. If they display less distress, etc, it is only because they deny existential reality. Faith in the self is effective as a superficial, temporary psychological defense but eventually it cracks open, leaving a person defenseless. The author's experience with hitherto long-term "self-believers" has been that at some point, a severe stressor will thrust them into a deep depression, anxiety state, or even psychosis.

At that point, no longer able to deny the reality of death and experiencing an intense sense of doom, only hearing the message of the gospel will enable the person to recover. However, this needs to be substantiated by more systematic study of faith and what happens to it over the life cycle.

FAITH AND THE LIFE CYCLE

There is, in fact, a line of research on religiosity over the life cycle.[65] We would expect people to be more interested in God as they approach death, and this turns out to be true. The findings show that religiosity increases with age,[66] and that religious attitudes and behavior are positively related with adjustment to aging.[67] However, we do not know whether this apparent benefit is psychologically defensive or whether it stems from a true sense of eternal security.

FACTOR ANALYSIS OF RELIGIOSITY

Research has shown there are a large number of factors in religiosity. This has led social scientists to pay more attention to how to define it.[68] As many as 21 factors have been found, but most research finds only two. However, factor analysis of religiosity is only as valid as the measures it is analyzing. So far this research is flawed by the fact that in no case has any measure of grace been included.

RESEARCH ON GRACE

Is there any research on grace? Yes, and its findings are promising. Up to this time, the one exception to the "grace-blindness" of the scientific community has been a program by a group at the University of Tennessee.

In a series of studies, this group investigated the roles of both guilt and grace in relation to mental health and general adjustment among Christian students of various denominations. The intention was to show that the awareness of guilt and sin, so widely attacked by the secular mental health profession, is only dysfunctional if it is not accompanied by knowledge of grace.

Using a self-report measure of guilt[69] and another one of grace (which also included items on sin),[70] the first individual study in Part One of a five part series found that grace generally displayed significant positive relationships with healthy functioning. Guilt was not uniformly associated with maladjustment. Where it displayed negative associations with healthy functioning, these were largely erased by partialling out grace. In other words, grace cancelled out guilt.[71]

Similar findings for the statistical effects of grace were obtained in the third and fourth studies of Part One. Guilt was only harmful without grace--just what this book has been saying all along.

However, the second study in Part One produced mixed findings on grace. Although the grace measure was negatively associated with depression, it displayed some positive relations with social anxiety and personal distress. Perhaps this was due to the sin items in the measure. However, there was also a difference in the religiosity of the student subjects in the second study, which did not include the Pentecostals present in the other studies. Evidently the relationship between grace and healthy functioning was mediated by the religiousness of the subjects. Pentecostal students measured higher on grace. For them, the grace measure was more positively associated with all aspects of healthy functioning than for others. Also for the

Pentecostals, guilt alone was positively related to healthy functioning.

Evidently the fact that the Pentecostal students had a deeper sense of grace enabled the guilt and sin/grace measures to unequivocally tap positive functioning. For others less steeped in a sense of grace, the awareness of guilt and sin/grace was related to anxiety.

Many Christian preachers promote, at best, only an intellectual understanding of grace. They preach against sin rather than communicating the forgiveness of God. Our universal problem is that the perception of sin is inherent, but the perception of grace is not. Humans need an intellectual and emotional grasp of grace to reverse the downward pull of guilt.

Part Two found that a negative relationship between intrinsicness (on the Allport measure) and depression was attributable to grace. Such a finding supports the idea that grace is a more relevant measure of a true relationship with God than intrinsicness. This interpretation is also supported by the fact that with grace partialled out, intrinsicness produced ties with an internal locus of control and self efficacy, i.e. faith in the self.[72].

Part Three of the series showed that whereas extrinsic attitudes and guilt were linked to problematic self-functioning, intrinsicness and grace were associated with less depression.[73] Part Four of the series showed that intrinsicness and grace were related to emotional empathy; grace was predictive of less distress and depression.[74] Part Five found grace to be positively related to a belief in authority and egalitarianism; it was negatively related to narcissistic exploitiveness, machiavellianism and excessive individualism.[75]

This research program certainly points to the benefits of grace. It also says secular psychology is partially correct about the harmfulness of an emphasis on sin and guilt. Religion is damaging to mental health if it raises the spectre of sin and allows guilt to surface without the accompaniment of God's gift of forgiveness. Merciless legalism reminds the person he cannot meet the mark of perfection and is therefore doomed. Since no "out" is offered under legalism, this deepens the innate terror. The result can be a psychotic flight from reality.

A potent example of this occurred in the past of one of my clients, who has a manic-depressive disorder. She listened to a legalistic Christian preacher on the radio one evening and panicked. Believing she was sure only of eternal damnation because of her short-falling, she began to scream and throw things out of the window...a sudden manic episode. This led to a night in the psychiatric emergency ward.

It must be added that this woman did not have her feet planted on the foundation of grace in the first place, nor anywhere near it. She belonged to a branch of Christianity which departs in some significant ways from the Bible, one of the cults. Now that she does have her feet on that foundation, she is doing much better. There have been no hospitalizations in recent years.

PRAYER

It is no easy matter for us that the remedy for our basic dilemma is dependence on an invisible means of support. In spite of all the astounding evidence for a master planner and designer of the universe, we cannot absolutely prove the existence of God. If we could, belief would be easy. Faith would be unnecessary. Answered prayers deepen faith, but praying requires at least a willingness to put aside disbelief.

As we consider research on prayer, we are going to see that it, too, suffers from a failure to differentiate requests to God through Christ from other approaches. It does not recognize the essentialness of a sense of grace.

Of the two types of petitionary prayer, the personal kind, focusing on one's own needs, and the intercessory kind, making requests to God for others, neither has been the focus of much scientific research. One reason may be that scientific investigation on prayer suffers most strongly from the feeling of transgression present in all research on the effects of religion. Is this "testing God"? Jesus was angered when his followers persisted in asking for "a sign" (Mark 8:12). If they had not believed what they read in the law and the prophecies, they would not believe even if they saw him come back from the dead.

A problem with research on prayer involves the null hypothesis, that prayer has no effect. This is not a valid conclusion for one who believes in the God of the Bible. The example of Paul and his "thorn in the flesh" (II Corinthians 12:7) shows us that God will refuse prayer for his own good reason. He knows what we need far better than we do ourselves.

PERSONAL PRAYER

Unless we claim God's pardon, our basic sense of unworthiness interferes with our ability to pray, particularly for ourselves. It just feels wrong to ask God on our own behalf. Perhaps we try it in a dire emergency but not at any other time. Many find less difficulty in asking someone else who seems less sinful to pray for them. All this changes when we realize God is "no respecter of persons" (Acts 10:34); his gift of Christ gives us equal access to him at all times and we cannot ask for too much or too often. Most of us ask for too little.

There are many testimonial books and articles on the way prayer, through the freedom of Christ, changed a person's life in a way that personal efforts could not have.[76] I have had numerous experiences of answered prayers in my own life. My psychotherapy clients often relate powerful experiences they have had with prayer. These are the straws which build the nest of faith, mine along with theirs.

The Bible gives us examples of God answering personal prayer. In one striking account, when King Hezekiah was taken sick, the prophet Isaiah informed him what God had to say about it: it was time for Hezekiah to die. But after Hezekiah's entreaties to him, God changed his plan and told him through Isaiah that he would be healed and allowed to live fifteen more years (II Kings 20).

As an area for scientific investigation, personal prayer is problematic. On a technical level, the impossibility of using a randomized, double-blind research design gives rise to potential sampling, experimenter and subject bias. Moreover, the dependent variable must be one that is completely outside of the control of the subject. If I only start taking my medicine after I pray for recovery and I get better, who is responsible? Believers would say the recovery is completely attributable to God, the source of both the pills and "my" will to take them, but this would not convince a skeptic.

A study on prayer and psychiatric recovery

One study on the effects of personal prayer used forty-five volunteer subjects with moderate to severe psychiatric symptoms. The volunteers were assigned to one of three groups. For nine months, a) the first group was treated with individual psychotherapy alone; b) the second "random" group, consisting of professing Christians, was asked to pray individually every day in whatever fashion had been their usual habit; and c) the third was assigned to a weekly two-hour "prayer therapy" group.

After the nine months, it was found that sixty-five percent of the patients treated with psychotherapy, none of the so-called "random" prayer group, and seventy-two percent of the regular "prayer therapy" patients had improved. Although the psychotherapy and "prayer therapy" groups both improved and the difference between them was not significant, it is worth noticing that there was healing without any specific psychological intervention in the prayer group.[77]

However, these findings are contaminated by the non-randomized distribution of participants; they were allowed to chose which group they were in. Thus outcome differences could be influenced by pre-existing characteristics of the volunteers.

Why such a poor outcome among the professing Christians in the so-called "random" group? Compared with the "pryaer therapy" group, participants in the group of Christians reported that they saw God as punitive and unforgiving. Thus they lacked the experience of Christ that would free them in their relationship with God.

Also, we know little about what actually occurred in the "prayer therapy" group. The apparent positive effects of prayer could have been the result of other factors, such as peer support. The group did engage in regular prayer but it is not clear to whom: to God through Christ or to one of Satan's minions. The reason for doubt is that group leaders appear to have promoted some suspiciously occultic concepts.

INTERCESSORY PRAYER

Praying for someone else can feel easier than personal prayer, especially someone we identify as a "good" person. For many, God's response to a prayer for another was critical in revealing him. Often this revelation is forgotten only too quickly, or reinterpreted as a coincidence. There is probably nobody who is not familiar with this "open/shut" phenomenon. Perhaps Satan gives us amnesia for all our answered prayers.

Intercessory prayer is less problematic as a field of investigation than the personal type in that it offers the possibility for a randomized, double-blind design. It happens that the only study on prayer conducted with anything approaching scientific rigour has provided evidence for the effectiveness of Christian intercessory prayer.

A study on prayer and physical recovery

In a 1988 University of California experiment, the "prayed-for" group in a large sample of coronary care patients made significantly better progress in recovery than the "non-prayed-for" group.

The experiment used a "double-blind" technique: although participants knew they were in a study involving prayer, neither the staff nor the subjects of the study knew who was assigned to the experimental and control groups. Each member of the "prayed-for" group was assigned three to seven intercessors, "born-again" Christians with an active prayer life, who prayed for them daily for several months. The "non-prayed-for" group was not given any special attention, and may have benefitted from the intercessory prayers of family members or friends. In fact, given the nature of the study, and the fact that patients could chose not to participate, we might expect participation would increase intercessory prayer for all subjects, and diminish outcome differences between the two groups. However, the difference in favor of the "prayed-for" group on an overall measure of progress was highly significant.[78]

Biblical examples

There is no latterday research indicating that only praying to the God of the Bible works, i.e., through the shed blood of Christ. Of course, the Bible contains reports of empirical demonstrations of the incomparability of God's power. There is the account of the plagues God inflicted on Egypt versus the minor feats of the Pharaoh's magicians. Apparently the magicians were able to pull off some stunts that had the appearance of magic, but in each case, God demonstrated his infinitely superior ability. God's final act was right out of the magician's league: the killing of all the firstborn by the angel of death (Exodus 12:29).

The most graphic biblical account is the story of Elijah and the 450 prophets of Baal. Two bullocks were prepared on

Mount Carmel as a test between God and Baal. Elijah and the prophets of Baal were each to call on their deities to consume their respective bullocks with fire. Even though Elijah soaked his bullock and its altar several times with water, when called upon, God obliged with a dramatic conflagration. The Baal-worshippers' dry bullock and altar remained unburned after all their entreaties to Baal (I Kings 18:21-39).

SUMMARY AND CONCLUSIONS

Salvation by grace is the true basis for mental health and other forms of well-being. This chapter sought for empirical evidence for this by touring large-scale scientific research.

In doing so, one thing that became apparent is that despite the claims made by Freud, Ellis and others that religion has adverse mental health effects, religiosity generally displays positive associations with physical and psychological well-being. In fact, religion has been proposed as a mental illness preventive measure.[79]

However, there is also evidence that much of this may derive more from the psychologically defensive role of religion than from peace within the spirit. Researchers in this area admit that it is very murky, especially in terms of the operational definition of religiosity.

The much-investigated intrinsic/extrinsic religiosity distinction may differentiate between those who act in faith and those who do not, but this is not necessarily faith in God. In fact, intrinsic religiosity is often confounded with salvation by works, of which the secular version is faith in the self. So in no way does this dimension tap the personal relationship with God only possible through Christ.

In general, the research on religiosity is muddy due to: failure to differentiate grace as a factor; imprecise operational definition of religiosity and "outcomes;" use of the wrong outcome measures; incomparability of research populations; poor experimental design; and lack of longitudinal studies that might establish causality.

Though largely ignored, grace has not been completely overlooked by the scientific community. One research program clearly demonstrates its positive links with mental health. In general, this program displayed superior psychological functioning for those scoring higher on a "grace" self-report measure. Moreover, grace mitigated the negative effects of guilt and was a stronger predictor of psychological adjustment than intrinsicness.

Investigation of the relationship between faith and mental health through the study of prayer is a little-explored but fertile area, also not without its problems. It appears that prayer works, but again, the role of grace is unclear in research carried out up to the present. The investigation of intercessory prayer offers more potential than personal prayer in the sense that factors such as self-control are ruled out.

In sum, the research shows that a self-report measure of grace is feasible and that such a measure is a powerful predictor of mental health. All in all, more needs to be known about grace and mental health.

Notes

1. Nesbitt, Maurice (1966). <u>Where no Fear Was: A study in neurotic personality related to the Christian experience.</u> London: Epworth Press.

2. Alwin, Duane (1988). "From obedience to autonomy: Changing aspects of religious behavior and orientation in American society." Paper presented at Changing Societal institutions Conference, Notre Dame, Indiana.

3. Princeton Survey Research Associates (1991, Jan 17-20). "The Great American TV Poll," Lifetime television show.

4. Rokeach, M. (1973). <u>The nature of human values</u>. New York: Free Press.

5. James, William (1958). <u>Varieties of Religious Experience.</u> New York, New York: New American Library, Inc.

6. Wundt, Wilhelm (1911). <u>Probleme der Volkerpsychologie,</u> (2nd ed). Stuttgart: Alfred Kroner, 1921. (First edition, 1911).

7. For example:
Batson, C. D. and Ventis, W. L. (1982). <u>The religious experience: A social-psychological perspective</u>. New York, New York: Oxford University Press.

Spilka, B., Hood, R. W., and Gorsuch, R. L. (1985). The psychology of religion: An empirical approach. Englewood Cliffs, New Jersey Prentice-Hall.

8. Wulff, David (1991). Psychology of Religion. New York, New York: John Wiley and Sons.

9. Freud, S. (1961). Civilization and its discontents. (J. Strachey, Trans.). New York, New York: W. W. Norton. (Original workpublished 1930).

10. Ellis, Albert (1962). Reason and emotion in psychotherapy. Secaucus, New Jersey: Lyle Stuart Press.

11. Sunderland, Luther D. (1988). Darwin's Enigma. Santee, California: Master Book Publications, p.37.

12. MacDonald, Coval B. and Luckett, Jeffrey B. (1983). "Religious Affiliation and Psychiatric Diagnosis." Journal for the Scientific Study of Religion, 22, 1, pp. 15-37.

13. Lindenthal, Jacob J. and Myers, Jerome K. (1970). "Mental status and religious behavior." Journal for the Scientific Study of Religion, 9, 143-149.

14. Stark, Rodney (1971). "Psychopathology and religious commitment." Review of Religious Research, 12, 3, 165-176.

15. Buckalew, L.W. (1978). "A descriptive study of denominational concommitants in psychiatric diagnosis." Social Behavior and Personality, 6, pp. 239-242.

16. Burgess, E. W. and Wagner, R. L. (1971). "Religion as a factor in extrusion to public mental hospitals." Journal for the Scientific Study of Religion, 10, pp. 237-240.

17. Murphy, H. B. M. and Vega, G. (1982). "Schizophrenia and religious affiliation in Northern Ireland." Psychological Medicine, 12, pp. 595-605.

18. Hunt, Dave (June, 1991). "A Cult is a Cult." Christian Information Bulletin, pp. 1-3.

19. In his book, <u>Rise of the Cults</u>, Walter Martin defined cultism as "any major deviation from orthodox Christianity relative to the cardinal doctrines of the Christian faith." Catholicism rejects salvation (i.e., complete forgiveness of sin) by the shed blood of Christ. The <u>Basic Catechism</u> Indulgentiarum Doctrin, #1687, urges Catholics to carry "each his own cross in expiation of their sins and of the sins of others..."

20. Levin, J. and Vanderpool, H. (1987). "Is frequent religious attendance really conducive to better health? Toward and epidemiology of religion." <u>Social Science Medicine</u>, <u>24</u>, pp.589-600.

21. Comstock, G. W. and Partridge, K. B. (1972). "Church attendance and health." <u>Journal of Chronic Disease</u>, <u>25</u>, pp. 665-672.

22. Argyle, m. and Beit-Hallahmi, B. (1975). <u>The Social Psychology of Religion</u>. London: Routledge and Kegan Paul.

23. Glenn, N. D. and Weaver, C. N. (1978). "A multivariate, multi-survey study of marital happiness." <u>Journal of Marriage and the Family</u>, pp. 269-282.

24. Larson, L. E. and Goltz, J. W. (1989). "Religious participation and marital commitment." <u>Review of Religious Research</u>, <u>30</u>, 4, pp. 387-400.

25. Ellison, C. and Smith, J. (1991). "Toward an integrative measure ofhealth and well-being." <u>Journal of Psychology and Theology</u>, <u>19</u>, pp. 35-48.

26. Lindenthal, J. J., Myers, J. K., Pepper, m. P. and Stern, M. S. (1970). "Mental status and religious behavior." <u>Journal for the Scientific Study of Religion</u>, <u>9</u>, pp. 143-149.

27. Chu, C. and Klein, H. E. (1985). "Psychological and environmental variables in outcome of Black schizophrenics." <u>Journal of the National Medical Association</u>, <u>77</u>, pp. 793-796.

28. Galanter, M., Rabkin, R., Rabkin, J. and Blatsch, A. (1979). "The "Moonies": A psychological study of conversion and membership in a contemporary religious sect." American Journal of Psychiatry, 136, pp. 165-170.

29. Ross, M. (1985). "Mental health in Hare Krishna devotees: A longitudinal study." American Journal of Psychiatry, 125, pp. 65-67.

30. Wilson, W. P. (1985). "Problem solving in crises." In G. Rekens (Ed.) Family Building. Ventura, California: Regal Books, 1985

31. Graham, T. W., Kaplan, B. H., Cornoni-Huntley, J. C., et al. (1978). "Frequency of church attendance and blood pressure elevation." Behavioral Medicine, 1, pp. 37-43.

32. Gurin, Gerald, Veroff, Joseph, and Field, Sheila (1960). Americans view their mental health. New York, New York: Basic Books.

33. McSherry, E. (1987). "Modernization of the clinical science of chaplainacy." Care Giver, 4, pp. 1-13.

34. Sherrill, K.A. and Larson, D. B. (1988). "Adult Burn Patients: The Role of Religions in Recovery." Southern Medical Journal, 81, pp. 821-825.

35. Willits, F. K. and Crider, D. M. (1988). "Religion and well-being: Men and women in the middle years." Review of Religious Research, 29, 3, pp. 281-294.

36. Johnson, M. A. (1973). "Family life and religious commitment." Review of Religious Research, 14, pp. 144-150.

37. Hunt, R. A. and King, M. B. (1978). "Religiosity and marriage." Journal for the Scientific Study of Religion, 17, 4, pp. 399-406.

38. Williams, C. M. (1983). Marital Satisfaction and Religiosity. Unpublished master's thesis, University of Utah, Salt Lake City.

39. Tavris, C and Sadd, S. (1977). The Redbook report on female sexuality, New York, New York: Delacorte Press.

40. Lorch, B. R. and Hughes, R. H. (1985). "Religion and youth substance abuse." Journal of Religion and Health, 24, 3, pp. 197-208.

41. Adlaf, E. M. and Smart, R. G. (1985). "Drug use and religious affiliation, feelings and behavior." British Journal of Addiction, 80, pp. 163-171.

42. Mandle, C. L. (1984). "Suicide: A human problem." Educational Horizons, 62, 4, pp. 119-123.

43. Lester, D. (1988). "Religion and personal violence (homicide and suicide) in the U.S.A." Psychological Reports, 62, pp. 618-630.

44. Levin, J. S. and Vanderpool, H. Y. (1991). "Religious Factors in Physical Health and the Prevention of Illness." Prevention in Human Services, 9, 2, pp. 41-64.

45. Bergin, A. (1983). "Religiosity and Mental Health: A Critical Reevaluation and Meta-Analysis." Professional Psychology: Research and Practice, 14, pp. 170-184.

46. Judd, D. K. (1985). Religiosity and mental health: A literature review - 1928-1985. Unpublished master's thesis, Brigham Young University, Provo, Utah.

47. Watson, P. J. et al. (1988a).

48. Gartner, J., Larson, D. B., and Allen, G. D. (1991). "Religious Commitment and Mental Health: A Review of the Empirical Literature." Journal of Psychology and Theology, 19, pp. 6-25.

49. Allport, G. W. and Ross, J. M. (1967). "Personal religious orientation and prejudice." Journal of Personality and Social Psychology, 5, pp. 432-443.

50. Hannay, D. R. (1980). "Religion and Health." Social Science and Medicine, 14, pp. 683-685.

51. Pargament, K. I., Steele, R. E., and Tyler, F. B. (1979). "Religious participation and individual psychosocial competence." Journal for the Scientific Study of Religion, 18, 4, pp. 412-419.

52. Kahoe, R. D. (1974). "Personality and achievement correlates of intrinsic and extrinsic religious orientations." Journal of Personality and Social Psychology, 29, pp. 812-818.

53. Pollner, Melvin (1989). "Divine relations, social relations, and well-being." Journal of Health and Social Behavior, 30, 1, pp. 92-104.

54. Batson, C. D., Naifeh, S. J., and Pate,S. (1978). "Social Desirability, Religious Orientation, and Racial Prejudice." Journal for the Scientific Study of Religion, 17, pp. 31-41.

55. Cline, V. B. and Richards, J. M. (1965). "A factor-analytic study of religious belief and abehavior." Journal of Personality and Social Psychology, 1, pp. 569-578.

56. Pines, R. (1989, January). "Why do Israelis burn out: the role of the intifada." Paper presented at the International Conference on Psychological Stress and Adjustment, Tel Aviv, Israel.

57. Spilka, B., Stout, L., Minton, B., and Sizemore, D. (1977). "Death and Personal Faith: A Psychometric Investigation." Journal for the Scientific Study of Religion, 24, pp.1-20.

58. Patrick, J. W. (1979). "Personal faith and the Fear of Death Among Divergent Religious Populations." Journal for the Scientific Study of Religion, 18, pp. 298-305.

59. Ross, Catherine E. (1990). "Religion and Psychological Distress," Journal for the Scientific Study of Religion, 29, 2, pp. 236-245.

60. Wilson, Glenn and Lillie, F. J. (1972). "Social Attitudes of Salvationists and Humanists." British Journal of Social and Clinical Psychology, 11, pp. 220-224.

61. Struening, E. L. (1963). "Anti-Democratic Attitudes in Midwest University." In H. H. Remmer (Ed.), <u>Anti-Democratic Attitudes in American Schools.</u> Evanston, Illinois: Northwestern University Press, pp. 210-258.

62. Bock, D. C. and Warren, N. C. (1972). "Religious Belief as a Factor in Obedience to Destructive Commands." <u>Review of Religious Research</u>, <u>13</u>, pp. 185-191.

63. Hood, R. W., Jr. (1976). "Mystical Experiences as Related to Present and Anticipated Future Church Participation." <u>Psychological Reports</u>, <u>39</u>, pp. 1127-1136.

64. Shaver P., Lenauer M., and Sadd, S. (1980). "Religious Conversion and Subjective Well-Being: The "Healthy-Minded" Religion of Modern American Women." <u>American Journal of Psychiatry</u>, <u>137</u>, pp. 1563-1568.

65. Worthington, E. L. (1989). "Religious Faith Across the LIfe Span: Implications for Counseling and Research." <u>The Counseling Psychologist</u>, <u>17</u>, 4, pp. 555-612.

66. Princeton Religion Research Center (1982). <u>Religion in America</u>, Princeton, New Jersey: Gallup Poll.

67. Blazer, D. and Palmore, E. (1976). "Religion and Aging in a Longitudinal Panel." <u>Gerontology</u>, pp. 82-85.

68. King, M. B. and Hunt, R. A. (1975). "Measuring the religious variable: A national replication." <u>Journal for the Scientific Study of Religion</u>, <u>14</u>, pp. 13-22.

69. McConahay, J. B. and Hough, J. C., Jr. (1973). "Love and guilt oriented dimensions of Christian belief." <u>Journal for the Scientific Study of Religion</u>, 12, pp. 53-64.

70. Watson, P. J., Hood, R. W., Morris, R. J. and Hall, J. R. (1985). "Religiosity, sin and self-esteem." <u>Journal of Psychology and Theology</u>, <u>13</u>, p. 116-128.

71. Watson, P. J., Morris, R. J., and Hood, R. W. (1988a). "Sin and Self-Functioning, Part 1: Grace, Guilt, and Self-

Consciousness." <u>Journal of Psychology and Theology</u>, <u>16</u>, 3, pp. 254-269.

72. Watson, P.J., Morris, R. J. and Hood, R. W. (1988b). "Sin and Self-Functioning, Part 2: Grace, Guilt, and Psychological Adjustment." <u>Journal of Psychology and Theology</u>, <u>16</u>, 3, p. 270-281.

73. Watson, P. J., Morris, R. J., and Hood, R. W. (1988). "Sin and Self-functioning, Part 3: The Psychology and Ideology of Irrational Beliefs." <u>Journal of Psychology and Theology</u>, <u>16</u>, 4, pp. 348-361.

74. Watson, P. J., Morris, R. J., and Hood, R. W. (1989a). "Sin and Self-functioning, Part 4: Depression, Assertiveness and Religious Commitment." <u>Journal of Psychology and Theology</u>, <u>17</u>, 1, pp. 44-58.

75. Watson, P. J., Morris, R. W., and Morris, R. J. (1989b). "Sin and Self-functioning, Part 5: Antireligious Humanistic Values, Individualism and the Community." <u>Journal of Psychology and Theology</u>, <u>17</u>, 2, pp. 157-172.

76. Nesbitt, op. cit.

77. Parker, R. (1957). <u>Prayer Can Change Your Life</u>. Englewood Cliffs, NJ: Prentice-Hall.

78. Byrd, R. (1988). "Positive Therapeutic Effects of Intercessory Prayer in a Coronary Care Unit Population." <u>Southern Medical Journal</u>, <u>81</u>, pp. 826-829.

79. Payne, I. R., Bergin, A. E., Bielema, K. A. and Jenkins, P. H. (1991). "Review of Religion and Mental Health: Prevention and the Enhancement of Psychosocial Functioning." <u>Psychologists Interested in Religious Issues Newsletter</u>, <u>16</u>, 3, 3-11.

Part Three

HELL AND MADNESS;

GRACE AND SANITY

This section applies the sin/death equation to the mental disorders defined in the DSM-III-R. In each case, it shows how sanity is restored only when humans grasp the grace of God. Therefore mental health counseling must have its basis in the Gospel, the good news of God's gift of a rescue from hell.

Chapter Fourteen

THE BIBLE AND THE DSM-III-R

Hell and grace...how do they apply to the many different varieties of mental disorder? That is the subject of this chapter. Chapters Seven and Eight highlighted schizophrenia, a striking showcase for the spiritual dilemma that affects all of us. The present chapter focuses on all the non-schizophrenic mental disorder categories, many of which are relatively common. We will see how each derives from existnential guilt.

HELL, GRACE, AND THE DSM-III-R

Heidegger said it is only when we accept the inevitability of death that we are fully alive.[1] But there is no way to accept death when we are separated from God and face the prospect of hell. Every moment is foreshadowed.

A friend of mine, never big on small talk, had an interesting response to people who enquired "How are you?" at parties. He would ask in reply: "How can I acquire the awareness of death and retain the will to live?" The host began to warn other guests that they should not ask how my friend was because he would *tell* them. Nevertheless, the question would come out and several events were ruined. So my friend stopped going to parties and stayed home reading his Bible. There, of course, he found the answer to his question. Through Christ we can embrace both life and death.

Jung considered neurosis "the avoidance of legitimate suffering."[2] There is truth to this. Undeniably, mental illness, neurosis, or whatever it is called, grows out of the avoidance of pain. But suffering is only legitimate if it leads to a cure. Certainly Jung could offer no true remedy. He offered a form of the Satanic lie, stating that cure came from the divinity existing within humans. He believed that if we would confront the pain instead of avoiding it, our divine nature would heal us. But we are not gods; we are separated from divinity in our natural state. We do need to confront the pain, but until we are sure of our connection to God through Christ, we cannot. Solomon told us that "fear of the Lord is the beginning of knowledge" (Proverbs 1:7). The knowledge is the Gospel.

If we fail to take the escape God gives us, we can be no more than defense-bound emotional cripples. This puts us at risk for one or more of the pathological symptom constellations defined by the Diagnostic and Statistical Manual of Mental Disorders (DSM-III-R),[3] the "bible" of the mental health profession. Either sophisticated, "healthy" defenses give way to more primitive ones under stress or the defense network completely malfunctions.

Since human faith is smaller than a mustard seed, all of us display some degree of psychopathology. The boundaries between normality and mental illness are quantitative rather than qualitative.[4] Each of us can recognize some of our own tendencies in each of the afflictions we will look at.

Freud and Jung described all forms of psychopathology as "neurosis." The DSM-III-R uses the term for only a subset of the increasingly vast array of identifiable psychological disorders. However, description is not understanding..."hath not God made foolish the wisdom of the world?" (I Corinthians 1:20).

WHY SO MANY DIFFERENT MENTAL DISORDERS?
Why are there so many different mental disorders if there is only one root problem? This is attributable to the fact that different types of genetic and experiential environment affect the types of psychological defense employed, the severity of the disorder, and the intensity of affect (the emotional climate). There are complex interactions among these factors, but each disorder grows out of the same awful crisis.

GUILT, SHAME, FEAR, AND RAGE
At the bottom of every mental disorder is existential guilt: the awareness of deserving eternal punishment. This

creates potentially overwhelming emotional pain in the form of shame, terror and rage.

The Genesis account describes fear and hiding, an outgrowth of guilt, to be the consequence of Adam and Eve's disobedience (Genesis 3:10). But Solomon, following the Torah, describes "the fear of the Lord" as the "beginning of wisdom" (Proverbs 1:7). Suffering is legitimate if it takes us to God. David asks why the "heathen" rage (Psalm 2:1). The reason is the heathen's sense of existential powerlessness.

This chapter will show that in the depressive disorders, shame and guilt are out on the surface ("I'm to blame"). In the anxiety disorders, a diffuse, unidentified, conscious form of fear predominates: the so-called "free floating anxiety." Rage predominates in disorders involving some type of defiant or explosive acting out, found notably in Mania, the personality disorders ("You're to blame"), and disorders of impulse control.

THE SPECTRUM OF MENTAL DISORDERS

The DSM-III-R is a classification system in a constant state of revision so as to better achieve its thorny task. Its breakdown of mental disorders is based on a behavioral analysis that ignores underlying psychodynamics. This makes for some anomalies in its groupings. Nevertheless, its map of human insanity provides the means to organize the present chapter.

This chapter describes the many psychopathological offshoots of our crisis. In each case, we point out how the knowledge of saving grace specifically applies to the healing process. This Bible-based interpretation of the DSM-III-R is not fully comprehensive, but it does cover the major classes of mental disorders, their subgroups, and many of the individual disorders. These are the major classes:

A) psychotic disorders;
B) neurotic disorders;
C) personality disorders;
D) substance abuse disorders;
E) a catch-all group of disorders of impulse control;
F) the psychosexual disorders;
G) factitious disorders;
H) psychological factors affecting physical condition;
I) central nervous system impairment; and

J) disorders of a more transitory nature precipitated by external stressors.

Differences between psychotic, neurotic and personality disorders

The major difference between psychotic disorders (the focus of Chapters Seven and Eight) and neurotic ones concerns the degree of contact with tangible reality (to be contrasted with existential reality), and the relative intactness of defense armour.

Although the psychotic person may have a clearer sense existential reality than "normal" people, he has no insight into the gross distortions in his thinking, perception, or behavior. He has lost touch with tangible reality.

The neurotic does have insight into his generally less distorted thought and behavior; at least he often knows when he is acting inappropriately even if he feels unable to control this behavior. He has a clearer sense of tangible reality than the psychotic but less sense of existential reality. Delusions and hallucinations are rarely part of his experience.

Psychotic and neurotic disorders can occupy relatively short time periods and present with broad, acute dysfunctionality. On the other hand, most personality disorders are chronic patterns of self-blindness typically associated with dysfunctional social relationships. According to the DSM-III-R, such patterns must last at least two years in order to be classed in the personality disorder category.

A) PSYCHOTIC DISORDERS

The psychotic category in the DSM-III-R includes:
1) the schizophrenia family;
2) the affective or "mood" disorders involving depression in some way; and
3) the disorders organized around specific prominent delusions.

1) SCHIZOPHRENIC DISORDERS

Schizophrenia is a family of disorders described in Chapters Seven and Eight.

2) AFFECTIVE DISORDERS

Affective disorders are primarily disturbances of mood. They come in all grades and many have a cyclical quality, the depressive lows alternating with upswings; valleys and peaks.

At the psychotic end of the continuum are two disorders. One is Major (or Clinical) Depression with or without psychotic features. The psychotic features consist of persecutory and other mood-congruent delusions or hallucinations. Most of these were discussed in Chapter Seven. The other is Bipolar Disorder, with its alternating crazy highs and deep, dark lows.

In the middle of the continuum are the neurotic depressions in which psychotic features are absent, and the Cyclothymic disorder, a milder version of the Bipolar disorder. These disorders are less debilitating but they still tend to be pervasive and lasting.

At the other end of the continuum are the more temporary situational (or adjustment disorder) depressions.

Depression

God cursed Adam with "sorrow" (Genesis 3:17), but promised Eve a double dose: "I will greatly multiply thy sorrow" (Genesis 3:16). This was no idle threat. Among males, the lifetime prevalence of all the recorded types of depression throughout the world is between fifteen and twenty one percent; for women it is almost double, from twenty five to thirty nine percent.[5] Nobody knows what the unrecorded figures for this very common disorder look like.

Depression is like being inside a big black cloud full of hopelessness, despair, and darkness. In Major Depression, despondent thoughts go along with "vegetative" symptoms: low energy; too much or too little sleep; and either overeating or loss of appetite. Even movement and thinking are slowed, a condition called "psychomotor retardation." Psychotic features are common but not always present.

Due to the darkness of thought patterns and the vegetative symptoms of Major Depression, a person loses the ability to function except on a basic level. The will to take action is missing. Getting up out of bed, bathing and eating become formidable chores. The person feels constantly tired and disoriented. With nothing to look forward to or hope for, why make the effort to do anything?

Guilt is more apparent than fear or rage in depressive disorders. Research shows that depressed people report more dysfunctional guilt than "normals."[6] In fact, they are often highly verbal about their extreme worthlessness and deservingness of death. Depressives are only too aware that they miss the mark of perfection and they express this frequently.[7] They are generally oblivious to the fact that their dark thoughts about themselves consume them--a malevolent, self-injurious form of narcissism.

The secular world of psychotherapy tends to regard this negative thinking as distorted, a departure from reality. But according to the Bible, the preoccupation with being unworthy, guilty, and deserving of punishment is anything but unrealistic. "The wages of sin is death" (Romans 6:23).

There is, however, a delusional element in the self-attribution of blame that depressed people often heap upon themselves. They falsely perceive that they are the cause of the ills of everyone and everything around them. It is not hard to see why they feel responsible for the misery of the whole world. As they slip deeper into depression, their gloom certainly is likely to be a stressor for others. Yet their sense of being toxic way outstrips their actual influence. A friend loses a job because of a lay-off, yet depressives suspect they, themselves, are the cause. Anyone whose life they touch must be tainted.

The depressive's belief that he is a blight on himself and others unavoidably leads to thoughts of suicide. It looks like an escape, an act of good riddance for the world. If he is having "command" auditory hallucinations, the voices, which have every appearance of the demonic, will try to drive him to kill himself.

Even those who believe in God can find themselves weakening to suicidality. At those times their faith is not strong enough to reassure them that God would get them out of the hole they find themselves in. Yet they may not take that step of committing suicide because it feels wrong. In the moment of "ending it all," there would be a repudiation of God. Would a momentary repudiation of God lose a person salvation? The answer to this is not clear, and it would be a big risk to take.

Suicidal preoccupation keeps our eyes off God. It can be reassuring to think that if things get too tough, we can go for the exit. Reassuring but paralyzing. The ace in the hole is really a joker. Only confronting the inadequacy of suicide as an escape route brings us to seek the true one. Jesus said: "I am the way, the truth, and the life" (John 14:6); his death enables us to escape hell, and thus, all the fear and guilt that underlies depression. I have found that those assured of salvation through grace may become depressed, but do not go into clinical depression.

<u>What causes depression?</u>

There is evidence that depression and other affective disorders have a genetic basis.[8] But twin studies indicate that, as in the case of schizophrenia, genes alone are not sufficient to produce the disease. The concordance rate of affective disorders among identical twins is still less than fifty percent, and the effects of shared environment, even during prenatal development, cannot be ruled out.[9] Clearly, other factors must play a significant role.

Affective disorders are associated with physiological and chemical changes in the brain.[10] Research shows that the "good mood" neurotransmitters, serotonin and norepinephrin, are rapidly depleted in depressed individuals.[11] This is indicated by the tendency towards mood elevation when drugs blocking the re-uptake (or depletion) of these brain chemicals are taken. It has led to a reliance on drugs for the treatment of depression, a remedy which addresses only the symptoms. The underlying guilt remains.

Although the psychiatric profession tends to regard neurotransmitter imbalance as the cause of depression, this cannot be so. If the problem were only physical, it would make no sense that certain types of psychotherapy reduce the symptoms of depression as well as drugs in the short-term,[12] and better in the slightly longer term.[13]

There are two recognized sources of depression. The "exogenous" type, which is usually less severe, appears to have an environmental trigger. "Endogeneous" depression seems to have an internal trigger. But in fact, both stem from a sense of powerlessness over existential reality; the only difference is that endogeneous type simply has a more direct connection to it.

Given the widespread rejection or misinterpretation of the Bible in the United States, it is hardly surprising that

depression is increasingly common in its population. At
bottom, it is a disorder of the spirit, a universal genetic
disorder inherited from our ancestors in the Garden of Eden.
If a depressed person feels a connection with God, it is only a
weak one. The essential experience of grace has either never
had a chance to penetrate deeply enough or it has not had the
support to remain. At best, it is a superficial concept, possibly
applicable to others, somehow not applicable to self. Satan's
role as accuser takes over: "You're no good. You're
unforgiveable." The experience of unworthiness is so
overpowering that it is impossible for depressed people to
believe in God's love. The truly existential nature of this
disorder is supported by research which shows that an increase
in depression is associated with a decline in belief in a higher
being and in salvation.[14]

A biblical hypothesis

A causal hypothesis about depression incorporating
research findings and the Bible is as follows:

Due to genetic and environmental deficits, the depression
sufferer lacks defenses towards existential guilt. He knows he
is doomed and cannot exclude hopeless, despairing thoughts
from consciousness. These thoughts affect the brain and
deplete the "positive mood" neurotransmitter chemicals:
serotonin, norepinephrine and others. Once the chemical
imbalance gets under way, it maintains or enhances the
despairing thoughts and mood of hopelessness.

Environmental events can trigger or exacerbate depression,
but this is not just a one-way effect. The depression-prone
individual often seeks an unpleasant, punishing environment in
an unconscious attempt to expiate guilt.

There is a downward spiral. Depressive thoughts trigger
self-punishing behavior and neurotransmitter depletion which, in
turn, darken thoughts and increase vegetative symptoms.

What cures depression?

Secular therapy attempts to completely change the realistic
perception of unworthiness and convince depressives that they
are worthy. Much as they might want to, nobody can swallow
this schema; it is simply untrue.

Although the so-called cognitive and interpersonal
approaches of therapy have been found to reduce symptoms of

depression by superficially changing what people think about themselves and how they interact with each other, there is no evidence for their long-term effectiveness.[15] Only a knowledge of saving grace will produce lasting change. A Bible-based cure takes the "unworthy but forgiven" approach. It emphasizes the undeserved, unearned nature of God's rescue, the payment for the sins that the depressive is only too aware of.

As we saw in Chapter Thirteen, large-scale research does not specifically address the role of the Gospel. It does, however, show religious belief to be associated with less depression.[16]

In my own practise I have found that individuals with a diagnosis of Major Depression or Bipolar Disorder show improvement over time as the message of the Gospel penetrates. One indication is that several clients who were previously hospitalized twice a year have avoided hospitalization since they began therapy that was Gospel-based. They are happier now they have begun to walk in faith; that is, faith in God and everything it implies about eternity. Their Bible study and answered prayers help build that faith. Depressions may come, but do not go as deep as they previously did, nor last long. My personal experience with depression attests to that. I am no longer immobilized for periods of several days as I was during my agnostic days.

The facts are not yet all in, but I have found that medication continues to be beneficial if not absolutely necessary for Christian long-term sufferers of severe affective disorders. This is due to what appear to be lasting physical changes in the brain. However, their increasing sense of grace keeps them on a relatively even keel.

Manic disorder

Bipolar Disorder (and its gentler cousin, Cyclothymic disorder) consists of alternating phases of highs and lows, sometimes interspersed with periods of relative normalcy. The wild and crazy euphoria of the Manic phase of Bipolar Disorder is a 180 degree turn from depression. The swings from one pole to another appear to be associated with switches in brain chemicals. Sometimes outside stressors precede the onset of Manic disorder, sometimes the trigger is clearly internal.

Whereas everything slows down during a depression, Mania is life in the fast lane. Thoughts race; ideas in the mind lose focus and fly off at tangents; speech is pressured; energy is superhuman; sleep becomes almost inessential; inhibitions disappear; spending sprees run up huge bills; irritability is high; and physical violence and sexual promiscuity are common. Yet communication is sought keenly, and creative Bipolar people often have their most productive periods at this time if the swing does not take them too far off balance.[17]

In many ways, Mania is much farther from reality than its opposite. The mental health profession recognizes that Mania functions as massive defense towards depression.[18] The grandiose delusions typical of this disorder evoke the Satanic theme of supernatural identification. The person acts as if he truly believes he is a law unto himself, delighting in sin. For a while, he has bought Satan's lies in an unconscious attempt to deny existential reality.

Yet until he hears the Gospel, a Manic phase is often the only time the person feels excitement or joy. Even previously-Manic Bible believers sometimes describe a sense of mourning for the crazy euphorias of the past.

3) DELUSIONAL DISORDERS

Before the third version of the DSM, this category contained only one disorder: paranoia. Now several other types of delusional disorder are recognized. These disorders generally have no symptoms of psychosis other than one prominent delusion, such as jealousy or paranoia.

As discussed in Chapter Seven, from a biblical point of view, the underlying existential truth in most delusions is striking. One curious type we did not mention is erotomania.

Erotomania

The erotomanic has an obsession with some famous person he has never met. Deluded that the person returns the affection, he attempts to carry on a relationship with them as if that were the case. What true message underlies this? It is that somebody powerful out there loves us. The delusion is a distorted version of the sense that the God we have never met face to face already knows and loves us.

B) NEUROTIC DISORDERS

The species of mental disorder within the general neurotic category are widely divergent in their symptoms. This category in the DSM-III-R includes the 1. Anxiety, 2. Somatoform, and 3. Dissociative disorders. These are three different ways that humans run, make walls, and hide from impending doom.

What all neurotic disorders to have in common are acute, disturbing symptoms that prevent or hinder social or occupational functioning.

1) ANXIETY DISORDERS

Existential guilt is accompanied by overwhelming terror. It produces a response so intense that our psychological defenses can crack under its pressure. In the anxiety disorders, guilt is more effectively "bound" (kept out of consciousness) than in the case of depression, but there is a failure to bind terror.

Aaron Beck, a major proponent of cognitive therapy, notes that the anxious person's thinking process differs from the depressive's. The depressive hears himself making global criticisms, whereas the anxious type hears himself making specific criticisms which produce fear. It is "as though the individual were simply warning himself about the dire consequences of his deficiencies."[19] Dire, indeed! Completely against the teaching of the Bible, Beck's treatment aims to reprogram the anxious person with the message that there is no dire consequence.

In this general category, the fear of eternal punishment is very close to the surface. Anxiety disorders consist of:

a) Phobias;
b) Panic Disorder;
c) Generalized Anxiety Disorder;
d) Post-Traumatic Stress Disorder; and
e) Obsessive Compulsive Disorder.

a) Phobias

Phobias are irrational fears of specified areas of human experience. Our deepest fear is displaced and projected onto some facet of this world.

Simple Phobia

A Simple Phobia is a fear attached to just one type of anxiety-arousing object or event. However, the fearful experience is only a trigger for the existential terror coming from the innate sin/death equation.

As we saw in Chapter Four, this contention is supported by research on snake phobia. The objective facts about the relative dangerousness of this animal are not sufficient to explain why fear of snakes is the most common simple phobia in the United States.[20] Yet the prevalence of this phobia makes perfect sense in the light of God's curse on the serpent (Genesis 3:15). Snakes trigger our sense of Satan and doom.

Fear of flying is another common simple phobia. It triggers a sense of vulnerability to the dark abyss. One client had Christian leanings at the outset of therapy but lacked a personal relationship with God through Christ. Initially terrified of flying, he was able to make several flights in a state of calm as grace became more real to him. The source of his fear had been a sense of eternal damnation. Now he saw he was assured of eternal safety through the shed blood of Christ. One idea he found particularly helpful was that he was in a win/win situation in the event of either safe arrival or a plane crash: "Absent from the body, present with the Lord" (II Corinthians 5:8).

Social Phobia

Social phobia is a fear of standing out among a group of people, particularly when it involves speaking or performing. The fear goes beyond any likely potential for harm from the human audience. The audience is perceived as condemnatory, out to destroy the person. The person is paralyzed by an adrenalized fight-flight response. All his attention is on his failure to meet the mark. The existential fear coming from a realistic sense of Satan's accusing and attacking role has been displaced onto the audience.

Social phobics sense the real danger resulting from their inadequacy: it dooms them forever. They often feel ashamed about being so scared; they have no idea of its unconscious source. The sense of inadequacy, which they may not be consciously aware of at other times, can be overwhelming when they know the eyes of others will be upon them. The cure is knowing that God forgives; he does not demand perfection.

He also protects them from Satan. He has provided Jesus to take all the condemnation humans know they deserve. God's assurance to the judges he selected to assist Moses was: "Ye shall not be afraid of the face of man." (Deuteronomy 1:17). This applies to all of us on a basic human level. With God on our side, our inadequacy need not preoccupy us when we are in front of others.

This phobia grows out of social hypersensitivity, or shyness, which has a genetic basis.[21] This means that to some degree, it is likely to continue to be part of the functioning of sufferers. Yet with a sense of God's compete pardon, they can feel comfortable enough to "be themselves" in social situations.

A client with this phobia had only recently perceived the true role of Christ. All his life he had typically been paralyzed in front of even a small group of people. He came for help after being unable to sleep for two weeks. He was worrying about an upcoming speech in front of five thousand people. As he assimilated three facts about God this changed: 1) unearned existential forgiveness, 2) God would carry him through this event, and 3) all credit belonged to God. His paralysis left and he was able to perform well.

Agoraphobia

Agoraphobics lose their defenses towards existential terror when away from the safe comfort of their own home. They may be able to go out if accompanied by another person but the fear is still there. As time goes on, they tend to become increasingly housebound.

I have found that the symptoms disappear when sufferers perceive that they have a continuous connection with God through Christ. For example, a realtor client had become afraid of leaving the house alone and was no longer able to work. She was especially terrified of driving across bridges and on lonely stretches of road. All this changed over the space of six weeks as she perceived the eternal safety she had through Christ. As a Catholic, she had been unaware of how directly she could go to God. Now she knew she could talk to him and be protected while at the steering wheel.

God promised: "Be strong and of a good courage, fear not, nor be afraid of them: for the Lord thy God, he it is that doth go with thee; he will not fail thee, nor forsake thee." (Deuteronomy 31:6).

b) Panic Attack Disorder

Sometimes agoraphobia grows out of a person's history of having panic attacks. Panic is aptly named after its noted association with terror over the horned "god" Pan, i.e., Satan. A panic attack is a sudden upwelling of archetypical terror from a part of the psyche that is usually unconscious. The agoraphobic may fear having an attack in a place where he feels particularly exposed. In reality, he is in constant danger if he has no relationship with God, but he does not feel that lack of protection all the time.

Although the attack may be triggered by some stressful real life event, nothing that is happening in the person's present environment nor anything that has happened in the past explains the severity of the terror. The adrenalized bodily response can feel like a heart attack, sharp and overwhelming. Tachycardia and hyperventilation may cause fainting. It is the panic of being at the brink of falling into the bottomless pit with no personal means of forestalling it.

Systematic desensitization is the secular treatment of choice for phobia and panic attack sufferers.[22] This is a behavioral technique which requires a person to picture himself coping positively with a series of increasingly threatening situations.

However, this visual rehearsal or "visualization"[23] approach can only have lasting effectiveness if it addresses the source of the fear. It must be used biblically, building on God's promises. Like everyone else, panic attack sufferers need a sense of saving grace. God gives us pictures in the Bible that chase fear away, or at least make it manageable. Biblical metaphors for God's eternal protection through Christ are tangible and they reach our hungry spirit, the ultimate influence on all our behavior. As we hear God's assurances that we can lean on him, that he will shield and put a hedge around us on our journey in the world, fear diminishes.

Visualization of images straight from the Bible helped the agoraphobic realtor. Her panic attacks subsided as she pictured herself being in God's hands at all times.

c) Generalized Anxiety Disorder

Generalized Anxiety Disorder is a more pervasive form of anxiety dysfunction than the previous ones. Sufferers find fear permeating every aspect of life.

Many of us are familiar with the feeling that by being hypervigilant on an airplane, we keep it airborne. Although we know this is irrational, we still cannot stop ourselves from being on the alert at all times, as if "helping" the pilot.

Generalized Anxiety is like this, only sufferers do not think their hypervigilance is irrational. In one sense it is not: disaster is ahead. Yet human vigilance will not stop it. Despite this, they are constantly braced against imminent doom, always adrenalized, expecting the unmentionable to arrive at any moment. Unable to let go, their minds are always racing, preventing them from being able to sleep at night until exhausted by hours of rumination over all the bad things that could happen. Relaxation is too risky because even though they know they do not have the necessary control to stop "it" from happening, they delude themselves into thinking they do.

Peace of mind can only be attained when they see that they are forever in the loving hands of God, who has total control of "it."

d) Obsessive-Compulsive Disorder

The defense mode of Generalized Anxiety Disorder involves being braced to fight the enemy at all times. By contrast, the Obsessive-Compulsive Disorder (OCD) sufferer attempts to eliminate the enemy's power by changing himself or his environment. Whereas Generalized Anxiety is a paralyzing state of unending dread, OCD is an action-oriented mode.

In OCD sufferers, fear is repressed. Guilt is closer to the surface[24] and actions display the psychological defense of pseudo-atonement. Freud was right in calling this disorder a "private religion."[25] Its goal is atonement for sin so as to escape from doom.

OCD sufferers spend a long time each day literally trying to clean themselves. Their daily routine may begin several hours earlier than necessary to enable them to follow a compelling purification ritual. Other compulsions concern the safety of the environment. For example, they check numerous times each day to see that the door is locked to keep the enemy out.

They have no idea why they are driven to do this but, at least initially, they do recognize the irrationality of it. The religious performance tends to get longer over time. New rituals are added in pursuit of the unattainable standard of perfection. Afraid to see the big picture, OCD sufferers focus on the minute details they have some hope of controlling. Yet violent, lustful, or other disturbing obsessive thoughts keep intruding into consciousness, telling them how ineffective the purification ritual is.

All of us have experienced obsessions and compulsions to some degree. Research has shown guilt lies behind intrusive thoughts in the general population.[26] We try to walk between the cracks on the sidewalk, but we sense a far more dire consequence for failing to do so than the breaking of Mother's back.

The problem is, we know unconsciously that we will always fall short. We have no way out other than to claim God's gift that wipes our slate clean. This cures the conflict responsible for OCD. A Jewish client reported that his obsessive thoughts about past sins receded as he recognised that Christ had paid for them. Productive, goal-oriented behavior gradually replaced repetitive compulsive rituals.

e) Post-Traumatic Stress Disorder

Post-Traumatic Stress Disorder (PTSD) has an obvious worldly precursor in the form of some type of acute trauma, like rape, extreme child abuse, witnessing a murder, or watching another die in combat.

The terrifying event exposed PTSD sufferers to their complete powerlessness in the face of the future punishment for which all humans sense they are destined. In a shocking situation from which there seemed to be no escape, PTSD sufferers were closer to the reality of hell than anything they had previously experienced. Flashbacks and nightmares keep reminding them of it. They feel utterly helpless against an unnamed terror.

The pervasive and lasting nature of the pathological response, which often intensifies over time, indicates that the deeper, archetypical guilt has been triggered by the trauma. PTSD sufferers escaped the punishment this time around but know it is still coming; they can feel it hovering. They may even seek punishment as a paradoxical defense. It provides temporary respite from the guilt and its attendant emotions that are so close to the surface. Five types of guilt, insidious and treatment-resistant (by traditional methods), have been identified in combat veterans: survivor, demonic, moral/spritual, betrayal/abandonment, and superman/superwoman guilt.[27]

Perhaps the trauma was an abandonment experience during childhood. This has reinforced existential guilt (they "deserved" this abandonment) and kept them emotionally closed. Consequently, what relationships they do form as adults tend to peter out. This, in turn, justifies and intensifies the constant sense of rejection they feel. Underlying this is the unconscious sense of separation from God and the fear of its consequence.

However, the more sure our connection with God through grace and our rescue from hell, the less we humans fear abandonment or trauma of any kind. We can open up and walk in faith instead of guilt and fear, looking at the future rather than the past.

2) SOMATOFORM AND PSYCHOSOMATIC DISORDERS

The body can produce physical symptoms as a distorted manifestation of existential guilt. If the physical symptoms are functional (behavioral) rather than formal (organic), they are categorized among the Somatoform disorders. If they do have a formal basis, they are classed in a DSM category called "psychological factors affecting physical condition," which is another name for psychosomatic illness.

In both cases, the basic conflict and the emotions around it are repressed from consciousness. There are no direct clues as to its root, only the indirect physical manifestation/s.

The physical symptom has one one or more of several potential functions: a preoccupation and distraction from the true dilemma; a "reason" for the unending anxiety; a futile self-punishment to reduce guilt; a way to obtain attention, sympathy, and someone to cling to in the absence of God; a means of escaping responsibility; and a means of prohibiting certain "sinful" thoughts and behavior that trigger the threat of eternal disconnection (as if only certain sins were subject to the punishment). This group of disorders express in a physical way the existential sense of being "not OK," inferior, and powerless.

SOMATOFORM DISORDERS
Somatoform disorders do not have a formal, physical origin. They are behavioral, i.e., "functional." Existential concerns are kept from consciousness and projected on the body in the form of somatic, or physical, defenses. This category includes a) Hypchondriasis, b) Conversion Disorder, c) Psychogenic Pain Disorder, and d) Somatization Disorder.

a) Hypochondriasis
Like sufferers of anxiety disorders, hypochondriacs have a strong sense of how vulnerable humans are when separated from God. Unlike anxious types, who fear something "out there," their deeper existential concern is distorted and projected on the physical part of themselves, a fear for the soul displaced on the body. They seek constant reassurance that the body is not about to fall apart, unconsciously aware that there is only that flimsy tent of flesh between them and hell.

Every slight symptom of illness, real or imagined, heralds destruction, just as the slightest infringement of the law does. No amount of feedback will entirely convince any of us of our soundness because we know we are not sound.

For hypochondriacs, preoccupation with the possible seriousness of every little ache and pain consumes increasing amounts of attention. This distracts them from the true dilemma and saves them from having to cope with the risky process of growth. Similar to depression sufferers, hypochondriacs have a pathological kind of narcissism. Only God's gift of an escape from hell enables them for take their eyes off their unsoundness and grasp the support God offers.

In working with them, I have found they are highly responsive to the promise of a new, immortal body.

b) Conversion Disorder
Conversion Disorder involves a psychogenic loss of use or alteration of some function of the body. Unlike hypochondriacs, sufferers from this disorder may express no concern about their blindness, loss of hearing, fainting spells, paralysis, or other impairment. This symptom is called "la belle indifference." Not only is the conflict repressed, but also concern about the symptoms. Life is simply adapted to the physical restrictions imposed by the disorder as if this were the most natural thing in the world.

The symptoms are generally more closely tied to a specific guilt-inducing thought or action than in the case of other Somatoform disorders. The specific guilt triggers the deeper existential guilt and the sense of its punishment. To be aware of it would be overwhelming, so repression and somatic displacement are employed instead.

The loss or alteration generally involves a part of the body that performs an action linked in some way with a guilt-provoking association: organ language. For example, throat problems may suddenly well up when a person thinks about speaking a guilt-laden statement.

Constriction of the throat is very common among incest victims, often intensifying during therapy as the threat of revelation surfaces. When treating incest victims, I have found that the most deeply repressed memories are the ones revealing some type of transgression of the victim, even a relatively mild one. Common guilt-laden themes in the victim are of two types: 1) hostile feelings and actions towards the abuser; and 2) regarding the incest, any sense of responsibility for it or enjoyment of it.

Outside of the "sin equals death" paradigm, it makes no sense that a person would have more difficulty dealing with some relatively inoffensive act of retaliation of his/her own than an act of brutal terrorism on the part of the abuser. But this is often the way the victim reacts. The fact is, any awareness of personal transgression stirs the fear of hell.

Existential terror, rather than stubborn, irrational fear of the abuser, is what really fuels the continued silence. Even the death of the once-threatening perpetrator is often an insufficient condition to allow the victim to disclose the abuse. What frees the incest victim to fully open up is knowing that he/she has God's complete forgiveness, the freedom from eternal condemnation.

c) Psychogenic Pain Disorder

The symptoms of Psychogenic Pain Disorder can be alleviated by anti-depressant medication.[28] This supports the idea that the felt pain is a metaphorical statement about the pain of living a life separated from God. The suffering has other functions: the avoidance of threatening events and responsibility, an excuse for dependency, and the alleviation of existential guilt through unconscious self-punishment.

d) Somatization Disorder

Somatization disorder uses the body to make a broad spiritual statement: outside of fellowship with God, we are sickly, in pain, and incapacitated in many ways... weak and helpless in the face of grave danger. This disorder involves multiple afflictions and incorporates symptoms of all three previous disorders. Uncomfortable as it may be to suffer in this way, facing eternal darkness is even worse. Even though Somatization sufferers whine and complain, it is easier to live the life of an invalid than face reality outside of Christ.

PSYCHOSOMATIC ILLNESS

Repression as a response to stress can cause lowering of the immune threshold.[29,30] This can lead to physical illness which, in turn, becomes a psychological refuge.

Let us use the example of anger. Adrenalin is released into the bloodstream when we are angry with someone. The anger triggers guilt and fear: "Thou shalt not hate thy brother in thy heart" (Leviticus 19:17). So the anger might be repressed, meaning it is not used to take the action for which the adrenalin was released. The reaction might have been a communication of some kind... asking someone to turn down a radio or stop some bothersome behavior. Therefore, the anger-provoking event tends to recur...the radio continues to blast, the person continues the bothersome behavior.

The adrenalized state also recurs, causing the person's system to become exhausted in time by the constant state of fight/flight arousal. This fatigue is accompanied by a lowering of the immune response and by various other physical symptoms such as muscular tension and gastro-intestinal disturbances.

But when physical illness appears, it may not be unwelcome. It can offer secondary gain in the form of psychological defenses such as regression and self-punishment. However, this mode of defense often backfires. Curling up in the womb of illness can present stresses of its own. One is an intensification of guilt: dependency and inactivity feel sinful. Compounding this is the loss of some of the action-oriented defense mechanisms. Self-purification rituals and "good works" are hindered by the sickness.

A more serious backfire happens when illness threatens survival. Then it is no longer a hiding place. However, survival threat can work to our long-term advantage by forcing us to think about existential reality. Either we go towards depression and despair or towards God.

Although many Christians maintain that God always removes sickness (and sin) from a believer's life, this is not true. We have the example of Paul's "thorn in the flesh" (II Corinthians 12:7). God is in control of biology, and he often uses illness to achieve his purposes. Sometimes he lets Satan's darts hit us. Often it is the only time we think about death and what might follow.

Yet it is true that adherence to God keeps us healthy. In the last chapter we saw research evidence that religiosity is associated with lowered incidence of physical illness. God promised that trusting in him "shall be health to thy navel and marrow to thy bones" (Proverbs 3:8). Rejection of him would result in "the emerods, and with the scab and with the itch, whereof thou canst not be healed...madness, and blindness, and astonishment of heart" (Deteronomy 28:27-28).

3) DISSOCIATIVE DISORDERS

Same root conflict, different type of defense yet: the massive use of repression, splitting, and isolation. Whereas the body is the arena for defensive strategizing in the Somatoform disorders, consciousness and the memory play that role in Dissociative disorders. This category includes a) Simple Amnesia, b) Psychogenic Fugue, c) Depersonalization Disorder, and d) Multiple Personality Disorder.

a) Simple Amnesia

The most common form of dissociation is Simple Amnesia: forgetting. The incest victim "forgets" an entire period of several years when the abuse was occurring. Everything that happened during those years is lost from consciousness so as to avoid triggering any of the painful memories which would, in turn, evoke guilt and a sense of doom.

b) Psychogenic Fugue

Other dissociative disorders involve a different kind of memory loss, a more drastic break from reality. Self-consistency is forfeited in the attempt to flee guilt and its

punishment. How creative is the human mind in finding ways
to "flee when none pursueth" (Leviticus 26:36)!

The relatively rare Psychogenic Fugue state has often
been the subject of movie fiction. One day a person suddenly
finds himself in a new geographic location with a completely
new identity and no recollection of the past. The new persona
is a defensive fabrication. It is an attempt to leave behind the
old person with its baggage of guilt and sense of doom.

However, the old self eventually returns. The only way
to be permanently born again and free from the consequence
of sin is to claim the coverage of Christ.

c) Depersonalization Disorder

Depersonalization is stepping back from the self, as if
partially living another reality. We do not find the total
memory loss characteristic of some other disorders in this
category. Rather, sufferers have a feeling that nothing is real,
including themselves. Life is like a movie they are viewing.

The idea that reality is an illusion is, of course, fostered
in many false religions. It is a flight from the underlying
reality, as if we can wake up and find it has all been a bad
dream. Only through Christ can we fully face reality.

d) Multiple Personality Disorder

How can one person acquire numerous different
personalities that speak with different voices fluent in unlearned
languages and use different styles of handwriting? How can
the personalities perform differently even at the minute level of
visual acuity and eye muscle balance?[31] Our theories of human
learning cannot explain this.

Past development can explain some of the symptoms of
Multiple Personality Disorder (MPD). Many of the
personalities seem to be fixated earlier stages linked to trauma
in the person's life. They may also be introjects of significant
others from the person's world, learned and expressed through
a particular talent for mimicry.

However, we had better be careful. The Western mind,
with its skepticism towards the notion of evil spirits, tends to
psychologize phenomena that are attributed to possession in
India,[32] China[33] and other parts of the East. The fact is, many
characteristics of MPD do suggest possession. Several interview
questions differentiating MPD sufferers from other psychiatric

groups suggest a family history of demonization: physical and sexual abuse as children, sleepwalking, childhood imaginary playmates, ESP, and supernatural experiences.[34]

The Bible mentions several instances in which one or more demons inhabit a human, using the person as a channel for speech and action. (I Samuel 16:23; Matthew 9:32; 12:22; Mark 7:39; Luke 4:33). In MPD, how do we know when these are possessing demons and when not? Testing the spirits, as described in the first epistle of John, would be one approach (I John 4:1-3). How does the person respond to the message of the Gospel? Is there a vehement repudiation of the name of Jesus?

One client described six different personalities plus one he called "me." Four of the personalities appeared to be earlier versions of himself, a fifth was called "the dog," and a more recent one was called "the stranger." This man had lately joined a legalistic pseudo-Christian cult. He attended services and Bible study regularly at his church. Nevertheless, he was unable to acknowledge that Jesus Christ was the son of God, the payment for sin. In fact, he refused to discuss Christ and insisted on his own purity according to a set of laws "revealed" to the founder of the cult in the mid 1800s.

It is likely that this man was possessed by at least one demon, because otherwise his repudiation of Jesus made no sense. It could not be explained by ignorance of the Bible. As false as the teachings are within his cult, there is still an acknowledgement of the importance Jesus, even if it is a grossly distorted one. However, none of his "personalities" stopped him from being involved in the cult as long as he did not have to say that Jesus is Lord. As long as this man thought salvation was due to works, Satan's aim was being achieved.

Standard therapy for MPD aims to eventually unify the personalities. If the personalities are really demonic entitities, they will not "fuse," integrate or unify. However, if one takes over and eliminates all the others during the process of therapy, it is difficult to discern that this is not unification.

Another client related that one of her former sixteen personalities had been a "very spiritual" girl of sixteen. Desperate and suicidal when her former therapist was away on vacation, she had called a leading expert and author on multiple personality for help. He graciously spoke to her on the phone for over an hour, giving her the advice to "join with the most spiritual member of the group."

This led to a resolution not to kill herself and a reduction in the number of personalities. However, without more information we cannot know whether this was fusion of personalities or the work of one demon who evicted all the others while posing as an innocent girl.

There is certainly something extraordinary about MPD whether or not it is a state of multiple possession. If the personalities really are parts of the person instead of possessing spirits, each can function as a refuge from the true self, a way to detach from the conscience. Demon or no demon, operating through a multiplicity of personalities is like being a ship going around in circles from port to port. The ship is unable to stay anywhere for long; nowhere is safe. The tour can only stop when a resting place is found in the God of the Bible. Much "prayer and fasting" (Mark 9:29) may be necessary if the person is truly demonized.

C) PERSONALITY DISORDERS

The long-standing patterns of psychological dysfunction called personality disorders have a wide variety of symptom patterns. One feature they have in common is blindness to the darker side of the self. The sin nature is heavily defended, along with the shame and guilt associated with it.

DEFENSE MECHANISMS IN PERSONALITY DISORDERS

Defenses tend to be the stubborn, primitive type that go along with persistently dysfunctional behavior. Massive repression keeps guilt below the surface of consciousness. Then deflecting defenses such as paranoid projection put the blame on external agents. Defenses employed on a less consistent basis include regression, acting-out, and the more dysfunctional of the compartmentalizers (idealization and devaluation), pseudo-atoners (self-punishment), and analyzers (unsophisticated rationalization).

Social relationships are always problematic. Personality-disordered individuals often hurl abuse at those around them. Criticisms from others are countered with denial, astonishment and blame of the critic. Interpersonal intimacy requires self-knowledge, and like all of us, these individuals dare not see the human depravity which condemns them. They deal with this in ways that are particularly harmful for themselves and others.

Under the surface lurks the sense of separation from God, which is translated into a fear of being abandoned by humans. This fear produces either extreme dependency ("I can't live without you") or counter-dependency ("I don't need anyone"). Lacking a sense of God's love, they have no basis for forward movement of any kind. Backward movement is likely; this is why personality disorders often precede symptoms of other disorders, particularly affective and neurotic ones.

However, if personality-disordered individuals begin to internalize God's compassion, it enables them to gain a sense of grounding, accept their flaws, learn from criticisms, and give and take in a relationship.

This is a broad and general statement about the varied category of personality disorders, and there are, of course, local variations. These disorders tend to form three clusters: emotional withdrawal and odd behavior; anxious and resistive submissiveness; and exaggerated, dramatic emotionality.

CLUSTER ONE: EMOTIONAL WITHDRAWAL AND ODD BEHAVIOR

One cluster involves emotional withdrawal and odd behavior: the a) Schizoid, b) Schizotypal, and c) Paranoid types. These types seem to be outwardly saying: "Since you are so rotten, I can do without you." Avoiding closeness protects them from confronting themselves, and from the pain of rejection by "them," which is really "God."

a) Schizoid Personality Disorder

Schizoid types are not conscious of needing love, nor consciously distressed about not having it. They have become numb to those feelings. If the Avoidant Personality types (see below) can be said to live inside a shell with their antennae out, Schizoids live inside a shell with their antennae drawn in. They are emotionally unavailable and spiritually dead.

Their work life may not be problematic; they sometimes have highly successful careers. Social life, however, is absent. Out of our fear of abandonment, suffocation, or abuse, Schizoids have accepted the notion that they can function without human companionship.

In Schizoids, we clearly see a principle that applies to all of us: our desire for survival is what opens us to God. The concept of God's love will not cut the Schizoid ice. They only thaw after they perceive the reality of hell and God's gift of a rescue. When they learn to trust the rescue, they begin to feel their need for love and come out of the freezer.

b) Schizotypal Personality Disorder

Schizotypals have much in common with schizophrenics, except that the features are less extreme. Symptoms are constant over a period of two or more years, chronic rather than acute.

Like schizophrenics, Schizotypals tend to be preoccupied with the spirit world. They seem to have a particular sensitivity towards it. Their speech and thinking patterns are religiously-oriented, filled with telepathy and other forms of psychic awareness. Ideas of reference are expressed in a digressive verbal style. However, they display none of the extreme aspects of a formal thought disorder. They experience illusions rather than hallucinations, and their paranoid ideation does not have the insistent quality of delusional thinking. Nor are they as lacking in insight as the true schizophrenic.

Their suspiciousness and fears of criticism or rejection lead them to isolate themselves. They present a cold front to humans like a Schizoid, but often seek spirit contact, not realizing that the entities upon whom they depend for companionship belong to the Satanic realm. Until they perceive the true nature of their spiritual contacts and come to know the God of compassion and mercy, they stay in a world of cold isolation, a foretaste of hell.

c) Paranoid Personality Disorder

Paranoid personality types have a pervasive sense that they are being plotted against. Cold and suspicious, they interpret the words, intentions and actions of others in a manner consistent with this fear. They do not have clear-cut delusions like psychotic paranoids, but a general feeling of threat.

Satan is definitely conspiring against us, so this tendency is not without a basis in reality. Their mistake lies in believing that the threat comes primarily from the human world rather than the "prince of the power of the air" (Ephesians 2:2).

CLUSTER TWO: ANXIOUS AND RESISTIVE SUBMISSIVENESS

A second group of personality disorders involves anxious, resistive submissiveness: the a) Avoidant, b) Dependant, c) Obsessive-Compulsive, and d) Passive/Aggressive types. In general, they convey: "I don't love you and you don't love me but I can't live without you."

a) Avoidant Personality Disorder

Avoidant types are aware that they want and need love but they avoid meeting new people out of a dread of rejection. They stay within the safe confines of family or one or two close friends, easily manipulated through fear of abandonment.

Avoidants are distressed about their isolation but feel powerless to do anything about it. They are afraid to make moves in any direction, social, educational, or vocational.

This disorder is a reflection of the approach/avoid conflict all humans have in their relationship with God. We desperately need God but we are terrified to approach him. Avoidants need to see the freedom they have to go to God. Under the umbrella of Christ, they are safe forever. It is essential they grasp that God will not abandon or punish them if they approach him through Christ. This knowledge will fill them with confidence and bring them out of their shell.

b) Dependant Personality Disorder

Dependent types cannot face the thought of being alone or functioning without a human crutch. Consequently, they sacrifice whatever needs and wishes of their own might interfere with their attachment to the humans they cling to. They are less afraid of making new human contacts than Avoidants, but this is definitely a problem. Dependants are superficially childlike, often to the point of extreme passivity and submissiveness. Relationships are unhealthy; either they open themselves up for exploitation or parasitically drain their hosts. Added to this is the poisoning, underlying resentment they feel about surrendering their own needs.

The truth is that they cannot make it alone, but Dependant types seek support from the wrong place: human relationships. Since they offer some comfort but cannot truly satisfy, human relationships take on an addictive quality.

However, when Dependents learn to lean on God, they no longer have to surrender their own needs to the needs of the other. They can follow their own unique pathway with God's support, unafraid to express feelings.

d) Passive/Aggressive Personality Disorder

Passive/Aggressives feel too powerless to assert their own needs and stand up for themselves. However, they will not comply with any "external" source of authority, particularly the other/s upon whom they depend. They unconsciously opt for the power of negation.

To smooth interpersonal relations, they adopt a facade of superficial cooperativeness. Behind this, they passively act out noncompliance. Sins of commission are replaced by sins of omission: procrastination, "forgetfulness," intentional inefficiency, dawdling, and stubbornness.

They resist all forms of authority, including ones they have sought to place themselves under. They establish a plan, then rebel against the feeling of constriction it produces by not following through with it. Sometimes it seems as if they make appointments just to break them. Unconsciously, they are trying to prove they are not doomed, they are above the law. Their rebellion is towards God.

The sense of utter dependency on God's rescue from hell is essential to cure this. The Passive/Aggressive is not the immoveable one, God is...immoveable and unconditional in his love. This knowledge makes the spirit of willing cooperation erase this trait.

c) Obsessive-Compulsive Personality Disorder (OCPD)

Here are the perfectionists, never satisfied with their own performance, nor with anyone else's. Driven by the desperate need to wipe away their guilt, they are continually finding one more flaw that needs to be corrected. They must be in control and on top of things at all times. Relaxation is not allowed. For one thing, it feels like sin. Even more importantly, it deprives them of a hiding place. It allows them to think and feel...far too dangerous.

Although this is fueled by existential guilt and psychologically defended by pseudo-atonement, the mechanism is sublimation, i.e., good works, rather than the more dysfunctional self-purification of OCD. The compulsive behavior, generally workaholism, and the obsessive thinking process that dwells on trivia are generally effective in binding existential dread.

Human relationships are cold and distant; emotions are kept under check through intellectualization and rationalization. Afraid to make a mistake, OCPD sufferers cannot make a decision alone. This means they depend on outside agents to decide for thems. Since they resent the power this gives others over them, they criticize these decisions constantly.

The cure begins with insight about the futility of striving to escape eternal damnation through numb perfectionism. The Gospel's message of God's complete forgiveness will replace the coldness with warmth, give room to make errors, provide freedom to relax, and build a foundation for decision-making.

Self-sabotaging Personality Disorder

This category is still under consideration for the DSM. The striking aspect of self-saboteurs is their obvious ability to achieve. They often go nearly all the way towards a major goal, then ruin the whole thing just before finishing. Years might be spent gaining expertise to do a certain type of work, yet the job interview is ruined by outlandish clothes.

Self-sabotage is an atoning defense mechanism. Success makes us all queasy, although not everyone goes as far as the self-saboteur. Unconsciously, self-saboteurs know they do not deserve success. They have a valid fear that it will make them even more corrupt than they already are. There will be a price to pay for it. Failure feels more comfortable; it temporarily seems to expiate existential guilt.

That is, until they learn about the gift of God's atonement and perceive that Christ takes all the blame. They need no longer seek failure when they know God has paid the price, that he will support and guide them every step of the way.

CLUSTER THREE: EXAGGERATED, DRAMATIC EMOTIONALITY

The third cluster involves exaggerated, dramatic emotionality. These types seem to be saying: "I deserve and must have your love but you cheat me of it, so I'll exploit and punish you." It consists of the a) Antisocial, b)

Histrionic, c) Narcissistic and d) Borderline personality disorders.

a) Antisocial Personality Disorder

There is a male/female difference in intropunitiveness/extrapunitiveness. Men tend to punish others; women punish themselves. We have already seen this in the psychological defense armament (Chapter Six) and depression (this chapter). Now we find it in the personality disorders.

The "acting out" Antisocial Personality (also known as "sociopath" or "psychopath")[35] and the new category of Sadistic Personality are rarely found in women. On the other hand, the Histrionic and Self-Sabotaging types are less common in men.

In a sociopath, the conscience appears to be completely buried. For this type of personality, the fear of God has to be the beginning of wisdom. Love and blessings can have no effect until his fear is aroused. The only thing that will cut ice with a person whose conscience and ability to love are in the deepest of deep freezes is dire threat. In view of the fact that the sociopath has a numbed sense of the future, this fear will not be readily woken up. Somehow the concept of eternal darkness has to strike a chord with him. It may not happen until he has spent considerable time in jail, particularly in solitary confinement. Then he might start looking at death, hell, and God's rescue. This will make him want to straighten up and give love instead of deceiving and manipulating others.

b) Histrionic Personality Disorder

The female counterpart of the Antisocial is the Histrionic Personality Disorder. She, too, is superficially charming and manipulative. However, she is never far from her basic sense of worthlessness. Her self-dramatization, seductiveness, interpersonal shallowness, and avoidance of blame are all facets of the existential guilt she is running from.

c) Narcissistic Personality Disorder

According to some of our leading secular experts on personality disorders, the Narcissistic type has been on the rise in the last twenty five years.[36] Either we look at God or at ourselves. Increasingly, we are doing the latter. This is the so-called "me" generation phenomenon. Today's popular religions and humanistic philosophies follow Satan in advising us to look to our own power and strength, the "god" inside us. But when we look at ourself realistically all we see is weakness and depravity.

Narcissistic types adopt a persona, a set of lies with which they delude themselves about how absolutely wonderful they are. They need the constant admiring attention of others in order to maintain the persona; they must be worshipped like a god.

Lacking compassion for themselves, they have none for others. Other humans are there simply to gratify their needs. Though deep inside they know they are doomed to everlasting contempt, they try to escape that knowledge by convincing themselves they are too important to be cut off forever...important, and possibly omnipotent and immortal. Layers of false pride cover the fear of seeing the true situation. The pride and fear are a barrier to a relationship with God. The only thing that will cut through those layers is a vivid sense of hell and its only escape.

d) Borderline Personality Disorder

Volatile Borderline types[37] sit on a huge vat of anger that is always ready to burst out. Missing are the ego control and defense mechanisms that could either channel or repress this anger and other painful, destructive emotions. The anger seems to be towards an undefined "them." This is God, upon close inspection.

Borderlines feel everything intensely and personally. They hate themselves and often engage in activity that is self-punishing, even mutilating. They may cover themselves in small cuts, a "blood sacrifice" of pseudo-stigmata unconsciously aimed towards atonement for existential guilt.

Typically, there was extreme abuse in their childhood. This led to a failure to internalize "healthy" defense modes or develop the interpersonal trust that might cosset them from the experience of separation from God. Consequently they feel the full impact of that separation but have no conscious understanding of it. There is a continual sense of meaninglessness, emptiness and boredom...a never-ending search for identity.

They cannot tolerate being alone. Like the Dependent type, they experience the need for God as a need for the other person. Yet they fear being suffocated and overwhelmed by that person, so relationships are unstable. Although they are often aggessors, they see themselves as only as victims. They certainly *are* victims in the sense that they are unable to differentiate where they end and another person begins. This leaves them wide open to another's influence.

Lack of boundaries means they jump into the deep end of a relationship too quickly. They see the other as an extension of themselves, a tool to be used. Failing to realize others are neither gods nor separate individuals, they ask too much of them. They resent others either for not caring enough or for caring too much. Relationships are demandingly stormy, leading to quick burn-out on both sides. Unconsciously provoking a fight to break up the relationship, Borderlines then blame the other person for this.

Borderlines' perception of others, which is truly a perception of themselves, is that they are either wonderful or terrible; there are no shades of grey. The first flaw is fatal. Their sense of the absoluteness of the penalty for the slightest degree of missing the mark shows itself in these extremes of idealization and devaluation. Deep inside they know grey is as condemning as black, and it shows in their behavior.

However, when their deepest fear is quieted and they know they are known to God, Borderlines lose their empty feeling and begin to see themselves as an "I." As a sense of God's mercy reaches them more and more deeply, they change in many ways. One transformation is the ability to tolerate imperfection in others. And no longer are they angry victims when they know God is on their side.

D) SUBSTANCE ABUSE DISORDERS

Alcoholism contines to be the biggest substance abuse problem in our nation, with approximately 15 percent of the population over 13 years fulfilling the DSM criteria for alcohol abuse, and another 35 percent regular drinkers in the moderate to light category. Besides the obvious problems with illicit drugs, prescription drugs also present enormous potential for abuse. Twenty percent of the population has at some time used one of the minor tranquilizers, which are highly addictive and can produce dangerous withdrawal symptoms.[38]

Why is chemical alteration of the brain so appealing to us? It helps us cope with the symptoms of our underlying conflict. Chemical alteration produces a change of mood, jolts us out of dysphoria, relieves boredom, relaxes, turns the channel, provides a preoccupation and distraction...all of which temporarily enable us not to feel the pain of existential guilt and terror. It gives us an excuse for not acting in faith, freeing us to shuck responsibility and give in to our rebelliousness. The chemical escape becomes an integral part of the defense equipment.

But substance abuse requires denial in order to maintain it. Denial and rationalization are common defense mechanisms for the alcoholic.[39] Nobody can stand to be aware that the substance is destroying them. Confronting that would mean having to quit. Quitting would mean not having that escape any more. The abuser cannot imagine life without it.

Deceit is also a common defense. It can be partly a function of the illegality of the substance but it is also an end in itself. It offers empowerment, the same kind of pseudo-independence as the drug. It also provides false existential reassurance. If the abuser can break the drug law and get away with it, then perhaps he can beat the hell rap which really plagues him. It gives a sense of control, the illusion--or delusion--of being above the law.

Certain drugs bolster this feeling of invulnerability. It is particularly true of stimulants like cocaine or alcohol in its early disinhibiting phase. These substances produce or enhance an illusion of omnipotence, a delusion of godhood. Cocaine addicts often refer to their drug as "the devil."

Only a sense of grace will replace the need for chemical escape. The substance abuser has to see his need for salvation from hell along with God's gift of that to him. He needs to experience a sense of God's mercy in a personal way. Then his relationship with God through Christ will enable him to envisage a better life and walk away from chemical dependency. (See a discussion of the Alcoholics Anonymous movement in Chapter Eleven).

E) IMPULSE CONTROL DISORDERS

This category includes several facets of human behavior that involve acting upon an impulse to perform an illegal, illicit, dangerous or highly imprudent activity:

a) Pathological gambling;

b) Kleptomania;
c) Pyromania;
d) Intermittent Explosive Disorder; and
e) Eating disorders.

Most of our basic impulses go against God and make us feel guilty. Guilt can exacerbate our propensity for rebellion. We rebel because we are angry about our situation. Deep inside we know the dire consequence of falling short. We are mad at the God who set things up this way. So when we break the law and eat the "forbidden fruit," for one glorious moment we feel above the law. There is temporary relief from the struggle to stay on the righteous path. It thrills us to do something bad and get away with it. That is, until we begin to realize that God sees everything. Every transgression puts us further away from God, steeps us in more guilt.

Transformation occurs when we see the God-given escape clause in the law. The more we know God sees all yet forgives and accepts us as we are, the less we want to rebel. Rebellion will still be in our nature, but we now no longer give ourself license to act on it. God sends the Holy Spirit to amplify our conscience and help us achieve restraint. Now if we rebel, there is a new dynamic to it. It is followed by shame and remorse, a sense of thankfulness for God's mercy, a desire to repent, and the recognition we can go to God for help in doing so. The change process has begun.

These comments apply to all disorders of impulse control. Now we pay close attention to the last type mentioned: eating disorders.

EATING DISORDERS

Two major eating disorders persist into adulthood, Anorexia Nervosa and Bulimia. These disorders involve somewhat similar ways of trying to exert control over the uncontrollable existential dilemma. Research has shown shame and guilt to be close to the surface in both disorders.[40] The driving force of these abnormalities is the defensive strategy of pseudo-atonement. Its focus is in the arena of fatness and food.

The illusion of atonement for sin is achieved, especially in Anorexia, by repression of the physical appetite and loss of body fat. The specific defense mechanism is "turning against the self." In Bulimia, "undoing" (purging) is also used. These two disorders, which may alternate over time in the same person, are paradigmatic of the unconscious merciless legalism present in all humans outside of a knowledge of God's saving grace.

Anorexia Nervosa

Anorexia Nervosa is a extreme form of impulse control. The appetite for food is repressed as a way to resolve the conflict over imperfection. To be perfect means to have no fat. This is reinforced by the cultural context which sees perfection "in the flesh" as being almost without it.[41]

The Anorexic, who is nearly always a female below the age of thirty, constantly strives to lose just a little more fat. Since this truly represents an unconscious need to reach the purity which avoids hell, it can never be met. If body fat is equated with sin, and losing fat is an attempt to eliminate sin and avoid eternal death, the cause is lost from the start. The person will die before achieving this aim.

Controlling body fat (i.e., sin) becomes the entire focus of the person's life, a distraction from the true state of affairs. All conversation tends to be around control of food/eating/not eating. The person's weight goes way below the ideal body poundage because the perception of being a sinner never goes away. The process of shedding fat even goes way past the point of culturally accepted slimness. It goes all the way to dangerous emaciation; loss of hair; drastic loss of muscle, including heart muscle; and even early death if there is no intervention.

There are secondary gains to emaciation. One is the reversal of secondary sexual characteristics that reduces guilt over sexual feelings. Breasts shrivel, menses stop, activity is restricted. These morphological changes and the physical weakness associated with them offer the escape of regression back into a second childhood. There is physical debilitation, often requiring entry into the safe structure of a hospital. The unconscious goal of this extreme dependency is to remove responsibility for sin.

Interestingly, a reverse anorexia is found in steroid users. Although they attain huge weight gains, they are never satisfied with their physique. The defensive nature of this perfectionism is proven by the fact that if they stop trying to bigger and better themselves, they often fall into deep depression.[42]

Bulimia

"Thou shalt eat, but not be satisfied" (Micah 6:14). This is the condition of the Bulimic. The increasingly prevalent Bulimia is estimated to affect between seven and eight million women in the United States.[43] It is a disorder involving periods of uncontrolled binge eating, which may or may not be followed by self-induced vomiting or some other means of eliminating the food before it is assimilated.[44]

As much as the Bulimic gives in to the impulse to gorge with food, she never seem to get full because food does not resolve her unconscious fear of hell. As a form of chemical dependency, the food has a numbing, antidepressant effect. It temporarily "stuffs" down the guilt, shame and depression due to existential reality, but the conflict remains.

Anorexia verus Bulimia

Research has shown that dietary restraint, growing out of a cultural value of slenderness for females, is closely associated with eating disorders.[45,46] For both the Anorexic and the Bulimic, eating feels illegal. Both are concerned with the changes in body shape related to food intake. The Anorexic exerts constant control over the entry gate to food. The purging Bulimic has found a way to be able to give in to the impulse to not only indulge, but overindulge, without damage necessarily being done to body shape. Purging damages the inside of the body but this unseen consequence is preferred over being fat.

The Anorexic's behavior implies a total repression of the existential conflict. As a perfect metaphor for her spiritual deadness, she is in a state of starvation but does not consciously feel hungry. Yet there is a tenacious, merciless clinging to perfectionism in the constant restraint of the impulse to eat.

It is not surprising that more psychopathology is associated with Anorexia than Bulimia. Anorexia is like a form of OCD with a prominent delusion about body size. Only a deep conflict of the spirit would explain why fasting to death would be chosen over facing the truth.

For the purging Bulimic, there is the superficial appearance of compliance with the law, a false front of perfection. Underneath this is repeated sin/atonement.

The Bulimic has more contact with reality than the Anorexic. The conflict is closer to the surface; she knows she is hungry. She is also closer to admitting she is a sinner, for the forbidden impulse to gorge breaks loose every so often. Then the pseudo-atonement mechanism of induced vomiting or some other type of purging can function: the psychological defense of "undoing."

Dietary preoccupations have always been a major element of legalistic religions, both western and eastern. Salvation is to be gained through food restriction or a correct diet. Occasionally members of the Jains in India starve themselves to death in a futile bid for salvation. Jesus cleared this up once and for all when he said "whatsoever thing from without entereth into the man, it cannot defile him;" (Mark 7:18) and "that which cometh out of the man, that defileth the man." (Mark 7:20). Only the sense of being a forgiven sinner, safe for eternity, can end this Anorexic/Bulemic bondage.

OTHER DISORDERS

A number of other disorders listed in the DSM-III-R have a more temporary or less pervasive nature, i.e the Sexual Disorders, Factitious Disorders, Sleep Disorders, Adjustment Disorders and the so-called "V Code" disorders that can be traced to external stressors such as death of a family member, marital problems, etc. In all cases, the problem is spiritual. Life is hard, and only a personal relationship with God enables us to thrive. The more we listen to God and follow his direction, the easier our lives will be. He is our problem-solver, the one to call on for help.

SUMMARY

In this chapter we applied our Bible-based diagnosis and cure to most of the DSM-III-R non-schizophrenic psychotic, neurotic and personality disorders. We also took a broad look at substance abuse and impulse control disorders. Eating disorders, a subclass in the impulse control category, received closer examination.

We saw the way in which all these disorders stem from one root. In each case, the sin/death equation makes the most parsimonious explanation. Therefore, only the Gospel will cure.

Notes

1. Heidegger, Martin (1962). <u>Being and time</u>. New York, New York: Harper and Row.

2. Jung, C. G. (1957). "The Undiscovered Self (Present and Future). In <u>Collected Works, 10</u> (2nd edition), 1969, pp. 245-305. (First German edition 1957).

3. American Psychiatric Association (1987). <u>Diagnostic and Statistical Manual of Mental Disorders, 3rd Edition, Revised</u>. Washington, DC: American Psychiatric Association.

4. Sabshin, Melvin (1989). "Normality and the boundaries of psychopathology." <u>Journal of Personality Disorders, 3</u>, 4, pp. 259-273.

5. Paykel, E. S. (1982). <u>Handbook of affective disorders</u>. New York, New York: The Guildford Press.

6. Jarrett, Robin B. and Weissenburger, Jan E. (1990). "Guilt in depressed outpatients." <u>Journal of Consulting and Clinical Psychology, 58</u>, 4, pp. 495-498.

7. Hewitt, p. L. and Flett, G. l. (1991). "Dimensions of perfectionism in unipolar depression." <u>Journal of Abnormal Psychology, 100</u>, 1, pp. 98-101.

8. Merikangas, Kathleen R., Spence, Anne M., and Kupfer, David J. (1989). "Linkage studies of bopolar disorder: Methodological and analytic issues: Report of MacArthur Foundation Workshop on Linkage and Clinical Features in Affective Disorders." <u>Archives of General Psychiatry, 42</u>, 12, pp. 1137-1141.

9. Nurnberger, J. I. and Gershon, E. S. (1982). "Genetics." In E. Paykel (Ed.) Handbook of Affective Disorders. New York: The Guilford Press, pp. 126-145.

10. Bower, B. (1991). "Schizophrenia, Depression Share Brain Clue." Science News, 138.

11. Paykel, op. cit.

12. DeRubeis, R. J., Evans, M. D., Hollon, S. D., and Garvey, M. J. (1990). "How does cognitive therapy work? Cognitive change and symptom change in cognitive therapy and pharmacotherapy for depression." Journal of Consulting and Clinical Psychology, 58, 6, pp. 862-869.

13. Barber, J. P. and DeRubeis, R. J. (1989). "On second thought: When the action is in cognitive therapy for depression." Cognitive Therapy and Research, 13, 5, pp. 441-457. Shows there is little difference between the short-term effects of cognitive therapy and medication. However, due to a hypothesized advantage in its teaching of compensatory skills, cognitive therapy is superior in relapse prevention.

14. Hole, G. (1977). Der Glaube bei Depressiven: Religionspathologische und klinisch-statistische Untersuchung. Stuttgart: Ferdinand Enke.

15. Robinson, L. A., Berman, J. S., and Neimeyer, R. A. (1990). "Psychotherapy for the treatment of depression: A comprehensive review of controlled outcome research." Psychollogical Bulletin, 108, 1, pp. 30-49.

16. Pressman, P., Lyons, J. S., Larson, D. B., and Strain, J. J. (1990). "Religious belief, depression, and ambulation status in elderly women with broken hips." American Journalof Psychiatry, 147, 6, pp. 758-760.

17. Paykel, op. cit.

18. Neale, J. M. (1988). "Defensive Functions of Manic Episodes." In T. F. Oltmann and B. A. Maher (Eds.) Delusional Beliefs. New York, New York: Wiley, pp. 138-156.

19. Beck, Aaron T. and Gary Emery (1985). <u>Anxiety Disorders and Phobias.</u> New York: Basic Books Inc., p. 103.

20. Doctor, R. M. and Kahn, A. P. (1989). <u>The encyclopaedia of phobias, fears and anxieties</u>. New York: Facts on File.

21. Herbener, Ellen S; Kagan, J. and Cohen, M. (1989). "Shyness and olfactory threshold." <u>Personality and Individual Differences</u>, <u>10</u>, 11, pp. 1159-1163.

22. Reid, William H. (1983). <u>Treatment of the DSM-III-R psychiatric disorders</u>. New York, New York: Brunner/Mazel Inc.

23. Some Christians believe visualization inherently occultic, to be shunned. This is going too far. God gave us the ability to visualize. We use this ability to make pictures in our mind when we think of, for example, the children of Israel crossing the Red Sea or Christ on the cross. When we visualize the future which God has promised us, it makes it more believable...the many mansions of our heavenly abode. We also make a spontaneous mental picture when we pray for somebody to be saved. We need to use all our faculties in our relationship with the God of the Bible.

Visualization is only occultic if we believe that our thoughts have magical power, the ability to produce the things our minds imagine.

24. McGraw, R. K. (1989). "Obsessive-compulsive disorder apparently related to abortion." <u>American Journal of Psychotherapy</u>, <u>43</u>, pp. 269-276. The disorder appeared subsequent to, and was apparently triggered by guilt feelings about three previous abortions stimulated by a routine medical procedure.

25. Freud, S. (1907). "Obsessive Actions and Religious Practices." In <u>Standard Edition</u>, <u>9</u>, 1959, pp. 115-127. Original German edition 1907).

26. Niler, E. R. and Beck, S. J. (1989). "The relationship among guilt, dysphoria, anxiety and obsessions in a normal

population." Behavior Research and Therapy, 27, 3, pp. 213-220.

27. Opp, R. E. and Samson, A. Y. (1989). "Taxonomy of guilt for combat veterans." Professional Psychology: Research and Practice, 20, 3, pp. 159-165.

28. Reid, William. H. Treatment of the DSM-III Psychiatric Disorders. New York: Brunner/Mazel, 1983, p. 149

29. Horowitz, Mardi (1984). "Stress and the Mechanisms of Defense." In H. H. Goldman (Ed.) Review of General Psychiatry. Los Altos, California: Lange Medical Publications, pp. 42-50.

30. Vollhardt, L. T. (1991). "Psychoneuroimmunology: A literature review." American Journal of Orthopsychiatry, 61, 1, pp.35-47.

31. Miller, Scott D. (1989). "Optical differences in cases of multiple personality disorder." Journal of Nervous and Mental Disease, 177, 8, pp. 480-486.

32. Adityanjee, R. G. S. and Khandelwal, S. K. (1989). "Current Status of Multiple Personality Disorder in India." American Journal of Psychiatry, 146, 12, pp. 1607-1610.

33. Li, Shengxian and Phillips, M. R. (1990). "Witch doctors and mental ilness in mainland China: A preliminary study." American JKournal of Psychiatry, 147, 2, pp. 221-224.

34. Ross, C. A., Heber, S., Norton, G. R. and Anderson, G. (1989). "Differences between multiple personality disorder and other diagnostic groups on a structured interview." Journal of Nervous and Mental Disease, 177, 8, pp. 487-491.

35. Reid, W. H. (Ed.) (1978). The Psychopath: A Comprehensive Study of Antisocial Disorders and Behaviors. New York, New York: Brunner Mazel Publishers.

36. O. Kernberg (1975). Borderline Conditions and Pathological Narcissism. New York, New York: Jason Aronson.

37. Kernberg, op. cit.

38. Chambers, Carl D., Inciardi, James A., and Siegal, Harvey A. (1975). Chemical coping: a report on legal drug use in the US. New York, New York: Spectrum Publishers.

39. Ward, L. C. and Rothaus, P. (1991). "The measurement of denial and rationalization in male alcoholics." Journal of Clinical Psychology, 47, 3, pp. 564-468.

40. Frank, Emily S. (1991). "Shame and guilt in eating disorders." American Journal of Orthopsychiatry, 61, 2, pp.303-306.

41. Bruch, H. (1978). The Golden Cage: The Enigma of Anorexia Nervosa. Cambridge, MA: Harvard University Press.

42. "Jumped Up." (June 1, 1992). US News and World Report, p. 59.

43. Dippel, N. M. and Becknal, B. K. (1987). "Bulimia." Journal of Psychosocial Nursing, 25, 9, 13-17.

44. Russell, G. (1979). "Bulemia nervosa: An ominous variant of anorexia nervosa." Psychological Medicine, 9, pp. 429-448.

45. Caulwels, J. M. (1983). Bulimia, the binge-purge compulsion. New York: Doubleday and Company.

46. Charnock, D. W. (1989). "A comment on the role of dietary restraint in the development of bulimia nervosa." British Journal of Clinical Psychology, 28, 4, pp. 329-339.

Chapter Fifteen

"FEED MY SHEEP"

A major issue in the counseling field is whether or not it is appropriate to deal with spiritual issues in psychotherapy, and if so, how. A particular concern for Christian counselors has been whether and how to "integrate" counseling and the Bible.[1] However, once the profession sees that grace is the foundation for mental health, the "if" question is eliminated. The "how" question begins to be answered too. The focus must always be on God's gift of the payment for sin.

Three times Jesus made a request to Peter: "Feed my sheep." (John 21:15-17). The food is the good news of God's rescue, the only route to mental health. The sheep are those who have "ears to hear" (Deuteronomy 29:4). For some of the reasons listed in Chapter Two, all those who seek counseling, including those who say they want Christian counseling, do not have ears to hear. They are hungry but may not be conscious of it. Yet the food must be offered to all in order to reach the few who will eat it up. I have found that those who do not want it leave.

I advertise counseling services through some secular channels which do not identify my Christian stance. Prospective clients are introduced to it when they call me for information. I ask God to send those with ears to hear, and I am frequently amazed at the receptivity of callers. Often clients who reach me this way are more receptive to a truly Bible-based approach than those who come through Christian channels.

This hard-heartedness results from merciless false teaching in the church and past counseling experiences in situations where psychology has made inroads into Christianity. It is typical of Christian counselors to keep all mention of the Gospel outside the counseling room. Several clients in my practise have said that their previous Christian counselors made no mention of God at all. Why? Well, here are some of the flawed arguments which have been used for not sharing the Gospel in counseling, and the rebuttals which destroy these arguments.

Argument 1.

The domain of psychotherapy is the emotional life, not the spiritual life. A person should go to his pastor for spiritual counseling.

Rebuttal 1.

The emotional life is dependent on the spiritual life. We cannot be mentally healthy when our hearts are heavy with the anticipation of hell. Besides, who says that the spirit and the emotions are two separate domains? By what authority? Certainly not the Bible. Do pastors and psychotherapists have exclusive territorial rights to different parts of the psyche, as if the psyche can be split? No.

There is an enormous degree of ambivalence and resistance towards "coming out" in the Christian counseling community. This is typified by two conflicting statements made by Benner,[2] who says "Psychotherapy is not a good place to talk about God, prayer, scriptural interpretation, or theology." He then goes on to say "Psychotherapy is also an excellent place to explore blocks in spiritual growth. Why is my prayer life so dead?" How we can explore such blocks without talking about God, prayer, scriptural interpretation, or theology is certainly mysterious.

There are now several accepted quasi-spiritual approaches in the mainstream of psychotherapy (see Chapter Eleven), so clearly there is a precedent for including the spirit in this work. But as we have seen, all of those other spiritual approaches convey the Satanic theme, just like any form of mental health counseling that is not Bible-based.

Argument 2.

Mental health can be achieved through secular means, so keep religion out of the picture.

Rebuttal 2.

Clinton McLemore is one Christian psychotherapist who believes "It is possible for an individual to be a paragon of mental health as this is traditionally defined, and yet be without faith in God through Christ."[3] Well, much hinges on how mental health is defined. If we define mental health as the short-term ability to bind anxiety and guilt through massive psychological defense, secular therapy is somewhat effective.

However, some of the humanistic mental health definitions we saw in Chapter Nine were: congruence, authenticity, emotional integrity, wholeness, and the ability to give and receive love. Psychodynamic approaches aim towards freedom from debilitating intrapsychic conflict. None of these goals can be met unless there is a sense of reprieve from the consequence of sin.

Argument 3.

Religion should only be a topic in psychotherapy if it is causing problems.

Rebuttal 3.

Absolutely right. It so happens that the root of all problems is a religious one: existential guilt. The fact that this root is not immediately apparent does not mean we can ignore it. If a car has engine trouble, a tune-up may help, but not for long. Sooner or later, the engine has to be dealt with.

Argument 4.

APA ethical guideline #2 requires that a psychologist operate within the limits of his competence.[4] A psychotherapist is not trained to deal with religious issues, so he should leave them alone.

Rebuttal 4.

True, preparation for dealing with the religious context of the client is notably absent in clinical training programs, even though it has been shown to be of major importance to a person's outlook on life.[5]

The clear purpose of this book is to show that clinical training without Bible training is useless at best, terribly dangerous at worst. But at the present time, if religion were to be included in standard clinical training, it would be likely to have a strong anti-biblical bias, just as the mental health profession has.

Currently, mental health licensing examinations require familiarity with a wide range of techniques and ideas which run in direct opposition to Bible teachings. Since there are many different and conflicting clinical orientations, examinees are not expected to espouse all these techniques and ideas, but merely display knowledge of them all. However, the Christian counselor can easily be led astray by this unless his training involves a strong emphasis on the Bible.

Should Christian counseling involve a specific training and credentiallying process beyond the generic license? Jungians can practise Jungian psychotherapy without necessarily having had any specific clinical training in it. Why should Bible-based therapy be treated any differently? Obviously Bible-based therapists need to be thoroughly grounded in God's Word, but should they have to prove that in a certification process beyond licensing? It might actually be advisable for them to do this. A Bible study requirement could make Christian counselors less likely to shy away from the truth. Of course, if the Bible were made central to mental health just as it should be, it would not be necessary to ask these questions. Bible training would be the core preparation for all counselors and psychotherapists.

Argument 5.

A psychotherapist's training, even if it included the Bible, would not provide as thorough a preparation in it as the training of a minister. To avoid confusing the client, a psychotherapist should refer his client to a trained minister for spiritual concerns.

Rebuttal 5.

Although it is clear that counselors do need thorough Bible preparation, the fact is that the message of the Bible is very simple: we are saved from hell by the blood of the sacrifice that God made of his only son, Jesus. How hard is it to communicate that? Besides, God has told us he will put the words in our mouths when we share the Gospel. However, a therapist has the responsibility to encourage his client to search the Scriptures for himself, not rely on what anyone else tells him.

It may help if the client talks to a minister, but many ministers lack time for intensive one-on-one counseling. More importantly, ministers in this age generally have little real help to offer. They have increasingly moved away from emphasizing hell and grace. With some highly notable exceptions, they are either legalistic or liberal (for a discussion of this see Chapter Twelve).

Argument 6.

If the minister is doing his job, there should be no need for a member of his flock to have individual counseling.

Rebuttal 6.

Even with good preaching, a person's blind spots can persist. We return to the example of David and the counseling God gave him through Nathan, the prophet. David loved God. He knew God's law but still was in need of individual counsel. The Holy Spirit will work through any means available, and a one-on-one counselor has a prime opportunity.

Argument 7.

This is an argument very common among "Christian" therapists maintaining a secular practise: A psychotherapist has no right to challenge a person's spiritual belief system. To do so would be an ethical violation. He should respect the person's freedom of choice. Evangelizing has no place in psychotherapy.

Rebuttal 7.

Where do we get this crazy notion that a person's spiritual belief system is sacred? The APA ethical guideline 3.c that psychologists be "sensitive" to the religious background of their clients[6] is actually wide open to interpretation. We can be sensitive to our clients' religious beliefs without considering them sacred. Did God ever say that Baal worship was sacred? Any spiritual belief system that is not based on the Bible is demonic, leading right into hell, and must be challenged. Sensitivity is involved in the "how" issue, not the "what" one.

With regard to freedom of choice, whatever the psychotherapist tells a person about God, the ultimate choice will always lie with the individual. That is the true purpose of free will, that we come to God willingly.

However, we can only exercise true freedom of choice when we have the full range of available information. Without the truth before us, we can only chose among bad alternatives.

A standard practise in the mental health profession is to challenge the delusions (or false beliefs) of clients. It is of the utmost importance that religious delusions be challenged with the right information and, given the dire consequence of ignorance, it is inethical not to do so.

Even if the Gospel were not essential to mental health, there is another reason why it should be part of psychotherapy. Saving life is the supreme ethical principle of the mental health profession. No Bible-believer worth his salt can say this applies merely to the prevention of suicide or homicide. The issue at stake is eternal life.

Argument 8.

Therapists should be value-free and belief free. They should in no way attempt to foster any spiritual belief system.

Rebuttal 8.

As Victor Frankl says: "There is no psychotherapy without a theory of man and a philosophy of life underneath it."[7] Research has shown this to be the case.[8] Psychotherapy is never value free. Any practitioner who believes his work is not absolutely riddled with spiritual values and beliefs is blind to what he is doing. The issue is how to use values in a way that does not abuse the therapist's power or the client's vulnerability.

There is no way to address mental health without also including religion. It is impossible to avoid taking a position vis-a-vis God. If we avoid talking about God, we are taking a position against God. If we talk about God without mentioning Jesus Christ, we are also taking a position against God.

The secular psychotherapeutic community often states that the client must find his own way to a religious position. Somehow it is ethical to force-feed anti-godly ideas but inethical to even mention God unless the client raises the issue. Even when he does, conversation is usually steered away.

There is a glaring inconsistency here. Obviously, the client is not expected to find his own way to mental health. Although he may not initially realize it, he has come for assistance that extends beyond his behavioral, cognitive, and emotional life into the all-important spiritual terrain. The therapist can be a guide in the client's spiritual investigation. He does not have all the answers. Only the Bible does. Several chapters in this book have shown that only the Bible holds up under scrutiny. It cannot be force-fed. The freeing truth in the Bible, if given a chance, will shine through the merciless legalism and delusionality in every other existential belief system.

Argument 9.

In their guidelines for APA ethical principle #4 on public statements, Spiegal and Koocher state: "Advice should have a scientific basis."[9] Where is the evidence that Bible-based psychotherapy works?

Rebuttal 9.

Obviously it is desirable to have evidence. But the fact of the matter is, there is no hard scientific evidence for the effectiveness of any form of therapy, per se. Personal qualities of the therapist have been shown to be the major determinant of treatment outcome.[10] At this point, other than case studies, there is no modern empirical research demonstrating the effectiveness of Bible-based therapy. Nor is there evidence that it is harmful. The guilt/grace research by Hood, Taylor and associates described in Chapter Thirteen indicates the mitigating effects of grace, but we need substantiation of that in a clinical setting.

However, the Bible itself has several examples of case studies of individuals who become insane when they go into idolatry and are healed when they turn to God. Saul, king of Israel (I Samuel) and Nebuchadnezzar, king of Babylon (Daniel 1-5), are cases in point.

Argument 10.

APA ethical principle 3:c states: "In their professional roles, psychologists avoid any action that will violate or diminish the legal and civil rights of clients or others who may be affected by their actions."[11] Is the promotion of a Biblical perspective any type of legal or civil rights violation?   How about separation of church and state?

Rebuttal 10.

"Freedom of speech" and "freedom of religion" are constitutional rights of both therapist and client. Is it a violation of religious freedom if religious ideas are explored in therapy? Surely not. If religiously-rooted ideas are excluded from psychotherapy, there is nothing of value to talk about.

Is it a violation if the therapist gives advice that conflicts with a person's religion, or attempts to change it? If so, the entire psychiatric profession is in violation of the constitution. This is the typical situation: the therapist determines a person has a basic Judaeo-Christian affiliation yet advises him to look to himself as a change agent rather than God.

If the client does not wish to hear about God, nothing compels him to listen. The therapist is obliged to take note of this and help him find alternative treatment if the client so wishes.

Interestingly, "separation of church and state" is frequently invoked to stop Bible proponents from speaking about the Bible in public places, even at public meetings in Christian churches.[12] What a warped interpretation of a law that states that government cannot enforce a religion!

On the other hand, "freedom of speech" is invoked when a member of an anti-Biblical spiritual discipline wants a public platform. For example, the San Francisco public library speaker program turned down a talk I proposed because the Bible would be brought into it. The grounds of separation of church and state were used. Soon after this, a program on witchcraft was offered at San Jose public library, defended on free speech grounds.

In fact, separation of church and state is not in the constitution. It was a notion devised to differentiate the controlling interests of two different bodies. It was not devised to prevent anyone from talking about God in public places. After all, we declare ourselves a nation under God. Curiously enough, the "separation" clause is never used to prevent clergy from talking leftist politics. It only seems to be used to fight the Bible.

Argument 11.

When a client refuses to listen on a spiritual level, should the Christian therapist not just deal with him on that human, secular level? Or if he will hear about a generic god, but not about the God of the Bible, should the therapist not accept this?

Rebuttal 11.

God tells us not to lie. The counselor must not be an instrument of Satan.

Argument 12.

If the therapist treats the person with enough love, he will experience Jesus through the therapist, and will be drawn towards him without the therapist having to mention the Gospel.

Rebuttal 12.

Many, if not most, Christian therapists work under this assumption. It may lead some clients to the recognition of God's grace. Howewver, it is far more likely to foster a secular humanistic perspective centering on how good we humans are, how much love we can give one another, and how much healing we can give one another through our love.

SUMMARY AND CONCLUSIONS

When Jesus told Peter and, by extension, all Bible believers to feed his sheep if they love him, he made it abundantly clear that this "food" was the spiritual message of the Gospel. This contradicts the stance taken not only by the traditional mental health profession but also the Christian counseling one. The present chapter has presented rebuttals of arguments used for omitting mention of the Gospel in the counseling room.

Christian counselors and psychotherapists are in the priveleged position of the sheep dogs used by the good shepherd. Either due to false teaching or like the greedy, selfish dogs described by Isaiah, "every one for his gain" (Isaiah 56:10-11), they have gone to sleep on the job. Maybe they think they can get away with working for two masters. We know what Christ had to say about that: "Ye cannot serve God and mammon" (Matthew 6:24).

Notes

1. Benner, W. (1989). "Toward a Psychology of Spirituality: Implications for Personality and Psychotherapy." Journal of Psychology and Christianity, 8, 1, pp. 19-30.

2. Benner (1989), op. cit., p. 27.

3. McLemore, Clinton (1982). The Scandal of Psychotherapy. Wheaton, Illinois: Tyndale Publishers.

4. American Psychological Association (1987). Casebook on ethical principles of psychologists, 2nd edition. Washington, DC: American Psychological Association.

5. Bergin, Allen E. (1983). "Religiosity and Mental Health: A Critical Reevaluation and Meta-Analysis." Professional Psychology: Research and Practice, 14, pp. 170-184.

6. American Psychological Association, op. cit.

7. Frankl, Victor (1975). The Unconscious God: Psychotherapy and Theology. New York, New York: Simon and Schuster.

8. Bergin, A. E. (1980). "Psychotherapy and religious values." Journal of Consulting and Clinical Psychology, 48, pp. 95-103.

9. Keith-Spiegal, P. and Koocher, G. P. (1985). Ethics in Psychology: Professional Standards. New York, New York: Random House.

10. Smith, M. L., Glass, G. V. and Miller, T. I. (1980). The benefits of psychotherapy. Baltimore, Maryland: Johns Hopkins University Press.

11. American Psychological Association (1987). Casebook on ethical principles of psychologists, 2nd edition. Washington, DC: American Psychological Association.

12. The author was asked not to bring God into a discussion of ways a neighborhood can become safer at a meeting held in a Congregational church in South Berkeley, California in September, 1989. "Separation of church and state" was the rationale for this request.

Chapter Sixteen

SUMMARY AND CONCLUSIONS

Fear of hell causes insanity; grace leads to sanity. Our mental health diagnosis is found in the Bible; so is its cure. The Gospel, or good news of God's gift of a rescue from eternal darkness, is the *only* source of mental health, that is, true peace of mind. Though clear from the Bible, this connection has not previously been made in Christian mental health literature.

At this point, there is no way it can be proven conclusively. Yet this is the most parsimonious explanation of the phenomena found in psychopathology, mythology, "normal" patterns of behavior, and the structure of religious belief systems. The presence of a profound fear about eternal survival in the spirit-thirsty human psyche...this is the missing piece to so many puzzles.

SUMMARY

Part One of the book was called "Hell and Madness." Its eight chapters presented the evidence that our universal fear of hell is the one root cause of all psychopathology. Chapter One showed how knowledge of a terrifying death sentence entered the human psyche when Adam and Eve ate the forbidden fruit in the Garden of Eden. The chapter went on to define the God-given reprieve of this death sentence as the only source of mental health.

Chapters Two and Three looked at the way science, often unwittingly, validates the Bible. The fact is, all psychological research and theory can and must be reinterpreted from the perspective of our innate existential dilemma.

How could inherent knowledge of our imminent and eternal demise not profoundly affect us? The fact that we may not be conscious of this conflict does not mean it is not there. It influences us in an unseen, deadly way until we know of our rescuer.

This is where Freud and Jung come in. Chapters Four to Six focused on the biblically-supporting aspects of Jungian and Freudian theories concerning the structure and workings of the psyche. The Jungian concept of inherent archetypes in a collective unconscious gives us a way to see how God's law, prophesies, blessings and curses are written in our genes. Freud's concept of a dynamic unconscious shows how this material creates an internal battle. His elaboration of psychological defense mechanisms describes what we do to try to both resolve the war and flee from it. Freud helps us understand how we humans are capable of hiding our heads in the sand for a lifetime.

Chapters Seven and Eight showed psychosis to be a showcase for our sense of doom. The inherent time-bomb is detectable in the phenomenology of all psychotic disorders, particularly the most severe one, schizophrenia.

Humans go crazy trying to escape hell. Only grace will cure this. Part Two, entitled "Grace and Sanity," showed grace to be absent from the non-biblical religions and traditional treatments for mental illness. Chapters Nine to Twelve journeyed on the sinking ships of secular psychotherapy, religions based on the misleading doctrine of perfection, counterfeit spiritual therapeutic approaches, and some Christian approaches that miss the mark. Finally we reached a discussion of the literature on religion and mental health. It is clear that researchers in the area are coming closer to finding grace to be the determinant of mental health. There is still a long way to go.

Part Three focused on application. Chapter Fourteen showed how our Biblical diagnosis and cure apply to the Diagnostic and Statistical Manual of Mental Disorders (DSM-III-R). Our conflict with Satan is variously manifested in the different types of mental illness classified by the DSM-III-R. Chapter Fifteen demolished the arguments typically made against bringing the Bible into mental health.

CONCLUSION

Jerome Frank[1] states that "Great evangelists of previous eras, like Jonathan Edwards and John Wesley, dwelt on the horrors of damnation, while some modern evangelistic movements, such as the Salvation Army, stress the joys of salvation." He then states that Wesley made a much higher percentage of converts than today's evangelistic revivals. This he attributes to God's wrath being more vivid to man in the eighteenth century than it is in the twentieth. Why? Not because the Bible has changed, clearly, but because preaching has changed. Today's lovey-dovey preaching does not address our deepest fear. It misconstrues salvation, applying it only to this lifetime, only as a rescue from sin. But if eternity is not at stake, many would just as soon forget God. Only if eternity in hell is at stake will humans scurry for God's cover.

Mental health is attained only when we recognize that hell is real, that we are destined to go there, and that God has gone to great pains to give us an undeserved rescue. Peace of mind involves a fundamental change in belief from negative to positive at the existential level: from doomed to rescued.

There is no peace of mind without reconciliation with God. It is the cornerstone and source of inspiration for all other changes in the human psyche, including the aims of secular psychotherapy and non-Biblical religions mentioned Chapters Nine to Eleven. These changes include: the experience of unconditional love, wholeness, relationship, congruence, individuation, ego control, self-acceptance, positive coping, optimism, actualization, meaningfulness, and enlightenment.

Without factoring in Satan's ability to blind us not only to the true reason for all our guilt and fear, but also to the conscious experience of these emotions, it makes no sense that we would not recognize our dilemma. Also, only the influence of Satan explains the obtuseness of the psychological profession. For example, Victor Frankl is not only concerned with the broad existential perspective; he is also knowledgeable about the Bible. Yet he is able to make the statement: "A religious psychotherapy in the proper sense is inconceivable because of the essential difference between psychotherapy and religion, which is a dimensional difference. To begin with, the aims of

the two are different. Psychotherapy aims at mental health.
Religion aims at salvation."[2]

But mental health is only possible when salvation is
assured. Outside of the act of atonement accomplished on our
behalf by the Lord God of the Bible, there is nothing to hope
for and everything to fear.

Grace is unmerited favor, salvation for free, God's gift of
the shed blood of Christ that pays the price for human sin, so
buying us out of hell. Only this unconditional love from God
melts the human heart of stone. It inspires us to love God
and desire to please him.

In conflict with what God says, psychology tells us to
love ourselves. It so happens that when our hearts melt, we
do soften towards who and what we are. We cannot admire
ourselves, but we become unafraid to face our depravity and
transgression. We learn to accept the beast that we are
because we know God does. The "guilt-based" self-loathing
called "low self-esteem" is replaced by an internalized sense of
God's forgiveness.

Seeing our shortcomings with the sureness of God's
unending mercy leads to repentance. This is the true basis for
what Freud called "ego control." Knowing God loves us, we
feel ashamed of our wrongdoing. We want to change.
Confession and repentance are outgrowths of salvation from
hell, two sides of the same coin. The paradox is: we have
the responsibility but not the control. We have the
responsibility for confession about our law-breaking but none
of the control to stop it. Only God can change us, and the
only way to connect with God is through Christ.

As we perceive God's unconditional love for us, the
basis for all our relationships changes. Security with God
makes our dependency on others lose its death grip. We can
love our neighbors, not expecting them to be any less than the
very imperfect human beings that we are. Realizing we do not
deserve salvation any more than the next person, we are
inspired to share the Gospel.

No longer held back by the guilt and uncertainty which
cause inaction and self-sabotage, we are freed to develop to
our God-given potential. Our lives take on meaning. This is
not the faltering so-called meaning that existentialists tell us we
can determine ourselves. It is the solid knowledge that we are
part of God's plan.

Do we really need scientific proof to support this? It is impossible to say. First person testimonials abound in the literature, but we do not yet have the large scale research that would prove grace to be the only genuine and lasting source of sanity.

If God wants us to have that, he will give it to us. For those who accept the Bible, no more proof should be needed: "So then faith cometh by hearing, and hearing by the word of God." (Romans 10:17). It may just be the case the for those who do not accept the Bible, nor will latter day scientific evidence of God's power convince them.

Notes

1. Frank, Jerome (1974). "Religious Revivalism and Thought Reform" in Persuasion and Healing. New York, New York: Schocken, p. 82.

2. Frankl, Victor (1969). The Will to Meaning. New York, New York: New American Library, p. 143.

INDEX